Praise for *We Are All Shipwrecks*

"Moving and complex, this is an exquisitely written tale of perseverance and unconditional love."

—*Library Journal*, Starred Review

"Readers who appreciate thoughtful memoirs will be charmed by Carlisle's generosity and easy, open reflections...a wise, contemplative, forgiving memoir by a likable narrator."

—*Shelf Awareness*, Starred Review

"A turbulent childhood is accurately rendered in this gritty, raw memoir of Carlisle's family and her search for the truth about her mother's death."

—*Kirkus Reviews*

"Although the initial intrigue in Carlisle's engrossing memoir is that of her mother's murder, quite possibly by the Hillside Strangler, the real story is what came after... Carlisle writes from her current perspective, questioning the implications of a life marked by death from the start and exploring how the adults in her life... shaped who she was and who she became."

—*Booklist*

"Rich and complex memoir... Carlisle captivates the reader in this tender, warts-and-all narrative of her attempt to unravel her mother's murder and of the man who helped to create an adventurous, if confusing, childhood for her."

—*Publishers Weekly*

"Stunningly powerful memoir…"

—*BookPage*

"A stunning piece of work—a wrenching, beautiful exploration of the author's struggle to solve the mystery of her mother's murder."

—*Fourth Genre*

"Every so often a book arrives that slaps you like an incoming wave. Powerful, briny, and brimming with the flotsam and jetsam of an uncommon life, *We Are All Shipwrecks* is a dazzling debut."

—*The Dallas Morning News*

we
are
all
shipwrecks

we are all shipwrecks

kelly grey carlisle

Published by Sourcebooks, Inc.
P.O. Box 4410, Naperville, Illinois 60567-4410
(630) 961-3900
Fax: (630) 961-2168
www.sourcebooks.com

The Library of Congress has cataloged the hardcover edition as follows:

Names: Carlisle, Kelly Grey, author.
Title: We are all shipwrecks : a memoir / Kelly Grey Carlisle.
Description: Naperville : Sourcebooks, [2017]
Identifiers: LCCN 2016040632
Subjects: LCSH: Murder--California--Case studies. |
   Daughters--California--Case studies.
Classification: LCC HV6533.C2 .C37 2017 | DDC 362.88/13092 [B]
--dc23 LC record available at https://lccn.loc.gov/2016040632

Printed and bound in the United States of America.
VP 10 9 8 7 6 5 4 3 2 1

For Milly and Callie

"Life is a shipwreck, but we must not

forget to sing in the lifeboats."

—*Peter Gay (often attributed to Voltaire)*

Prologue

The Yankee Whaler

BRUNCH AT THE YANKEE WHALER WAS A BIG DEAL IN OUR family. The Yankee Whaler was a restaurant on a boat at Ports O'Call, a tourist-trap-cum-old-time-New-England-fishing-village in the Los Angeles Harbor. We went once or twice a year. My grandfather, Richard, would wear a tie—his Old Etonian; his second wife, Marilyn, would wear a dress instead of slacks; and I would wear my Easter dress with white sandals. Marilyn would order mimosas or champagne cocktails, a sugar cube trailing silver bubbles down the long flute, and my grandfather and I would drink Shirley Temples or virgin piña coladas. I loved going there because I could stare out the window while I ate and watch the hulking container ships—Matson Line or Evergreen—glide by on the Main Channel, pulled along by scrappy little tugs. I loved the tug boats, how their sides were covered in tires that looked like big, black zeros, how they chirped and barked at each other with their shrill whistles, the thunder from their massive engines vibrating through the water and up through the restaurant's floor, sending my bones all aquiver. Sometimes a sea lion would swim by on its way to a buoy, or a line of pelicans might skim along the water's surface, looking for fish. Once in a while a true motor yacht would come along, all white paint and varnished teak and shining chrome, and my grandfather would make guesses as to its make, vintage, and owner. That was the kind of boat my grandfather had hoped to buy, but he'd had to settle for the *Intrepid*, a secondhand Coast Guard cutter, currently a stripped-down hull sitting under a blue tarp at Donahue's Marina.

But on the day when we waited for Detective Varney to join us at our table, we didn't sip coladas and mimosas. The channel was empty as I stared out the window; a lone seagull circled lazily above the dark water. I was eight. I had my report cards from school clutched in my lap: a stack of thin, stapled blue booklets marked *Carnet Mensuel* on the front, my grades handwritten in cursive inside. They were good report cards. I was proud of them. My grandfather had told me to bring them to show the detective. My dress was stiff, and its tag scratched the back of my neck. The glass goblets of ice water on our table sweated. I took a small sip from one, careful not to spill, then put it back, precisely over the water ring on the white cloth. My mouth was soon dry again.

When the waiter showed him to his seat, Detective Varney shook my grandfather's plump hand and patted his back, as if they were old friends. This puzzled me because I'd never met the detective before. He shook Marilyn's hand, and when he saw me standing beside the table, Detective Varney grinned. He stooped down to put his hands on my shoulders. His tie grazed my nose.

"You sure did grow up to be a pretty little girl, now, didn't you? Last time I saw you, you were just a bitty thing." He held his hands a foot or so apart to show me.

My mother had been murdered when I was three weeks old. This was the detective who'd found me nestled in a pulled-out dresser drawer in a Hollywood motel room. My grandfather had explained these things to me a few weeks before, the first time I'd ever heard the truth about her death.

When I remember that day and Detective Varney, I picture

Dennis Franz from *NYPD Blue*—balding, kind of pudgy—but I know that isn't right. A portrait from the beginning of Detective Varney's career in the sixties shows an attractive man, clean-shaven, with intense eyes and full lips. In newspaper pictures from the Hillside Strangler investigation in 1977, he is tall and thin and sports a plaid coat and thick mustache. He is older than in the first picture, a little stooped as he walks next to Kenneth Bianchi, but still handsome and distinguished.

The adults began to talk about the detective's family, retirement, boats. I listened quietly. I used my best table manners, holding my fork the English way, taking small bites.

Halfway through lunch, Marilyn nudged my arm gently and whispered, "Don't forget to show Mr. Varney your report cards."

"Yes," said my grandfather in his English accent, not whispering. "She goes to a Frog school. Le Lycée de something-something. In Redondo Beach. What is it, love?"

"Le Lycée Français de Los Angeles," I said softly. Speaking French embarrassed me. I hoped he wouldn't ask me to say it again.

"Yes, that's it. She's doing very well there. They teach her French."

I'd placed the stack of report cards to the side of my plate when our food came, and now I pushed them across the white cloth to Detective Varney. He took them and glanced over each one, his glasses pulled slightly down his nose. He nodded and smiled. "Very good."

I smiled back. I wanted him to like me because somehow I felt as if he were connected to my mother, as if he'd known her. I was about to ask him what she had been like, but then it occurred to me: they'd never actually met.

I thought I should ask him questions about her murder. I looked out the window and tried to think of some while the adults resumed their conversation, but I couldn't come up with any. I already knew the answer to the most important ones anyway.

A red and white Catalina Cruises boat came by, headed back to the terminal. It was almost empty; you could see through its windows to the other side of the channel.

Who killed her? No one really knew. My grandfather had explained this to me. How had she been killed? I knew that too. She'd been strangled. *Why* she'd been killed didn't seem as important, and who could answer that question anyway? Why did people die? They just did. People died all the time. Other questions seemed excessive, nosy—like the people who slowed down to stare at car crashes on the 405.

I twisted the cloth napkin in my lap and looked at the table covered with white linen, the china plates with gold rims and shiny silverware, the goblets of water, the vase of flowers. This wasn't the right place to talk about things like that anyway. None of the adults had mentioned the murder. My grandfather's chair was pushed close to the table, its edge digging into his round, hard belly. Marilyn smiled pleasantly, nodding as the detective spoke about his travel plans. She sat straight in her teal dress, her smooth hands folded delicately in her lap. Perhaps there would be some other time I could ask questions. Maybe when I was older. I imagined interviewing the detective when I was a grown-up, a teenager, dressed immaculately in navy silk, white pearls, and high heels, looking like Nancy Drew. Nancy's mother had died too.

After dessert and coffee—the bill paid by my grandfather—we all walked out together. We stood by the channel in the bright afternoon sun, the smell of warm tar from the pier mixing with salt air and the intermittent waft of crab cakes and dumpster smell from the San Pedro Fish Market. The cannery down the channel chugged away. The adults talked the way adults did, carrying on conversations long after my interest had waned. I wandered over to the rail by the water. I watched Detective Varney for a moment, the way he towered over my grandfather's fat frame and Marilyn's slender one, how he looped his thumbs in his belt and nodded his head without saying anything. Then I turned my attention to the water over the rail, how black it was in the shadows made by the dock, how you could see nothing in it but your own vague reflection, dark, almost sinister. I climbed one rung of the wooden railing, my shoe pushing gray paint flakes into the water. I wondered how deep the water was and what things might be hidden at its bottom. Big grumpy crabs, scallop shells, dropped tools, tin cans, pirate ships. Then it was time for Detective Varney to leave.

"Kelly, come say goodbye," Marilyn called.

I gave him a hug, my cheek resting against his yellow shirt.

"Goodbye," I said. "Thank you for helping my family." I said this because it sounded grown-up and because I didn't know what else to say.

I would never see the detective again, would never get to ask my questions, but I'd think of him once in a while, as if he were some benevolent spirit or a guardian angel, the man who'd taken me out of a motel dresser drawer when I was a baby and saved me from harm.

I've never understood why my grandfather arranged this meeting when I was so young, or what he thought I could gain from it. But when I ask Marilyn about it years later, she says the brunch wasn't for me, but for the detective. In fact, that was why my grandfather had told me about her murder in the first place. He and the detective had stayed in touch in the years since my mother's death. Mr.

Varney was retiring, and the brunch was my grandfather's retirement gift to him. He knew that the detective had seen only the bad endings of stories, the lives that ended in death, wives made widows, children made orphans. Detective Varney had worked on the Tate murders, the Hillside Stranglers, and Bobby Kennedy's assassination, as well as my mom's murder and hundreds of other nameless cases like it. When my grandfather invited Detective Varney to lunch, it was to show him a happy ending. *I* was the happy ending, eight years old, still alive, doing well in school, loved. All these things were true.

If that had been the plan, to show the detective a happy ending, I don't think my grandfather would have left his thoughtfulness unmentioned. And so now, as I remember that brunch at the Yankee Whaler, I imagine the conversation on our way back home to Palos Verdes, twenty minutes from the harbor and just south of Los Angeles proper.

"Well," he would have said, speaking louder than he needed to over his Mercedes's diesel engine and looking back at me in the rearview mirror, although he was really talking to Marilyn. "That went well, I think. Good thing to do, show him a happy ending. God knows what he's seen."

And perhaps that conversation—experienced then but imagined now, when my recall of it fails—is why this memory of meeting the detective is a happy one for me, one colored more by the golden light of that afternoon than by its shadows.

I

When We Lived in a House

1

MY GRANDFATHER'S BEDROOM, DIM WITH AFTERNOON
shadows, was the smallest room in our small house, tucked
behind the kitchen and furnace. The floor creaked as I walked in,
and I held my breath a moment at the sound, then exhaled again.
His room smelled of cedar from his closet, the Yardley's oatmeal
soap and lemon-lime Barbasol from his bath, and the sharp tang
from his unmade bed. He had diabetes and often left his electric
blanket on its highest setting, so that, although he never stopped
being cold, he sweated constantly under the covers. When I was
seven, I didn't mind the smell. In fact, when I was sick, I liked to
sleep in his twin bed, precisely because it *was* smelly and always
warm. His bedroom smelled exactly like him, and I loved him.

His desk was a lawyer's desk—massive, wooden, ornate—that
took up a quarter of his small room, but he wasn't a lawyer. His
desk chair was a corporate president's chair, a brass-studded leather
armchair on a swivel. Technically, he *was* a corporate president—of
a tiny Nevada corporation called alternately Delta Publishing and
Portola Investments, whose sole interest was a video store on
Century Boulevard in Inglewood, just east of LAX. A messy pile
of papers several inches thick covered the desk; a smaller stack sat
on the floor where they had slipped off the pile, gathering dust and

fur. It was the favorite napping place of our tabby, Klutz, and as I
moved the chair, she gave a small grunt.

If one were to explore the papers on my grandfather's desk—
something strictly forbidden, but which I often did anyway—one
would invariably find illegible notes on yellow legal pads, overdue
bills, unopened notices from the Writer's Guild, copies of *Yachting*
and *The Economist,* a creased black-and-white spanking magazine,
folded to the Readers Write section, as well as old classifieds
from the LA Harbor *Log,* in which my grandfather had circled
certain boats in blue ballpoint, pressing the pen so heavily that the
newsprint tore. Sometimes at the bottom of the pile, or sometimes
in the top drawer of the desk, I'd find my grandfather's gun—a
black metal thing with a brown plastic grip. Under no circumstances was I to touch the gun, but kneeling on the chair, with my
legs tucked under me and the chair-back hiding my body, I often
did, rubbing my fingers along its barrel. There was also a bayonet,
given to my grandfather by one of the clerks who worked in his
video store, who got it from a friend who'd served in Vietnam. It
was 1984; the war had ended before I was born, but grown-ups
still spoke of it in hushed tones. I didn't often touch the bayonet.
Its dull metal was streaked here and there with rust-colored stains,
which I imagined was someone's blood.

But that particular afternoon, six months or so before I would
find out about my mother's murder or meet Detective Varney, I
wasn't looking for the gun or the bayonet but for things that felt
almost as dangerous: pictures of my mother. I knew my grandfather had them because, the night before, he'd shown them to me.
Marilyn had been out teaching ESL at Harbor College, as she did
every Tuesday and Thursday night. After dinner, my grandfather
had called me into his bedroom, then drawn two photographs
from the papers on his desk. He held them in front of me with

his sausage fingers, putting his fingerprints all over the image, something Marilyn always warned me not to do with photographs.

One picture was of the back of a little girl petting a cat, and another was of her blowing out candles on her birthday cake. There were nine candles. I had just enough time to count them before he turned the pictures around to look at them himself, his bushy eyebrows furrowed over his thick glasses.

"That's Michele when she was a little girl. She looked like her old man, poor thing," he said. He meant himself.

I squeezed around next to his chair so I could see them again. I couldn't see my mother's face in those pictures; her back was turned toward the camera. The little girl had red hair, and in both pictures, she had on the same dress. She was chubby, with stubby arms and legs. Before I saw those pictures, I'd always thought of my mother as a tall, graceful woman with long hair and soft, cool hands, the way Marilyn's hands were cool on my forehead when I was sick. Marilyn, so much younger than my grandfather, was the right age to have been my actual mother, and so I'd always thought of Michele as being Marilyn's age. I'd never thought of my mother as a nine-year-old, someone not much older than me.

My grandfather rarely talked about my mother, and so I had all sorts of questions saved up for him, all variations of *What was she like? Would I have liked her? Would she have liked me?*

"Did she like to draw?" I asked. I loved to draw.

He leaned back in his chair, his dark blue dressing gown barely reaching across the fat tummy encased in the red flannel nightshirt Marilyn and I had given him for Christmas. His legs beneath were bare, hairless, pale like milk, and marbled with blue veins. His elephant-like feet were shoved into burgundy slippers.

"I suppose. Doesn't every child like to draw?" He sounded bored by my question.

"Did she like dogs?" I reached toward the photographs again.

"Well, she had a cat," he said, nodding toward the picture.

"What was its name?"

"I can't remember."

In spite of Marilyn's careful training, I traced a finger along my mother's back. "What was her favorite color?"

"How the hell should I know?"

"I bet it was green. Mine's green. What did she want to be when she grew up?"

"I have no idea." He was quiet a moment. "She always knew you'd be a girl, though." He took off his glasses and cleaned their thick lenses with the edge of his dressing gown. "She'd had your name picked out since *she* was a little girl, not much older than you are now. You were named after a steak house. Kelly's."

I was disappointed to hear this. I thought I'd been named after the *Kelly,* a famous battleship he'd told me about.

"I'll always remember it. She was just a little girl—eight, nine. We were driving along the freeway and she saw a sign for Kelly's, and she said, 'That's what I'm going to name my little girl.' And I said, 'How do you know you're going to have a little girl?' And she said 'I just do.' She was stubborn that way."

That story made me feel better, that she'd known I was going to be a girl years before I was born, as if by magic.

He slipped the two photos into the pocket of his dressing gown. "It's getting late," he said and stood up. "You need to get in bed. Mommy will be upset if you're still awake when she comes home."

I knew Marilyn wouldn't be mad; she never was. But I knew, too, to get up and go brush my teeth. While I brushed, I counted how many naked women and men were in each row on the wallpaper in Marilyn's bathroom. I counted them all the time, the rows of men drawn in a variety of mustaches and poses, cartoon women fat and thin, their nipples pink or black dots. It was something our landlord had picked out.

I was in bed when Marilyn came home. When she leaned over to kiss me good night, I fiddled with her wooden-bead necklace, the one with the small goat's horn charm that came from somewhere in Africa. I breathed deeply the dry-cleaning smell of her wool sweater, her minty breath, and the cigarette behind it.

"Good night, sweetheart," she whispered. "Go to sleep."

The next day when I got home from school, before my grandfather came home, I decided to look for more pictures of Michele, ones that would show her face. I was certain they were somewhere in his desk, that my grandfather had simply misplaced them. Marilyn had hundreds of pictures of me, after all, carefully labeled and filed in specially purchased photo boxes. I assumed the same had to be true of my grandfather and *his* daughter.

My hands shook as I sorted through the pile, careful to leave each paper in its original spot, careful to put the gun back where I found it. I sifted through bills and old magazines, scratch pads and newspaper inserts. There was nothing.

A few days later, I searched my grandfather's desk again and finally found some pictures. But they were the same two that he'd already shown me, tucked in the top drawer, creased and covered in fingerprints, as if he'd often touched them.

"Blood is important," my grandfather would sometimes tell me on those nights when Marilyn taught ESL and we were left alone. "Where you come from is important. It's who you are."

He'd sit at the head of the dining room table—a repurposed

boardroom table—in his dressing gown, sometimes with his street clothes beneath, an empty ice cream bowl in front of him, a few drops of French vanilla spattered across his shirt. I'd sit sometimes in a chair, but more often than not on the red carpet beneath the framed technical drawings of German U-boats, next to Marilyn's electric typewriter on its stand, which rested in the corner by my grandfather. I liked to sit on the floor, where sometimes Klutz the cat or Ugly the dog would deign to visit me. Across the living room, visible from the table, the TV would be set to a wildlife documentary, the volume turned low so that bugs ate other bugs in silent, slow-motion pantomime.

My grandfather didn't see very well, and when he didn't have his contacts in, he wore thick glasses with lenses that looked like the bottoms of Coke bottles. It was hard to tell what he was thinking when he wore his glasses, because you couldn't see his eyes. You couldn't tell if he was looking down at the table or at you, but you could always tell when he wanted you to believe what he was saying, because he took off his glasses when he said it and looked straight at you with blind eyes. He always took off his glasses when he told me the stories of my family.

"Your grandmother, Yvonne Spencer," he'd sometimes begin. "You know, Spence."

Spence was his ex-wife, my mother's mother. They'd divorced long before I was born, when my own mother was a child. I'd lived with Spence and her friend Dee until I was four years old.

"Well, she was half Hawaiian, on her father's side. He was full-blooded. Cliff diver. Can't remember his name." This, he explained, was why I liked to swim and why I turned so dark in the sun. "He was an alcoholic, though. Lost all of his money on some water deal in Palm Springs. Married to an absolute bitch. Spence's mother. She hated me, of course."

My grandfather, who spoke with the accent of English movie stars, told me he was related to the Earl Grey of tea fame and Lady Jane Grey of beheading fame. Somewhere, in England, our family had a house named Fallodon. This was important, he told me, because it meant we had noble blood. "Blue blood, they call it. Don't know why. *Everyone's* got blue blood. They do! Your blood's blue until it comes out of your skin." He pulled his sleeve up to his elbow, exposing his forearm and tracing the blue vein under his wrist.

"Of course, you've got Norman blood too. All over England, little old ladies go looking through churchyards to see if their ancestors are Frogs. You know the Normans, right? 1066? King Harold got his eye speared by an arrow. Bloody fool. Shouldn't have looked up."

I did know, but only because he'd told me before and because I'd read about the Bayeux Tapestry in one of his books. Our house's entire southern wall was lined with my grandfather's books: thrillers and spy fiction, the adventures of Hornblower and Hollywood biographies, Miss Marple and Poirot, tomes on navigation and marine architecture, books on the Louvre, pirates, and English castles. Up on the highest shelf was a lone car-racing trophy from the Paramount Ranch Racetrack, engraved to "Richard 'Dick' Grey, Second Place." I asked to see it sometimes, and my grandfather would obligingly bring it down and let me run my finger along the pewter car. "I quit racing not too long after I won this trophy," he'd say. "Too many near misses."

Sometimes my grandfather told me he was a baronet, which I knew must be true because his checks and credit cards were all imprinted with "Sir Richard Grey." I wasn't sure, though, if he was called "Sir" because of the baronetcy or because he'd been knighted for his bravery by the Queen herself after World War II.

"You look at the ceremony and you think she's just tapping them lightly on the shoulder," he'd tell me. "But, no, she gives you a bloody good wallop."

When we went shopping, sales clerks would sometimes call him "Sir Richard" or "Sir Grey." Sometimes they called Marilyn "Lady Marilyn" or "Lady Grey," although she hated it and would ask them to *please* not call her that.

On some nights, my grandfather told me the story of his own childhood, how he was an orphan, how his parents had been killed in 1918 by the Spanish flu when he was a baby, just after the First World War. The Spanish flu sounded exotic to me—something prettier, rarer than the regular flu. He'd tell me how he was raised by many different people—a bishop in the Church of England, an uncle, a cousin—moving again and again all over England.

"I had a nanny once," he said. "Her name was Frieda. Good old Frieda. Taught me German."

To show me how he spoke German, he'd run his fingers along my side and whisper a rhyme in German about a mouse: *Here creeps a mouse, without a house...*

"Frieda taught me that," he'd sigh. "It's why I ended up in secret operations during the war. I could speak it fluently."

All of these things were important to know, he told me, because where you came from was important to know. Of my English, Hawaiian, and "blue" bloods, the most important was the English: the blood of Shakespeare, Nelson, and Churchill ran in my veins, and I must always remember that. On some nights, he'd tell me that I was half English, because he'd forget I wasn't really his daughter; he'd forget that my mother, Michele, his dead daughter, had ever come between us.

When I was little, before he'd finally told me the truth about her death, my grandfather would tell me how my mother had been killed in a car wreck. I was three weeks old when it happened. It was a story I'd heard for so long, I couldn't remember a time when I didn't know it.

"She never knew it was coming," he assured me. "It was painless, fast. You were just a baby, so of course you can't remember it."

And then, after he'd finished telling me stories, he'd put his glasses back on, his eyes once more obscured by the lenses.

2

A FEW WEEKS AFTER HE SHOWED ME THE PICTURES, MY GRAND-
father picked me up from school. "We're going to Bristol
Farms," he announced as I got into the Mercedes. "You can help
me pick out dinner."

A married couple was coming to dinner that night, and my
grandfather was eager to impress them. A week or so earlier, we'd
had cocktails on their boat, a large motor yacht docked at the
Long Beach Marina. It had a fiberglass hull and expansive tinted
windows. Marilyn had drunk a glass of pink wine, which our hosts
also drank, and my grandfather had a gin and tonic.

"Heavy on the tonic and light on the gin," he'd told our host,
who'd made a great show of mixing drinks at the wet bar. "The
diabetes, you know."

I'd been given a Coke, shown a place to sit on the plush, white
carpet, and then ignored, so I passed the time watching the adults.

The man's bald spot was sunburned, which looked painful
to me. When he'd first met us on the dock, he'd been wearing a
captain's hat. His mustache was a pale ginger, bushy and unkempt.
He wore a white Izod shirt and khaki shorts and Top-Siders
without socks. My grandfather wore almost exactly the same outfit,
which I would come to recognize as a kind of yachtsman's uniform,
but my grandfather wore no captain's hat. "Never trust idiots who

wear captain's hats," my grandfather said. "It's a sign they don't know what they're doing."

The man's wife perched on a stool next to him at the bar, leaning in to the conversation as if she were supremely interested, but I could tell she was bored by the way she kept looking at her red fingernails. She was wearing white Bermuda shorts and a white and navy striped sweater, and her long legs stretched down the bar stool. In her earlobes were red plastic earrings that, upon closer inspection, turned out to be anchors. Like Marilyn, she was much younger than her husband.

My grandfather talked expansively while Marilyn sat demurely on the couch next to him, fiddling with the stem of her wine glass. The couple was trying to sell my grandfather the very boat we were sitting on. In fact, this was exactly why we were having cocktails with the couple in their navy whites and nautical flair. My grandfather wanted to buy a boat, a motor yacht to take us through the canals of Europe and to Costa Rica, the Fjords and San Diego. He wanted a boat because he'd been in the navy and because he loved the sea. He wanted a boat so that we could make a quick escape—from what, he didn't say.

At the end of the night, he'd invited them over for dinner at our house. On the ride home, he was already planning the meal; he was going to pull out all the stops. Marilyn said nothing and stared out the passenger window.

The afternoon of the dinner, the Bristol Farms parking lot was bustling with BMWs and Jaguars. Inside it was swarming with Friday crowds: Palos Verdes wives—processed blonds fresh from the tennis courts, still dressed in pleated skirts and appliquéd windbreakers—kids just picked up from school, businessmen charged with bringing home something for dinner, and people who liked to eat, like my grandfather. Bristol Farms was his favorite grocery store. I knew we'd be getting much more than we needed for that night's meal.

My grandfather's trips to the grocery store were completely different from Marilyn's. Marilyn went shopping at Ralphs with a list she'd carefully updated all week. It was written in orderly cursive with her Pilot Razor Point pen and used unappetizing abbreviations like "chix" for chicken. Her list was composed of things we actually needed: staple foods, ingredients for recipes, paper goods, pet food. She had a nylon coupon organizer that she'd ordered from a newspaper insert, the same kind of insert from which you could order a thousand printed address labels or customized checks with five different American patriot eagle designs. Marilyn's trips to the grocery store were carefully orchestrated campaigns, military operations upon which hung the entire war effort. Keeping house was like war for her, an angry battle against the shoes that cluttered the floor, the dishes that piled up on the counter. Too often, it seemed, I was fighting for the enemy, putting my shirts inside-out into the laundry hamper, leaving my dirty socks under the dining room table and empty glasses on the floor by my bed.

When *she* went grocery shopping, Marilyn mapped her trip down the aisles so she'd buy canned goods first and end up at the frozen foods last so they would have less time to melt. She bought a predetermined number of cans of cat and dog food, stacking them in her cart in columns of eight high. She checked each egg in the carton and carefully calculated the price per ounce of cereal, cat litter, and frozen juice concentrate. At the checkout stand, she placed her items on the conveyor belt in the exact order in which she wished them to be bagged. She instructed exasperated baggers how to place them in the sacks: "Double paper, please. And pack them as full as possible—don't worry if they're heavy. You can get more in there," she'd say, placing a bag of celery and a box of crackers on top of an already-packed bag. "See?"

This was not how my grandfather went to the grocery store. My grandfather did not keep lists. He did not shop the aisles in a particular order.

The bakery was right by the entrance, and so that afternoon his first stop was to pore over the glass cases of fruit tarts, napoleons, cheesecakes, rum babas, and German chocolate cake.

"What do you think, Little Toad? Rum babas?" I was about to say napoleons, my favorite, when he told the lady, "Fruit tarts. Six, please. Yes, that will be very attractive." She filled a perfect, pink bakery box, while I was sent to fetch a baguette from a brass basket.

"No, best make it two," he said when he saw the loaf I'd brought, and I went back to get another.

Then we came to the sushi counter. He grabbed boxes of nigiri and maki—still exotic then, even in LA—tuna, mackerel, salmon, shrimp, roe—California rolls for me because I would not tolerate the others. At the butcher counter, he ordered steaks, chops, roasts; at the fish counter, salmon filets, swordfish steaks, tiger shrimp, clams, mussels, halibut. A short walk to a cooler, and then small rounds of Edam, Camembert, and a wedge of sharp cheddar dropped into our shopping cart, followed by half a dozen candy bars from a display on a farm table, then peanut brittle and Famous Amos chocolate chip cookies, some of which my grandfather would eat in spite of his diabetes and some of which would end up in my lunch box. (He packed my lunch full of candy and cookies every day so that I could trade to make friends, or, failing that, eat them myself. It was usually the latter.)

My grandfather consulted carefully with the green-aproned

wine merchant beneath the fake pergola in the middle of the store, moving on with four bottles of white. Then he gathered the foods from England, which he always bought when we went to Bristol Farms: Devonshire clotted cream in tiny glass bottles; Lyle's Golden Syrup; lemon curd; Bird's custard for trifles, its powder packed in a tricolor tin; and, of course, the kippers, flayed and snug in their plastic package.

On particularly unlucky Saturdays, my grandfather cooked kippers for breakfast. I'd wake to the pungent, salty, fishy smell that wafted into my nostrils, headed straight down my gullet, and squeezed my stomach in an iron vise. I was convinced there was nothing on earth—at least nothing edible—that smelled as bad as frying kippers, although now, as I try to think of the right words to describe them, I find only pleasant ones: sea, salt, savory; the smell of wood smoke and lanolin on a wool sweater; the smell of kelp freshly washed on shore. Perhaps it is only that sometimes I miss my grandfather.

He'd eat the fish slowly, pensively pulling stray bones from between his full, oil-slicked lips. He seemed to go to another world when he ate his kippers, lost in some cloud of kipper incense, transported to another place where there was nothing but the smoky fish melting on tongue and teeth. But really, it was just that he'd gone home.

Kippers were one of the strange things my grandfather ate because he was English. He didn't follow cricket scores or English politics; he didn't observe Guy Fawkes Day or Boxing Day. He never got letters from England, never made phone calls. The only way you could tell he was English, besides his accent, was by what he ate. His favorite meal to make for friends was roast beef and Yorkshire pudding—the pudding cooked beneath the roast so that it caught the dripping juices. He taught Marilyn to make bubble and squeak, which he made from leftover potatoes, broccoli, and onion, sautéed in plenty of oil and salt. He'd eat jellied tongue and blood sausage, which, of course, were in our shopping cart that day too, sliced and wrapped neatly in white deli paper.

Then, finally, we hit the freezer section (not, mind you, because he had planned it that way, but because some thoughtful person had placed it last on his way to the checkout). Into the cart went boxes of frozen rumaki, stuffed Cornish game hens, chicken cordon bleu, Häagen Dazs rum raisin, Dreyer's mint chocolate chip, frozen Belgian waffles he'd heat in the microwave and serve to me for breakfast with eggs, bacon, *and* toast.

"Want anything, Little Toad?" he asked.

I surveyed the overflowing cart. I couldn't think of anything we didn't already have.

At the checkout counter, we threw his booty haphazardly onto the conveyor belt, candy bars mixed with lamb chops, ice cream mixed with warm baguettes, sushi thrown between bottles of ginger beer. He didn't care how the baggers filled his plastic grocery sacks. My grandfather couldn't be bothered with coupons.

"Wow, are you having a party?" asked the very friendly checker, her curly red hair gathered into a ponytail at the top of her full face.

"Yes, love," my grandfather said. But I knew we'd be eating most of it ourselves.

She bounced a little as she scanned our items, so that the curls of her hair bounced too, like little springs. I decided she looked like a Cabbage Patch doll. I wanted a Cabbage Patch doll very much.

At the end, she breathlessly called out our total as if she were an announcer at a race, so that the whole store could hear, "Two hundred ninety-four dollars and fifty-two cents!"

My grandfather didn't bat an eye. He spread his checkbook open on the counter and creased it with a long fingernail.

"Got a pen, love?"

I stood beside him as he wrote, silently willing the checker not to ask me about my school uniform. I noticed her puzzling over the patch on my blazer, trying to make out the French and Latin.

"And what school do *you* go to?" she asked. Of course she did. Everyone did: the grocery store checkers, the postal clerks, the waitresses at Coco's.

"LeLyçéeFrançaisdeLosAngeles," I muttered, getting the long name out as fast as I could.

"What?"

"Le Lycée Français de Los Angeles," I said again, loudly and slowly this time, as if I were addressing an idiot, although *I* was the one who felt stupid. "It's a French school," I added quickly, before she could ask.

A small line had formed behind my grandfather, but no one at the counter seemed to be in a rush.

"So you learn French there? Can you say something in French for me, sweetie?"

I hated when adults asked me to say something in French. I never knew what to say or what they wanted me to say. I was shy and embarrassed that my uniform attracted so much attention, annoyed that my school couldn't have a normal, shorter name, preferably in English. Eventually I'd come up with something to say in French, like "The butterfly yellow flies in the sky"; or "It makes warm outside"; or "I like well the school." But I'd make them wait a long, awkward moment before I said it.

That afternoon, I said, *"Nous avons achété trop de nourriture."*

"Oh, that's wonderful," she said, smiling benevolently at me, "French is such a beautiful language. You're really lucky to be able to learn it so young!"

I didn't feel very lucky; I just wanted to hide. But my grandfather never wanted to hide.

"Yes," he said, as he signed with a flourish. "You've got to teach them a language while they're young. That's the way they do it in Europe, love. That's how they can all speak English over there. Meanwhile, you Americans can barely speak your own language."

The checker laughed. Everything sounded charming when my grandfather said it in his English accent.

The French school had been my grandfather's idea. When I was five and it was time for me to go to first grade, he'd decided that I should go to a private school. The money from the sale of my grandmother Spence's house had been placed in a trust for me, and my grandfather wanted to be sure I got the best education he could afford. He considered two options. There was Chadwick School in Palos Verdes—movie stars' children went there—and then there was Le Lyçée Français de Los Angeles, which had a campus fifteen minutes away in Redondo Beach, overlooking the ocean. The students were taught French and wore school uniforms, which appealed to his snobbery. On the other hand, my grandfather had an innate English suspicion of all things French. In the end, Chadwick had a waiting list, and Le Lyçée was cheaper.

"Besides," he said, "it's a Frog school, so they'll have good food."

He promptly signed me up for the cafeteria service. Classic French cuisine was the best food in the world, my grandfather said. He knew this because he'd once been a chef at the Savoy, mentored in the very kitchen Escoffier had made famous.

My grandfather told me he'd gone to private school too, although, he pointed out, in England, private schools were called "public" schools. After he'd been orphaned, he'd gone to Eton, the prestigious English school, on scholarship. He'd had to wear a uniform, just like I did, and had fond memories of going to a tailor for a fitting. In fact, just that year, he'd ordered an Old Etonian tie from the back of a magazine, just to prove he'd gone to school there.

"Only Eton graduates can wear this tie," he'd tell me as he twisted the silk about his thick throat.

My grandfather said that it was only because he was an orphan that he'd needed a scholarship to go to Eton because, of course, the Greys were a very prestigious family. He said it was because he'd been able to go to Eton that he'd gotten into Cambridge, also on scholarship, and from there gone on to medical school.

"A good school opens doors," he told me. "Keep your grades up. With an education, you can be whatever you want to be. Don't you forget that!"

This pronouncement, unfortunately, hadn't quite worked out for my grandfather because World War II had come along. He'd been drafted into the Royal Navy just before graduation and been made to give up doctoring, instead becoming a secret agent and war hero, then an immigrant to the United States, and a chef somewhere in between—I wasn't sure when.

Lunch at the French school, in which my grandfather had placed so much faith, left something to be desired. It consisted of Chef Boyardee raviolis and sauce from a can; tepid, anemic peas; Stouffer's food-service Salisbury steak, scalding on the outside and still a little frozen on the inside; mashed potatoes or corn dogs; soggy french fries, whose saving grace were several packets of ketchup. If he had been expecting me to be introduced to the miracles of coquilles Saint Jacques and foie gras, sole meunière and charlotte russe, he must have been marvelously disappointed.

That night, when the boat couple came over, my grandfather served bouillabaisse, a dish he usually reserved for friends. I set the table under his careful supervision: Marilyn's Imari china, salad and dessert forks, soup spoons and teaspoons, cloth napkins, red tapers, water and wine glasses. My grandfather sliced the warmed baguette. He poured cold white wine in four glasses—the wine he'd bought at Bristol Farms, not the bottle the couple had brought, which he'd dismissed with a shake of his head once he was in the kitchen. He carefully arranged fish, clams, shrimp, and mussels in each bowl and poured the delicate orange broth over them.

"Oh, it smells wonderful," the woman said from the table. I didn't like the way she lingered on the *n* in "wonderful." When my grandfather served her, she placed a red-nailed hand on his arm and said, "It's so kind of you to have us."

"It does smell good," Marilyn said when she sat down.

During dinner, my grandfather told his war stories, about serving on the *Kelly* with Lord Louis Mountbatten and going to India, working as a commando in World War II, being tapped for the Special Operations Executive.

"What did you do with secret operations, Sir Richard?" the man wanted to know.

"Oh, sabotage mostly. Lots of plastic explosives—Aunt Jemima, we used to call it. You'd mix it up like pancake batter, then stick it under bridges and what not. You could even eat it, if you had to."

He casually smeared an inch of butter onto his bread. My grandfather said he ate that way—the enormous quantities of butter, as well as ice cream, Camembert cheese, red meat, chocolate—because he'd almost starved to death in a concentration camp.

"Tell them about the piano wire," I volunteered. This was my favorite part.

"Piano wire?" the man asked.

"I'd string wire across the roads, just at neck height." He bit into the bread and chewed, butter still glistening on his lip, then continued. "The Huns'd come down the road on their motorbikes and slice their heads clean off."

The woman swallowed her soup and blinked a little.

"Tell them about Dunkirk," I said.

"I was at Dunkirk," my grandfather said, chewing his bread. "Back when I was still in the navy, before I was recruited."

"Oh, how interesting," the woman said. You could tell she didn't know what Dunkirk was.

"Tell them about where you hid!" I insisted.

My grandfather glared at me. "Perhaps another time," he said, his accent becoming just a hair snootier.

I hadn't realized that story was supposed to be a secret. He told it to me all the time. It was my second-favorite story—after the decapitations—wherein he'd hidden from the Germans in a latrine during the rout of the English at Dunkirk. Nobody had wanted to sit by him in the tiny rescue boat. I didn't ask him to tell the part about the concentration camp—even I knew not to do that—but he brought it up later himself, in answer to some question.

"I was at Buchenwald. German holiday camp, you know." My grandfather watched their faces when he said it. They looked impressed.

"My God," the man said. "What was that like?"

"Well, let's just say it wasn't a bloody picture show."

I knew this story was true because sometimes my grandfather screamed in his sleep, waking us all with his cries. In the morning, he'd reassure me: "Don't worry, love. I was just dreaming about the camps again."

But the couple looked puzzled, as if they did not understand the way you avoided speaking about something painful.

Marilyn stayed quiet during this conversation, eating her soup delicately, answering only when the woman asked, "And what do you do, Marilyn?"

"I help out with Richard's business, mostly."

"And you're a teacher!" I added.

"Yes," she said, smiling down at me. "I teach night school at Harbor College."

The way she said it made it sound like it wasn't something to be proud of, but I was proud of it. She got all sorts of presents from her students from all over the world—the necklace from Africa, the Japanese doll that sat on my highest shelf, brightly colored Peruvian cloth.

During dessert—the lovely fruit tarts and Marilyn's chicory coffee, liqueurs from my grandfather's collection of bottles on a small table by the door—we opened the dining room curtains for the skunk-and-raccoon show. One of my evening chores was to fill the kibble and water bowls every night. We'd started feeding the skunks for a science-fair project—a two-hour, unedited video of skunks and raccoons eating Purina Cat Chow—and had never stopped. We watched them every night through the slightly wavy glass windows. But tonight a possum sat in the chow bowl, ruining the show.

"You feed what? Oh," the woman said, in answer to my grandfather's explanation, peering out the window and fingering the neckline of her low-cut top.

The man asked, "Why is it you feed them, now? I'm not sure I understand. Why do you want to attract them?"

I took my fruit tart and snuck off to my room with Ugly, who was hopeful about sharing my dessert with me. If these people couldn't understand why you'd want to feed skunks and raccoons, I really couldn't be bothered with them.

That night, Marilyn and my grandfather fought after she tucked me in. I could hear their raised voices through my closed door. No sound made me feel lonelier; I hated it when they fought. I curled up beneath my blanket and looked at my night-light. My grandmother's friend Dee had mailed it to me shortly after Spence's death because she knew I was afraid of the dark. It was a ceramic farmhouse with white plaster walls and a thatched roof, red shutters, and a green tree that shaded it. It reminded me of the house Dee, Spence, and I had lived in together in the mountains. The house and tree were poked through with small holes to let the light escape. My tears refracted the light, making visible the beams shooting out of the tree and house, blurring my vision with light.

Sometimes on those lonely nights, I imagined what it would be like if I still lived with Dee and Spence in the mountains. I remembered little bits and pieces of our life together—fishing and making cookies for Santa and sledding in the snow. Sometimes I tried to imagine what it would be like if I still lived with Michele, but that was more difficult to do because I knew so little about her life. All I had of hers was a Bible she'd had as a child. It had a black, fake leather cover that zipped all around and pages with red edges. It was the King James version, filled with *thous* and *thees* and endless lists of names. But it had color illustrations of Moses in the rushes and Mary Magdalene weeping, and on the inside cover, my mother had written her name, Michele Ann Grey, in the big loops of someone still learning cursive. Sometimes I traced my finger along her name or along the ridges of the book's black binding. Sometimes I took the Bible to bed with me and tucked it beneath my pillow, my hand resting softly on its cover.

We didn't buy the couple's boat.

3

TWENTY FEET AWAY, ON THE COVE'S ROCKY BEACH, COLD waves rolled onto shore with a roar, then receded with the grumble of round stones clunking together in the foam's pull. Farther out in the cove, the Pacific broke against the bottom of the cliffs, exploding into white spray. But the water in the tide pools by my feet was glassy smooth, still. I squatted beside one while Marilyn kept walking, the wind whipping her hair this way and that. It was a big pool—two yards long—its own world of color and gentle movement: a drab fish darting through tufts of rockweed and sea lettuce, a purple urchin adjusting its spines contentedly. Tiny green anemones carpeted the middle of the pool, their tentacles almost imperceptibly swaying.

I stroked a chiton at the pool's edge, running my nail along the segmented chinks of its thick armor. The chiton looked prehistoric, a bit like a lobster's tail without the lobster, or like an overgrown, flat roly-poly. On the cliffs and hills behind me were hundreds of its fossilized relatives, frozen in similar rocks in similar positions as the live one beside me, *their* tide pools long vanished.

We lived in Rolling Hills Estates, one of the communities on the Palos Verdes Peninsula, which jutted south and west of Los Angeles, forming the southern border of Santa Monica Bay. Our side of the peninsula was built up with houses and malls, but the southwest side, overlooking the ocean, still had wide-open spaces, places where mustard and wild fennel grew tall. This was especially true along Portuguese Bend, where the edge of the peninsula was slowly slipping back into the ocean, taking with it chunks of land and abandoned houses. This was where we were now, at Abalone Cove, where the sea flowed in between Inspiration and Portuguese points.

Millions of years ago, the peninsula had been covered by the ocean; then, as it was uplifted out of the sea, it became an island, separate from Southern California. I knew a little about these things because of the books Marilyn read to me at night and the rock-hound hikes she took me on with the parks and rec department. All over the peninsula, it was easy to find geodes lying on the ground, rocks bearing the fossils of plants and fish. Even the stone benches at the Lutheran church Marilyn and my grandfather had sent me to briefly when I was four had fish swimming across their faces. No one else at the church seemed to notice them but me. Neither Marilyn nor my grandfather attended church themselves; she was a former hippie who objected to organized religion, and he was a bitter, lapsed Catholic. Instead, they would drop me off for Sunday school, and when it was over, I'd wait for them on those benches, one hand clutching a coloring page of Jesus and the other fingering the articulations of vertebrae, the curves of ribs and eye sockets, the miracles of fish and time.

The water in the tide pool was warm from the afternoon sun. A solitary anemone looked like a green flower penned by Dr. Seuss. I leaned over and ran my finger along its crown of tentacles, as Marilyn had shown me how to do when I was little. I felt the gentle tug of the tentacles' sting, then watched as they collapsed into its mouth. Satisfied that the trick still worked, I dried my hand on my shorts and walked in the same direction Marilyn had, stepping carefully between pools, trying not to crush barnacles and exposed anemones. As I walked, I gathered tiny clam and turban shells, spent limpets, pieces of mammal bone, bits of frosted, smoothed glass, and interesting shards of plastic. The waves roared in my ears. Once in a while I came across a fragment of an abalone shell, but never a whole one. Marilyn had a whole one she used as an ashtray. When it was clean, its inside looked as if it has been painted with quicksilver and sapphire. Archaeologists had found piles of abalone shells near Indian sites, but I'd never seen one at the beach. Marilyn said they were rare now.

It was always Marilyn who took me on adventures: trips along the Camino Real to see the California missions, weekends in Berkeley and Marin County to visit her old hippie friends, and closer places like the La Brea Tar Pits in downtown LA and the Getty Museum in Malibu. My grandfather never came with us, preferring to stay home. I'm not sure I would have wanted him to come anyway.

But some of my favorite adventures were only ten minutes from home, here at Abalone Cove or down at Cabrillo Beach in San Pedro, where they also had a marine museum. We never went swimming, because Marilyn didn't like how she looked in a suit, but that was all right. I could stay at the beach for hours looking at animals and collecting bits of flotsam. After the boat couple's visit, my grandfather had started looking for boats in earnest, visiting marinas and looking in shipyards, reading the classifieds and circling prospects. One of the reasons he said he wanted a boat was because he loved the ocean, but the part of the sea I liked was here, at the shore, where you didn't need a boat and there was so much to look at.

And when I got bored of looking, I'd find a patch of warm sand between the rocks to sit on and stare at the shining water until I could see the light like a stain when I closed my eyes. I'd daydream stories from the books Marilyn read to me at night, imagine the ships of Spanish explorers and Portuguese whalers anchored in the cove, Indians collecting fish and mussels in their reed baskets, smugglers landing at night, the tide pools in front of me stocked with abalone. The land behind me had once been farmed by Japanese Americans before they were taken away to internment camps. Sometime before that, it had been covered with Californio ranches and adobes, like in *Zorro*, and before that, it had been the home of Indians. There were no historical markers or signs, but everywhere you walked on the peninsula, you were walking in someone else's footprints. You'd never know it, though, without a Marilyn or a library book to tell you.

My other favorite trips with Marilyn were to the library. Together we'd browse for books by the d'Aulaires, *Norse Myths* or *Abraham Lincoln*, books of California history, illustrated stories about the Underground Railroad. Sometime in August, we'd check out costume books and begin the long planning process for Halloween. Every year, Marilyn and her friend Josette made me a Halloween costume: hand-sewn, elaborate affairs like Pallas Athena, Cleopatra, and Joan of Arc, characters I loved from books.

Marilyn didn't read as much as my grandfather, but she still checked out books and stayed up until one or two in the morning to read them—books of philosophy I couldn't understand, history that bored me, or, worse, books about how to make yourself a better or thinner person.

Marilyn's taste in books leaned toward the practical and sensible, but when I went to the bookstore with my grandfather, I picked whatever caught my imagination. Every few weeks, he and I went to B. Dalton at Peninsula Center. First we went for dinner at the Jolly Roger, where we wore pirate hats and dueled with plastic garnish swords, drank Shirley Temples, and finished with ice cream sundaes. At the bookstore, I wandered the aisles freely while my grandfather perused the latest in biography and spy fiction. He bought us each one book, and I could pick any book I wanted; he barely glanced at the covers before he paid. Sometimes my choices didn't work out so well, titles like *100 Coupons for Romance* or *The Journals of Lewis and Clark*, but fiction never disappointed. I had dozens of Nancy Drews; illustrated versions of classics like *Pride and Prejudice, Robinson Crusoe,* and *Heidi*; books on tape of Sherlock Holmes, James Herriot, and T. S. Eliot's *Murder in the Cathedral*, which I didn't understand but listened to over and over again because I liked the way the words sounded—the elegant cadences of the English actors, the chant of the monks, the mournful choruses of women.

In the evenings, Marilyn would read me the books we got at the bookstore or the library, long after I knew how to read myself. These, too, were my favorite adventures with her. We'd lie together in my twin bed, propped up next to each other against my pillows, her arm cool against mine, a book laid open on her lap. Lamplight surrounded us in a circle. Marilyn's whispery alto incanted the author's words, and suddenly, within the confines of the light, another world was conjured, and for an hour, we could live in it: the lush garden behind a wall, the Palace of Knossos, Jo March's attic, the sinister House of Shaws. For an hour, we were together— hearing the same words, seeing the same landscape, caring about the same people—as close as an adult and a child can be.

Sometimes after we read books about the Underground Railroad or slavery, I made her tell me stories from Mississippi, when she was a volunteer during the 1964 Freedom Summer. Marilyn wasn't like my grandfather; it took a lot of effort to get her to talk about herself, asking her question after question to get to the best parts: About the time in Jackson, Mississippi, when she was arrested and spent the night in a crowded jail cell. About the countryside—the flat cotton fields with their spiky stalks and white tufts, the red earth beneath the big sky. About the black sharecropper's family with whom she stayed while registering people to vote, and how they had had to douse the lights and huddle on the ground while white men took potshots at the house.

"Weren't you scared?" I wondered.

"Well, yeah. But I could go home at the end of the summer. They had to stay."

My grandfather's stories were the ones I told to classmates or adults I wanted to impress, but it was Marilyn I wanted most to be like, whose stories made me glow with a warm light.

Our days at the tide pools always ended too early for my taste. The cliffs' cool shadows overtook the south-facing cove, or the tide rolled in, and Marilyn called to me to pack up, worried we'd be late getting home. We climbed the steep, dusty hill back to the parking lot, passing sagebrush, lemon berry, and mustard plants taller than me. The sound of the crashing breakers got softer and softer as we got higher, their susurrations pierced by the seagulls' shrill cries. We always stopped at the top of the cliffs and looked back at the ocean spread out before us, sometimes sapphire blue and sometimes steel gray, its vast surface a mirror of the sky, impossible to see through.

4

Y OU KNOW," MY GRANDFATHER BEGAN, PUSHING AWAY FROM the dining room table. He took off his glasses and cleaned them with the hem of his dressing gown, exposing his hairy belly, alabaster legs and, to my alternate horror and detached interest, the points in between—he'd chosen not to wear underwear that night, which wasn't all that uncommon. "Robert Donat and I were cousins."

We'd just finished watching *The Ghost Goes West,* one of my favorite movies, starring the English actor Robert Donat, who is better known for his roles in Alfred Hitchcock's *The 39 Steps* and *Goodbye, Mr. Chips.* We had all of his movies on video. I didn't especially like the serious movies, though; I liked ghosts, bonnie Scotsmen, castles, and the occasional slapstick gag.

The table in front of us was covered in a pile of loose quarters and edged in rows of stacks of ten quarters each. The silver stacks reminded me of Roman soldiers, the endless lines of them from old movies my grandfather and I watched together, like *Spartacus* and *Cleopatra.*

My grandfather had bought a VCR a few years before, almost as soon as they'd come out, and had already amassed a considerable collection of tapes. In the living room, among the thirty shelves of books that lined the wall, a good three were devoted to tapes from the Magnetic Video Corporation or Disney. And as if those hadn't been enough, we'd trek to the neighborhood video store every couple of weeks to rent more. Together, my grandfather and I had watched Errol Flynn swashbuckle his way to Maid Marian, Maurice Chevalier croon about little girls, and Jeanette MacDonald warble her undying love to Nelson Eddy. History lessons at our house consisted of watching Laurence Olivier in *That Hamilton Woman* and Paul Scofield in *A Man for All Seasons,* supplemented by the children's books Marilyn read to me. We watched Bogart stride his way through the *Maltese Falcon,* float his way through the *African Queen,* and go off his rocker in *The Treasure of the Sierra Madre.* We watched Jimmy Stewart hang out with a rabbit, sass an angel, and faint during a filibuster.

On the nights when we watched old movies together, like that night of watching *The Ghost Goes West,* my grandfather told me about his own days in the film business.

"You know, I met Bogart once," he'd start the story, the name of the actor changing with whatever film we'd just seen. "Nice man. Very polite. Shy. He was quite a sailor. That was when I lived in that apartment building with...oh, what's her name?"

Her name might have been Claire Bloom or Vivien Leigh or Olivia de Havilland or any number of movie stars from the thirties, forties, and fifties, because my grandfather claimed to have known them all, even if he couldn't always keep them straight. He said he'd worked with Hitchcock in England just after the war. After he'd moved to America, he'd written scripts for *Perry Mason* and *The Twilight Zone.* He'd met Laurence Olivier and Vivien Leigh, was friends with Ava Gardner, and had lived in the same building as the woman who might have been Claire Bloom, Vivien Leigh, or Olivia de Havilland. He claimed to have known John Wayne well enough to call him "Duke." Living in LA, where movie stars lived across town and film shoots were a common sight, my grandfather's stories didn't seem like such a stretch. They were filled with details that made them seem real—the Duke's sailboat, Olivier's obsession with false noses, Vivien Leigh's instability, his cousin Robert Donat's asthma. Several of our bookshelves were filled with Hollywood biographies and autobiographies of stars my friends never recognized; their covers were always black-and-white portraits from the forties or fifties, faces I knew well. I never read them but I did pull them down to look at the pictures, always surprised to see Errol Flynn in street clothes or Vivien Leigh looking old.

The pile of quarters on the table settled a little. My grandfather pulled the flaps of his robe back over himself and cinched its belt.

"People used to mistake Bob and me for one another. They'd stop me in the street to congratulate me, buy me a pint in the pub—a pub's like a bar. Once I was going up the back steps of his flat to visit him, and he nearly knocked me over on his way down. He was running away from bill collectors or something." My grandfather took a sip of tea from the big mug I'd given him—English breakfast, with two tea bags and a splash of milk.

"He died of asthma, poor thing. His last role was as a Chinaman. 'We shall not see each other again, I think.' Those were his last words on film. He keeled over the next day. Imagine. *The Inn of the Sixth Happiness*—that was the name of the film. Your mother had asthma, you know."

I leaned closer for more of the story, for more about my mother, but it was finished. It was one I'd heard before, anyway. I was proud that I had a movie-actor relative, although none of my friends at Le Lycée had ever heard of him, and try as I might, I couldn't really see any resemblance to my grandfather in Robert Donat's handsome face.

We went back to counting quarters and stacking them. Then we placed them into the crisp paper wrappers from the bank, and then placed those into canvas sacks bearing seals from the Federal Reserve. When we were done, my fingers were greasy and smelled of metal.

In the middle of the night, long after Marilyn had come home and gone to bed, the phone rang. Someone had broken into our video store. Soon I found myself in the back seat of my grandfather's Mercedes, still in my pajamas and wrapped carefully in the afghan from the couch. We raced down the empty 405 toward the airport. Marilyn drove while my grandfather sighed loudly every few miles. Every once in a while when we flashed beneath a streetlight, I'd catch her looking at me in the rearview mirror.

"How much do you suppose they got?" my grandfather asked, finally.

"I told you, Richard, I don't know. Whatever cash we started with this morning, plus however much we took in during the day." She was mad, annoyed that we'd all had to tramp out in the middle of the night, annoyed at having to repeat herself. Our store was broken into at least once or twice a year.

"They broke the lock?"

"Yes, I told you that."

My grandfather often repeated facts he didn't like, as if repeating them might make them not true. We exited the freeway at the airport and drove east on Century Boulevard toward Inglewood and Watts.

"Try to go to sleep, sweetheart," Marilyn said gently, looking at me in the mirror. "We're almost there."

"It's okay," I muttered, my cheek resting against the cold window.

The parking lot was empty except for the alarm-company car; the police had already left. After my grandfather and Marilyn spoke to the driver, he left too, and they went inside. I sat in the locked car alone and wrapped the blanket more tightly around myself. The parking lot made me nervous at night, although I didn't mind it when I waited there during the day. Our store was on a corner lot, and so there were two driveways to keep an eye on, as well as the dark space behind the dumpster.

Moths banged into the floodlights that illuminated bits and pieces of the store's exterior: beige stucco and boarded-over windows, the No Loitering sign, fragments of red signs that read "Adult," "Vid," "ovelties," "XXX." The floodlights created as much shadow as they did light, and I kept waiting for someone to walk out of the dark. During the day, men always cut through the parking lot rather than walking around the corner. Sometimes they slowed down by the store's entrance, as if they might catch sight of what was being sold inside, but all they could see was a paneled wall and a notice about needing to be older than eighteen to enter. I knew because I, too, had often tried to see in, never having been allowed inside myself.

I'd known about the store for a long time, but I'd only understood what "adult videos" really meant for a few months. I'd been riding home from a sleepover with my best friend, Jill, and her dad, Larry. I loved Larry and thought he was God's gift to little girls, especially Jill and me. Larry worked in the Garment District downtown and always brought us back T-shirt and dress samples and autographed pictures of famous people, like the Incredible Hulk and Magnum, P.I. He cooked hamburgers on a barbeque grill and could fix his own car—two things my grandfather could not do. He and his wife, Kathy, snapped at each other all the time, but they also slept in the same bed and took vacations together—things Marilyn and my grandfather did not do.

Larry's car was dark except for the rhythmic flashing of the streetlights overhead. Jill and I stretched our legs straight out in front of us and dangled our feet off the red plush bench. The seat belts held us snug against the seat back, and we reached our hands behind us to feel in between the cushions for loose change, crumbs, Barbie heads, spoons; you never knew what would be back there. As we drove home, I watched the back of Larry's head—his brown and gray hair, his little bald spot above the burgundy seat.

Perhaps in the back of my mind, I knew I wasn't really supposed to tell anyone, but I didn't know what a real secret was yet. So when Larry said, "Marilyn and Richard probably get you all sorts of free movies from their video store, huh?" I answered, "No, they have an *adult* video store."

I was pretty proud that my parents owned an "adult video store." I knew an adult video store meant I couldn't see any of the movies because I was too young, but what I didn't understand was the difference between movies that I was too little to watch, like *Psycho* or *Rambo,* and the movies my grandfather sold in his store. I thought "adult movies" meant films that were more advanced and sophisticated than the G-rated movies Jill and I were allowed to see. Yes, it was a secret in our family, but I thought that it was a secret just because we were modest and didn't want to boast. I was proud of the fact my parents only had adult movies in their store the way I might be proud telling someone, "My parents only have science books and Shakespeare plays in *their* library."

I remember how Larry looked up in his mirror when I told him about our store, how even though it was dark and he wore glasses, I still saw his eyes widen.

"They own a what?"

"An adult video store." I was pretty happy to have impressed him with my parents' occupation.

"An *adult* video store?" he repeated, this time with a wide grin on his face. That grin made me nervous.

"Yes," I answered, but I was starting to look for a place to hide with the spoons and Barbie heads.

"What's an adult video store?" Jill piped up.

"Nothing," Larry said. "It's a store with videos only adults can rent."

"Like *Rambo*," I explained to Jill.

"Exactly," Larry echoed, and I let out a deep breath, relieved to see that he understood after all.

Larry came into our house when he dropped me off. As Jill and I stooped to pet Ugly, I heard him say to my grandfather, "So, Richard, I hear you have an *adult* video store."

I didn't like the way Larry pronounced "adult." It was the same tone of voice some kids used to make fun of other kids, and it was strange to hear it coming from a grown-up. There was a pause in the conversation, and I looked up from the dog to see my grandfather staring straight at me.

"I have no idea what you mean," my grandfather said. He used his best snobby voice, the one that made his English accent more pronounced. "Where did you ever hear that?"

"Kelly told me."

I could almost hear Larry wink when he said it. I kept staring at the oozy sore just above Ugly's tail. I could feel my grandfather's eyes boring into the back of my head. After Larry and Jill left, my grandfather sat me down at the dining room table.

"Don't you *ever* tell *anyone* what business I'm in *ever* again," he began in a low growl.

"Why?" I asked.

"Because no one will like you if they know what business we're in. Don't tell your friends because they'll stop being your friends. Don't tell your teachers because they'll give you bad grades. Don't tell anyone, or they'll hate you." The pitch and volume of his voice had risen slowly so that by the end he was shouting.

And even though I said "okay" in my tiniest voice, I still didn't understand. Why wouldn't adults like movies made for them?

I believed my grandfather, and I didn't tell anyone about our business again. I wouldn't until after I graduated college. But he had been wrong about Jill; she was still my friend, and so was Larry.

Headlights filled the Mercedes, and I was blinded for a moment. It was just a locksmith, his red truck covered in hand-painted letters: 24-Hour Service, *Fast*, Radio-Dispatched. I watched him get out of his truck, hitch up his pants, then go inside with a clipboard. He came back out and grabbed a box of tools.

I'd never gone inside the store, but by now I had a fairly good idea of what it looked like, just as I now knew the difference between *Rambo* and the movies my grandfather sold (those had naked people *doing IT!*). The store's front room was stuffed ceiling to floor with shelves of video boxes, like our neighborhood video store, only the boxes were more brightly colored and covered in naked bodies. I knew this because every six weeks Marilyn would make the two-hour trip to the San Fernando Valley to buy new merchandise. She'd return late in the afternoon with huge cardboard boxes packed with rainbow-hued video boxes I was not allowed to see. In the afternoons, when I was away at school, or late at night, when she thought I was asleep, she'd shrink-wrap and label the videos on our dining room table—hundreds at a time— the piles of boxes on the table taller than she was.

Those boxes fascinated me, although I never got close enough to examine them. The realm of sex—that thing adults were so secretive about—was merely a rumor in Le Lyçée's third grade; "sexy" was a taunt no one understood. But there on the table were artifacts from that world. I'd steal distant glimpses of them when I could: hot pink or canary yellow or electric teal backgrounds with cutouts of shiny, naked bodies, barely discernable in the moments from when Marilyn pulled the first video out of the cardboard box to when she looked over her shoulder and caught me peering around the corner of the hall.

"Kelly," she'd hiss. "For God's sake, go to your room."

Back in the parking lot, a man walked out of the dark and right toward the car. His hoodie was tight around his head, and his face was downturned, his hands in his pocket. I thumbed the lock on the door. He looked up at the noise and seemed startled, as if he hadn't expected a car to be there. He walked around; he was just cutting through on his way to somewhere else. I put my hand back under the blanket.

The carpet in our store was olive green, which I knew because my grandfather had used the remnants of our house's wall-to-wall carpet. The clerk's counter, where the cassettes and money were kept, was surrounded by bulletproof glass. My grandfather had had the glass cage installed after a female clerk had been raped at gunpoint and beaten. I knew that this had happened because she'd stayed in our home for a week or two to recover. As she lay on our couch, my grandfather had played videos of the Bolshoi Ballet for her, *Swan Lake* and the *Nutcracker*. When she started crying, he told me she had a migraine, and for a long time, I had "rape" and "migraine" swirled together in my head, so that the two necessarily went together: rape was something very bad men did; rape hurt a woman's head.

In my imagination, the back of the store was separated from the front by a tacky, red-bead curtain. I had no basis for imagining the red-bead curtain, except that I'd watched *Foul Play* with Goldie Hawn and Chevy Chase, and there was a bead curtain in the massage parlor Dudley Moore frequented. Behind the curtain were the arcades—viewing booths partitioned by pressboard walls, each containing a TV and a coin acceptor—where men sat watching movies, popping in quarters for five-minute segments of film. I didn't understand what the men did in there, or why they'd watch a movie in our store instead of their own home. The arcade was what made the most money, but the City of Inglewood kept trying to shut it down. Every once in a while, an official notice would arrive from the city about sanitation or code violations. My grandfather would bellow a stream of curse words, contractors or lawyers would be called, and after a while, things would settle down again.

———————————

By the time the locksmith had finished his work, I'd fallen asleep. I woke briefly when my grandfather opened the door and set a bag of quarters behind the driver's seat. I heard the familiar slink and clunk of thousands of loose coins. The burglars must not have been able to break into the arcades, and Marilyn had emptied them. The car rumbled to a start.

The next thing I knew, I was being carried by my grandfather back into the house.

"You're getting too big to carry, Little Toad," I heard him murmur in the dark, words warm with his fruity breath; I felt the gentle prick of his whiskers against my cheek.

In the morning, we were late for school.

5

OUR FAMILY WAS THE KIND THAT TOOK IN STRAYS: DOGS, cats, people—it didn't matter. My grandfather had acquired Ugly and Klutz that way. We'd had another stray, a cat named Comet, until he died of feline leukemia. We kept his ashes in a cardboard box, along with the ashes of Marilyn's old dog, Kim, in the linen closet at the end of the hall. My mother's ashes were in there too, her cardboard box significantly bigger than the cat's and wrapped in water-stained, yellowed paper, tied with a ribbon. For a while, they'd stored her in the garage, perched on a pile of cardboard boxes in a dark corner. I'd spotted the beribboned box one day when I was little and insisted it was a forgotten birthday present for me, and so they'd had to explain what it was. After that, they'd brought the box inside. Now I sometimes peeked in the closet to say hi; I'd open the mirrored doors and breathe the smell of clean sheets and towels, the nutmeg-and-orange-peel sachet I'd made in preschool. "Hi, dog! Hi, cat! Hi, Mom," I'd whisper softly, then close the door again. I had a kind of faith that she—or some part of her—was in that stained box. Some part that could still hear me. I didn't even have a picture of her.

That summer, we acquired a husky-shepherd mix named Lisa when she started wandering away from her house down the street. She'd come to our backyard and sniff around, wagging her tail. Once

I'd finished playing with her beneath our giant coral tree, we'd call the number on her tag, and the sandy-haired doctor who owned her would come and take her away again, apologizing profusely.

My grandfather started letting Lisa in the house and feeding her. He bought her her own large-size Milk Bones, much bigger than Ugly's. She came over more frequently, stayed longer and longer.

"Richard," Marilyn would say, her arms crossed and eyes narrowed, "you shouldn't do that. She'll keep coming back."

"So what if she keeps coming back?"

"I don't want another dog."

"It's not a question of what you want. She's decided she wants us."

"But she isn't ours!"

One afternoon, the doctor showed up carrying her leash and a manila folder of vet records. "Here," he said. "Since she likes it over here so much, you can keep her."

The metallic clunk of the leash on the table made my heart skip a beat. I lingered in the dining room, staring hopefully at the lead. *Please, please, please let us keep her,* I thought. Ugly was old, blind, and diabetic. Every morning and every evening my grandfather filled a syringe with 10 units of fast-acting insulin and 10 units of slow from their refrigerated vials, then plunged the needle into his own leg; then he'd use the same needle to give a dose of insulin to the dog. Ugly generally lay in the kitchen like a lump in her dog bed. She wasn't even good for petting because her greasy hair made my hands smell. Lisa, however, played with a tennis ball and ran around barking with it still in her mouth while I chased her. Her coat was clean, a pretty shade of tan, and her brown eyes clear. I looked up at my grandfather, where he sat in his chair after offering the doctor a drink.

"We'd be glad to keep her," he said, as if he were doing the doctor a favor. Marilyn, who stood by the kitchen door in her red apron, did not look so certain but said nothing.

"Well, okay," the doctor said slowly, as if he hadn't counted on my grandfather saying yes. "Well, here's her leash. Her shots and everything are all up to date. So is her license." He knelt down by Lisa and gave her a hug. Her tail swooshed along the carpet.

As the doctor started walking toward the door without his dog or leash or manila folder, my grandfather gently holding his elbow, he said, "It's funny. I wonder why she kept coming over here. It's not like you were feeding her or anything, were you?"

"Oh, no, of course not, chum. It's just that Kelly plays with her so, you know, with you being gone all day…" My grandfather moved his hand from the doctor's elbow to his back and gave it a pat. I felt bad for the doctor, who'd always been kind and now seemed very sad. Lisa moved toward the door to follow her master, but I held her back by the collar.

"Daddy, you lied," I said when my grandfather came back from walking the doctor to the curb.

"I didn't lie. What are you going on about?"

"You did too feed Lisa!"

"No, I didn't."

"You did. I saw you."

My grandfather was suddenly angry, his hand catching hold of my shoulder, his thumb pushing into the space behind my collarbone. "Don't you ever accuse me of lying again, or I'll take her away." He let go.

Marilyn called from the kitchen door, "Kelly, it's time to take care of the skunks, okay?"

"Lisa," I called, but Marilyn shook her head. "No, leave her here." I supposed she didn't want Lisa to eat the skunk food. I walked barefoot to the back porch, carrying the ten-pound bag of cat chow. Old kibble was scattered around the empty dog bowl; the cement was greasy from months' worth of dropped food. The curtains were drawn across the windows of our dining room, but Marilyn and Richard's raised voices bled through the thin plate glass. They were arguing over the dog. Marilyn didn't want to keep her; my grandfather called her a selfish cow. I felt sorry for Lisa, sitting there with them while they talked about her.

Bloated wads of orange matter floated in the metal water bowl from where the raccoons had dropped their food. I filled the plastic dog bowl, then took the water bowl to the spigot to rinse and fill. I stepped carefully over a piece of pale, soft scat—from skunks, possums, or raccoons, I didn't know.

As I filled the steel bowl, Roy came outside and sat on the back stair with a grunt; he was our other stray. He was an Englishman my grandfather's age, his friend from the harbor who'd been coming over for dinner off and on for years. He'd been sleeping on our couch for the past week or so. I didn't know why. People often slept on our couch, although they were usually store clerks or Marilyn's sister, sheltering from bad marriages or on extended visits between jobs, or sometimes Marilyn's nieces and nephews, running away from home.

"Understand you've got yourself a new dog now. Exciting, innit?" He smiled, and the sun-spotted skin of his face crinkled beneath his Greek fisherman's cap.

"Yes," I said. "They're fighting now, though."

"Ah. Won't last much longer, I think." He clasped his hands together, indicating he'd be waiting outside for it to stop too.

Roy was right, and after I put the water bowl back on the porch, the shouting stopped. Lisa could stay.

That night after dinner, we dimmed the lights in the dining room, turned on the porch light, then slowly opened the curtains.

A large skunk sat next to the orange bowl, crunching kibbles with white teeth, his little black paw draped on the edge of the bowl, his tiny claws curled against the side. Lisa tried to charge the window, but I reached up and held her by the collar. After a while, she settled down and watched them too, whining every once in a while and wagging her tail. Soon another skunk came, and after a little squeaking fight, they both settled down to eat. I wondered if there'd be babies soon.

We all watched together for a while, until Roy and my grandfather lumbered off to read and Marilyn went to her desk to work on filing rental contracts for the store. After I washed the dishes, I lay down on the floor with my head resting on Lisa's side. With the adults gone, it was quiet enough to hear the crunch, crunch of the skunks' teeth through the window, the rustle of their snouts in the kibble. Soon a raccoon lumbered onto the patio and carefully picked up a kibble in his elegant paw, considered it for a moment, then swished it around the water bowl before he popped it into his mouth and thoughtfully chewed. I loved the raccoons for their sleek faces and the soft bushiness of their tails that I wished I could touch. Instead, I ran my hands over Lisa's neck and head, the soft velvet of her ears, the downy fluff of her undercoat.

"You're going to live with us now," I explained, sticking my fingers up in the thick fur beneath her collar where I could feel her pulse. "No more running away or moving around, okay? This is a good home."

She wagged her tail and stared out the window.

———————————

Most of my grandfather's friends were strays—single men in their fifties or sixties who had no family or children in the picture, which isn't necessarily the same as not having a family or children. They were poorer than my grandfather, or lonelier, or less educated. Almost all of them owed him for something: a job, a loan, a place to stay, a paid medical bill. They'd come over to our house to eat dinner or live a while or maybe just to have a drink from my grandfather's well-stocked bar. Some of them worked for him. The people who took jobs at our porn store usually didn't have much going on in the way of family or friends. There was Bobby, a gigantic African American man, and his wife, Suki, a tiny Japanese woman who always smiled. When I was very little, they babysat me in their apartment sometimes, letting me watch video after video on a VCR my grandfather brought over for the occasion. But one day something broke inside Bobby, and he killed Suki, then turned the gun on himself, and my grandfather couldn't explain why. There was pale, six-foot-tall Virginia, with her long, dyed, black-as-death hair, who chain-smoked Virginia Slims without irony. There was Glen, who brought me crisp, glassine envelopes filled with colorful stamps from around the world.

Some were my grandfather's acquaintances from the harbor, like Roy. My grandfather still had friends from the harbor from the last time he'd owned a boat, the *Sirocco*, whose picture hung in our dining room. There had been a steady stream of harbor folk for the past year since he had started looking at boats again, but Roy was my favorite. He'd spent most of his life working at sea. While he stayed with us, he was helping Marilyn teach me to ride a bike, gripping the back end with a gnarled hand to keep me upright and running along while I pedaled. He told good stories and spoke French with an English accent, something I'd never heard before. When he'd come to stay, he'd brought me a beat-up copy of *Le Figaro* he'd saved from his last trip to France, sometime circa 1980. I didn't mind speaking French with him, because with him, speaking

French was like sharing a joke, something you did for a lark when you were bored. Sometimes when people slept on our couch, I couldn't wait for them to leave—Marilyn's teenaged nieces and nephews, with their stinky feet and ignorance of historical events and Nancy Drew, bothered me especially—but I would have been happy if Roy had stayed forever.

But Roy did leave, finding an open berth on a boat going south. He died in Central America the next year or the year after that, on a trip to hunt for sunken treasure. We didn't hear about it until long after it happened. Some harbor folk said he'd found the treasure and was killed for it; others said he was shot by the DEA while running drugs.

To hear my grandfather tell it, Marilyn had been a stray too, and he the knight in shining armor who'd rescued her. He'd met her in the early 1970s at a place he called the "Happy House," a rundown Victorian near Hollywood inhabited by a loose commune of hippies, druggies, and assorted hangers-on. The house's second floor was an impromptu factory where the hippies earned extra cash by making Pyrex smoking pipes they called "dream crystal." Marilyn was trying to hold on to a postal job she wasn't very good at; she was the only person in the house who didn't make pipes. She was poor and kind of lost, so much younger than my grandfather—a waif with messy, brown hair and big eyes, someone without a home. My grandfather came to the Happy House to visit a friend and fell in love with her instead.

Marilyn had grown up watching her mother work grueling hours at a bottling plant for not much money, then come home to keep house for Marilyn's drunken, abusive stepfather. So she'd gone away to UC Berkeley as soon as she could, then taken a break to register voters during the civil rights movement, then lived in Guatemala for a spell after college. She moved into the Happy

House when she came back and was trying to get over her first love, a man she'd met in Guatemala City.

"Of course, Mommy wasn't a virgin anymore," my grandfather liked to say, "so the boyfriend in Peru—"

"Guatemala," Marilyn interrupted, her delicate skin flushing pink.

"*Guateh-maala*, then. Well, of course he wouldn't have married her because of that—used goods, you know—and here she was pining away for him, so she ended up with me. Took her away from all that. All that dream-crystal shit."

Marilyn's marriage to my grandfather and her subsequent rise in class made her the most successful woman in her family: the one nieces and nephews stayed with, the one her sister came to for help.

Years later, it's easy to see that there wasn't much difference between my grandfather's relationship with Marilyn and the one with his friends. He picked people who had less than he did, who were—on paper, at least—his inferiors.

Their wedding portrait hung on Marilyn's bedroom wall. In it, she looked like a queen in her long, lace gown with its Tudor neckline and blousy sleeves, her short, dark hair setting off her elegant neck and unblemished skin, her slender fingers holding her bouquet. My grandfather, in a romantic gesture, kissed her graceful hand, although, as my school friends liked to point out, it actually looked like he was eating a hot dog. Unlike my grandfather's bed, Marilyn's bed was always made, its sheets fresh and smelling vaguely of fabric softener. Sometimes I'd lie on it and stare at their wedding picture, dwelling on the fairy-tale embrace, taking for granted that their marriage had begun in love, soft and fuzzy like the focus in that picture. I'd also search the photo for her wedding ring—a legend in our family, because Marilyn had lost it on their wedding night, taking it off at a restaurant to wash her hands and leaving it on the sink. Over the course of their years together, my grandfather would buy her two rings to replace it, each made of gold links holding a diamond. The second one was more like the original that had been lost, but neither seemed to make her fully happy. And although she didn't lose either replacement, my grandfather kept telling the story of her absentmindedness over and over again.

If you were to see that portrait today, how young Marilyn was compared to my grandfather, you might think that she was a poor man's trophy wife—young and interested only in his money, but without the fake breasts and big hair. But you'd be wrong; money wasn't the only reason she married him.

"Why'd you marry Daddy?" I'd asked Marilyn once. We were at Palos Verdes Park one breezy afternoon, sitting on swings that overlooked the Pacific. Marilyn's hair ruffled and fluffed in the wind. The question had just popped into my head. I suppose I wanted to hear a love story, something suggested by that romantic picture above her bed.

"Well..." She paused and dug the toes of her blue Nikes into the sand. Her sunglasses from Thrifty's looked straight ahead, her hands gripped the swing's chain. "He was stable. I really just wanted someone who was stable and educated."

"What's stable?" I asked.

"Well, he had a steady income. He had money. He didn't drink."

In the park in front of us, someone's kite crashed to the ground.

"I was almost thirty. It's not like I had any other prospects."

Marilyn was the most beautiful woman I knew. She wore her hair short and wavy, and its cut made her neck graceful, her shoulders delicate. Her skin was pale, the color of a white peach. Her blue eyes were tinged with gray, and if there was any fault to her face, it would be that her eyes were also always a little sad, even when she smiled. If you'd told her she was beautiful, she would have shaken her head and laughed, surprised that someone thought so.

"And Richard loved me, and no one else did."

"But you loved him too, right?"

It was just a moment's pause.

"Sure, I loved him too," she said evenly. Then she pushed back with her feet, and for a second, I thought she was going to start swinging and gliding through the air, the way she sometimes raced me to see who could swing highest and fastest. But all she did was hang for a moment above the ground, then put her feet down to stop.

6

I HAD LIVED WITH MY MATERNAL GRANDMOTHER, SPENCE, AND her friend Dee from when I was six weeks old until I was four. We lived in the San Gabriel Mountains, just northeast of Los Angeles, in a house on a hillside, surrounded by pine trees and oaks that rained acorns on our roof. The air there always smelled of chimney smoke and a cool, fresh wind, and sometimes deer came to our back door. I don't remember much about that time, only bits and pieces, moments without beginning or end.

I do remember this. One day they took me fishing. With her brown fingers, my grandmother pushed an orange marshmallow onto the barbed tip of a hook and dangled it in front of my nose. "See? See? That's what the fish sees."

I remember looking at the lake, trying to see the fish swimming in its depths, but I couldn't see past the water's surface. I imagined them teeming in the mysterious dark beneath, unseen, invisible even, until they bit a hook and were pulled into the sunny world above.

I remember the trout wrestling with the line as they came up, fighting the air and light that surrounded them. I remember the dark red behind their gills, the gaping of their mouths, the glossy wet of their skin, like varnished wood. I remember how beautiful they were even as they died, how I stroked my finger along their flanks and sang to them under my breath.

And, then, I remember this too: One morning we went out for breakfast. We ate waffles, and the syrup stayed sticky and sweet on my lips. Then we went to the grocery store; then we came home. Dee stood in front of me by the door, a paper grocery sack in one hand, her keys in the other. I was looking at my shoes, sticking their tips into the sticky sap that had fallen on to the wooden deck, wondering if it, too, were sweet. Spence was a little ways behind me, her arms full of groceries. I remember the golden sap and the light in the trees above and maybe a birdsong. And then.

Dee opened the door, and I heard my grandmother drop her groceries behind me, a whoosh and a crash. A can of soup rolled by my foot, the red and white of its label a blur. I turned around to look at her. I can still see her face, even now—an amazed look, her eyes wide open, her hands limp at her sides. Then she fell, face first, onto the deck.

Dee put me in my room while she called for help. Men's loud voices filled our house. After a while, I snuck out of my room. I went across the little hall and peeked into the bedroom where they'd taken my grandmother. They were all looking at her, and no one noticed me. I stared between the navy legs of the paramedics. I couldn't see my grandma's face, only her arm and chest. She was wearing a red windbreaker. It was covered in white vomit. I could smell it from the door. Even now, every time I see a red windbreaker, I smell that smell.

The next day, my grandfather and Marilyn took me away to live with them in their house in Palos Verdes, three hours away and on the other side of the city. Before they came to get me, Dee sat me on her lap. She was a big, soft woman, and I always felt safe in her arms. She held me tight, like she would never let go of me, and then she whispered a secret.

"I want you to know something," she said. "Even though Spence is gone and we can't see her, she can still see us. She's up in heaven, watching us down here. No matter what happens, she'll always be watching you, okay?"

I nodded.

"I love you," she said. And then she let me go.

As we drove down the mountains and through the high desert, I looked out the window of my grandfather's old, blue Thunderbird. Mormon Rocks and tumbleweeds whipped by, but the gray sky above us remained very still. I looked at the sky and saw my grandmother looking down at me from heaven. She peered through the clouds and had on a halo and wings and looked something like the crayon angels I drew at school, only better. She watched that big T-bird thread its way through the desert to the freeway, watched it take me far from everything I had ever known. For a long time after that, I felt her watching me, her eyes on the back of my neck, the top of my head. She watched me when I was good and when I was bad, when I went to the bathroom and when I slept.

The next morning, my grandfather told me again that Spence was dead.

"That means she won't be back," he said.

We were seated at the dining room table: him at one end, Marilyn at the side, me on her lap, her arms around my chest. I ran my finger along the edge of the table as I watched my grandfather. He was almost as big as Dee, although where her fat was soft, her body like a pillow, his was hard—a hard, round tummy, sturdy legs, and strong arms tan against his shirt. He was much older than Marilyn, and his hair was gray and thin. Silver hairs grew like wires from his eyebrows and nostrils; he had a wart above his upper lip. He said words strangely—a result, I'd soon learn, of his being English.

"It doesn't mean you won't see her again, like in heaven," Marilyn said gently.

"But not here," my grandfather said. "Do you understand?"

"Yes," I said, anxious to slide off of Marilyn's lap and be allowed to play.

"So you'll be living here from now on. With us," my grandfather said.

"Okay."

"Your grandma loved you very much," Marilyn said. "You know that, right?"

"Yes."

Her hand swept across my forehead and tucked a stray hair behind my ear, then returned to holding me. Her hands were pretty, pale and smooth, her nails painted a dark rose. She smelled good, and I liked sitting with her. We waited a little in silence; I didn't know if I was supposed to say something or not. Then Marilyn loosened her arms, and I slipped off her lap to go play in the yard.

My new home had a huge tree in the backyard, and that was where I headed, stepping carefully in that new place. The tree's trunk was wider than me, and it was taller than the top of the house's chimney. Its branches were as wide as the back of the house. I touched its bark. It was smooth except for tiny bumps that tickled the palm of my hands. I leaned into its trunk and gave it a hug. Spence died in January, so the tree must have been bare, but when I think of that day, I remember it in full leaf, the leaves rustling above my head, my arms dappled in sun and shadow. When I was little, I petted that tree and gave it hugs and whispered into its ears, which were always the same height as my mouth, no matter how tall I grew, until I became too old to whisper into the ears of trees. In the spring it put on bright orange flowers that in the summer turned to seeds of the same color. Marilyn called it a "coral tree," and I hoarded the bright seeds as I did the seashells she and I found together on the beach. If I close my eyes and reach into my pockets, I can still feel those seeds, smooth and cool like polished beads.

———————————

After Spence died, Marilyn and my grandfather took me to see a family therapist. Her office was in Beverly Hills on Wilshire Boulevard, in a tall black building. I've always called her Dr. Fork, though I'm sure that wasn't her name. She had black hair and blue eye shadow, and she knelt down in her skirt suit to play with me on the floor. We played with brightly painted wooden blocks and cars, and then we colored, and then she left me to go talk to the adults.

After their talk, Dr. Fork told them not to worry, that I was fine. I was handling Spence's death quite well, and I was a normal, well-adjusted four-year-old.

"But you two," she said, looking at them across the polished desk, "are another story. Save everyone some trauma down the line and get divorced now. Do it before she makes attachments."

Marilyn and my grandfather didn't heed her advice, and we never saw Dr. Fork again. And perhaps the good doctor's intervention had come too late anyway.

One morning a month or two later, as Marilyn and I walked down the driveway toward her brown Audi on our way to Montessori, a thought began to trouble me. I was staring at the ground, carefully picking through the cracks and chunks of asphalt caused by my favorite tree's roots.

"Is Spence my mommy?" I asked Marilyn.

"No," she said. "She was your grandma."

"Is Michele my mommy?" I asked.

"Yes," she said, "but she's dead now."

"She died in a car crash?"

"Yes."

"Are you my grandma?"

"No," she laughed. "I'm too young to be your grandma."

She was, in fact, thirty-six—twenty-six years younger than my grandfather.

"Are you my mommy, then?" I asked.

"Yes," she said, after the slightest pause.

"Well," I asked as we got into the car, "then can I call *you* Mommy?"

"Of course. I'd like that."

She buckled me into the front seat, carefully looping the shoulder strap behind me so it wouldn't get in my face, then kissed me on my nose.

I don't remember Marilyn being moved by that conversation on the driveway, but I think she must have been. Later, when I was in college, she told me how much she had wanted a baby of her own. She told me that when Michele died in 1976, she'd prayed and prayed that I would come to live with my grandfather and her. Instead, I had gone to Spence, and Marilyn was heartbroken.

What she didn't tell me was what I would later discover in my twenties, when I found a carbon copy of a letter Marilyn had typed to a friend shortly after Michele died. I didn't tell Marilyn about reading the letter, didn't ask her about those events so many years before. But the night I found it, I sat by the window of her apartment and stared out into the darkness and thought about how lucky I was.

"Richard is inconsolable," I read, the paper beginning to yellow, "because he blames himself for her death. But I keep thinking about the baby. I hope that she comes to live with us (she is in foster care now). Spence, Richard's ex, doesn't want the baby. Richard doesn't either—something about shitty diapers and bottles. But I want her. I want her so much."

Later in the letter, she asked her friend, who was a nurse, whether or not a baby might be affected by her mother taking quaaludes or "blue angels" during pregnancy, because Michele had apparently been on both.

As I sat staring out the window, I thought about the night when Marilyn had written the letter, that night when I was just a baby. I imagined she sat at a table with her typewriter, maybe also staring out the window into the dark as she wrote, and I thought about how I was somewhere out in that dark. How I was a little baby who needed a home, and my grandfather did not want me, and my grandmother did not want me. But a lonely woman, unrelated to me by blood, wanted me more than anything in the whole world, and the simple fact of her love made my childhood and my life better. Marilyn told me once that when I first went to live with Spence instead of her, she stopped believing in God. But when I came to live with her when I was four, she was so grateful, she started believing again. As I sat by the window and read her letter, it was easy for me to believe too.

Years later, the past is one of the few things I can still talk to Marilyn about. When I ask her about the time with my grandmother and Dee, she tells me that I remember it wrong. She says that Spence and I didn't live with Dee in the mountains. On the day Spence died, we were only up to Dee's for a visit, as we often were. She says that my grandmother and I lived in a nondescript, beige rancher in West Covina, in one of the smoggiest parts of the city. She says that when she and Dee and my grandfather went to Spence's house to clear out her things after she died, they had to wear face masks. The kitchen was filled with black bags of garbage; the floor was littered with trash that hadn't made it into the bags. The roof leaked, and there were buckets scattered throughout the house to catch the water. The floors in all the rooms were covered in dirty clothes and toys. My toys were everywhere, hundreds of them. Marilyn says she thinks Spence must have gone broke buying me toys; the closets were packed full of them, piles were in every room. She thinks Spence must have bought them out of guilt for what happened to Michele.

I barely remember Spence, but when I wonder if she loved me, I think of those mountains of toys, bought on an early retirement pension from the LA County Probation Department—an early retirement she took to raise me when my mother died. I don't remember that house. I don't remember those toys. I wouldn't believe Marilyn, except that I have a picture of the house I can't remember; I have a probate report reflecting its sale.

I do remember a swimming pool that was empty, its bottom covered in leaves and dust. I remember wishing for it to be full. There was a baker's rack nearby that was covered in spider plants. I played beneath their tendrils and clusters; I liked to feel their hanging leaves tickle my neck. Was that at Spence's house? I remember once lying in a bed and rolling over a lit cigarette. I remember the way my skin still burned, even after a hand had swatted away the ashes. Was that in Spence's bed?

Marilyn says that I *had* visited her and my grandfather before Spence's stroke. Spence knew that she might die before I grew up and that my grandfather would be the one I'd go to live with, so she wanted me to get to know him, just in case. I don't remember those visits either, but Marilyn has pictures to prove it to me:

two-year-old me brushing my teeth in their bathroom; a cake she made for my birthday; me hugging Ugly.

Marilyn says she and my grandfather picked me up from the mountains the night Spence collapsed, not the day after. I couldn't have seen those tumbleweeds through the Thunderbird's window because it was dark; in fact, she says, I slept the whole way to Palos Verdes.

"Poor thing," she says on the phone, static crackling in the thousands of miles between us. "You must have been worn out."

If I think really hard, I can remember that drive at night too: leaving the house in the dark, being half-asleep, the dirty, gray leather of the backseat soft against my cheek as I lay across the bench. I remember digging my fingers into the seat so I wouldn't slide off when we turned.

I have one more picture that proves I'd met my grandfather before I came to live with him. As I write, I take it out of the worn, blue folder I keep it in along with other pictures, birth certificates, death certificates, and a few important letters. It's a color snapshot from 1977. In it, I'm a baby, maybe eight months old. My grandfather holds me up to his face; it is quite possibly the first time he has ever seen me. I am brown-haired, chubby-cheeked, dressed in a frilly shirt and a puffy, pink diaper cover. My hands touch his cheeks, my lips brush against his big nose, my eyes stare into his. My grandfather seems young in that picture, younger than I ever remembered him, but already in those first few months of my life, he must have aged. The bags under his eyes are from sleepless, angry, grief-filled nights. The expression on his face isn't joy in his first grandchild; it is a look of weary sadness, a tired, wary look that says, "What next?" It is a look I remember only from his later years, always a fleeting look, one that fell over his eyes when he thought no one was watching and that vanished as quickly as it came.

I run my thumb over the back of that picture and feel the creases where my grandfather used it as a bookmark, carelessly jamming it between pages. "Kelly" is written in pencil on the back in his messy capitals, as if he thought he might one day forget who the baby was. I imagine him touching the photograph, long after I'd grown up. His hands were like those of a monster, big and thick, wrinkled and rough, brushed with fine black hair; his fingernails dirty and long like claws. I imagine him holding the photograph I'm holding, and it's almost like holding his hand again.

I wouldn't remember anything of that visit to Dr. Fork, the family therapist—our one and only—except for the way it entered our family lore.

"That quack said our marriage wouldn't last. She said we should get divorced," my grandfather would boast, slicking back his greasy hair with a thick hand, then pointing to his auditor—me, a dinner guest, an employee. "I walked out of her office right then and there because I knew a little girl needed a mother *and* a father, and I was right."

When I was little, I loved hearing this story of how he'd vanquished the evil Dr. Fork who'd wanted to destroy our family, who'd wanted to separate me from my mommy. But now, thirty-something years later, I wonder if the doctor wasn't right; I wonder if Marilyn would have been better off if she'd left Richard then.

I still call Marilyn "Mommy."

7

I HELD MY GRANDFATHER'S HAND AS WE WALKED THROUGH THE
marina's gravel lot, which was filled with old dusty cars and a
lopsided RV. A stand of eucalyptus trees shaded a crooked, dirty
yellow house. A sign in one of its cracked windows said Donahue's
Marina: Office, and that was where my grandfather led me. We
passed another sign, this one hand-painted onto pressboard and
hung crookedly on the chain-link fence: "If you'Re Dog shits here
YOUR to pick it up!"

"Look, Daddy," I pointed.

My grandfather didn't stop to read it, but I took the sign as
further evidence that something wasn't quite right. Surely this
wasn't where we'd be buying our yacht? My grandfather had taken
great pains to explain the difference between a boat and a yacht to
me. All summer he'd taken me to shop for *yachts*. We'd looked at
shiny, white ones with fiberglass hulls and huge, tinted windows;
antique Chris-Crafts with blue canvas awnings, chrome fixtures,
and teak decks—whatever caught his eye in the LA Harbor *Log*.
Those boats had been in marinas at the outer edge of the harbor
with a view of the open sea and a fresh breeze. Those marinas had
guard shacks, lawns, and palm trees; they had concrete pilings and
docks, nylon ropes coiled neatly by their cleats. My grandfather
and I had walked down wide, stable docks, his large hand engulfing

mine, while he talked to friendly men in golf shirts who gave me free key chain floats and koozies.

So when he took me to Donahue's for the first time, to sign the paperwork for our new yacht, I thought he'd made a mistake. To get there, we'd driven down a dusty, potholed road. We'd crossed three sets of railroad tracks and passed a cargo terminal. We had almost been smashed by a semitruck whose driver proceeded blithely along in spite of my grandfather's having called him a "motherfucking bastard" through the open window of our Mercedes.

You couldn't even really tell you were near the ocean until the road rounded a bend, and suddenly, there it was: a smooth channel of blue surrounded by a shipyard and docks, way at the back end of the harbor, on the border between San Pedro and Wilmington, as far from the open sea as you could get and still be on water.

In the dim shack, my grandfather sat down at a desk with Chuck, the marina's manager, while I was relegated to a greasy vinyl couch nearby. If I sat the wrong way, I slid backward, sinking into the dip between the cushions and the back; if I sat too close to the front of the cushion, I found myself sliding down toward the filthy linoleum floor.

The office was musty. Someone had dusted recently, but they'd missed big swathes on the end table, and a dead fly sat in the gold tin ashtray. As I looked toward the back of the building, behind Chuck, I could see where the scarred linoleum ended in a jagged line, revealing hard-packed dirt below. A few dead leaves had blown in through the gap between the bottom of the exterior wall and the dirt.

I sat as straight as I could so that my skin wouldn't make contact with the greasy couch, but also to be polite.

"I want you to make a good impression on Chuck," my

grandfather had said in the parking lot. "Remember who you are, where you come from."

I recognized this directive as part of being "Sir Richard," as much as the Old Etonian tie and imprinted checks. Being "Sir Richard" also meant that, on occasion, my grandfather's English accent would become slightly more pronounced, and I would be expected to be on my best behavior. "Noblesse oblige," he'd explained once and left it at that.

Chuck, red-faced and breathless, filled out a bill of sale. His body melted over the sides of his creaky office chair, and he wiped the sweat off his forehead with the same hand he'd used to hand me an old Brach's butterscotch he'd dug out of a desk drawer. The plastic wrapper had stuck stubbornly to the sticky candy, and after a while I'd given up and hidden it behind me, pushing it into the crack between the cushions of the couch. Chuck called me "sweetheart" and "darling" in a way that bothered me.

"Now, *darling*, are you excited to see your grandpa's new boat?" he'd interrupted their conversation to ask. "You're just going to love what your grandpa's bought for you. Just wait until you see it, *sweetheart.*"

He called my grandfather "Sir Richard" in the same tone, but my grandfather didn't seem to mind at all.

Finally, the men stood to shake hands, and then we went down to the dock to see our new boat. It was low tide, and the wooden ramp angled steeply over rocks coated with sea mud. The mud was olive brown, a color like the one I'd sometimes make on bad days in art class, a putrid mixture of brown and green and gray. The air smelled of the salty mud, of dead fish and, although I didn't recognize it at the time, of raw sewage. The ramp bounced beneath Chuck and my grandfather's heavy steps, and the weathered wooden dock rocked as we walked along it. Every now and then, part of a plank was missing, and I could see the shady, green water below. We passed a few dozen boats—all in various states of disrepair, painted in dirty shades of white or pastels—until we came to the end of the dock, where the biggest boat in the marina listed hard against the end tie. Its eighty-three feet of once-white paint was peeling; rust dripped like tears from the nails in its wooden hull. Its portholes were dusty and dark. The ropes that tied it to the dock were encrusted with black mussels. A thicket of sea squirts and algae grew peacefully just below the boat's waterline.

"Well, there she is. Isn't she beautiful?" Chuck said as my grandfather looked the ship up and down, end to end.

"Yes," he said, looking at her hull, "she is. She's got great lines. She's solid." I saw the pride blush slowly across his face, his bushy eyebrows raise with pleasure.

That night, my grandfather took Marilyn and me out to dinner at the Hungry Tiger to celebrate his purchase. Even though it was built in the middle of a shopping center parking lot, the Hungry Tiger looked like an old inn, the Admiral Benbow from *Treasure Island,* built of cobblestones and dark wooden beams. I was always disappointed when we went in, though, because it was just another restaurant inside: a large room packed with tables covered in goldenrod cloths, walls lined with framed prints of tigers, and bookshelves whose ancient-looking volumes were glued to the wood; I knew this because I'd tried once to pick one up.

We were seated in roomy leather chairs on wheels. Marilyn and my grandfather were handed heavy menus bound in leather, and I was given a paper child's menu. I ordered a Shirley Temple.

"Bring her extra cherries, if you would," my grandfather

commanded the waiter, a pale young man whose acne-scarred cheeks were studded with sparse, black hairs. "We're celebrating!"

When our drinks came, we clinked glasses and said cheers, my grandfather and I more loudly than Marilyn. Wreck that it was, I was excited about the boat. The way my grandfather described it, owning a boat meant trips to exotic places, whale watching anytime I wanted, living the pirate-buccaneer-sharpshooter-swashbuckler lifestyle to which I seriously aspired. I'd watched every Errol Flynn film on video and ridden my spring horse in the backyard, using a broom handle as a lance, until it had collapsed beneath my weight. I wanted him to name the boat "Athena," after the warrior goddess from my book of Greek myths.

As Marilyn took a sip of wine, she gazed at something farther away than the restaurant's wall.

We ordered: my grandfather, steak; Marilyn, red snapper; me, fried shrimp. Another Shirley Temple was commanded without my having to ask.

My grandfather began to talk, his voice happily bombastic, about what would be done to the boat, what items purchased, what trips were to be made—the Panama Canal, perhaps? The canals in Europe? Yes, the canals in Europe. Hawaii. Mexico. Alaska.

Marilyn grunted in assent once in a while, but if you actually paid attention to her, you could see she wasn't listening. She was still staring across the restaurant, her hands folded in her lap, her eyes shinier than normal. I reached a hand under the table to hers and held it. Her soft fingers squeezed mine for just a moment, then went limp again.

"What's the matter, Mommy?"

"Nothing, sweetheart, I'm fine," she said.

"What? Something's the matter?" my grandfather wanted to know.

"Nothing, Richard," she said, her voice a little harder.

I couldn't imagine why she was upset. I replayed the short ride to the restaurant in my mind. Had we said something to hurt her?

My grandfather started talking again, about engines we'd need to overhaul and the anchor and chain we'd buy, trips to Seattle and San Diego.

"Are you okay?" I whispered. She didn't answer, but instead turned her head a little toward my grandfather, as if she were paying attention. He kept talking.

Across the restaurant, an amorous couple held hands and looked soulfully into each other's eyes, the side of the woman's bare foot sliding slowly along the man's leg. I looked back at Marilyn and my grandfather—his annoyance with her sadness slowly rising—and tried to gauge who would explode first. I prayed silently and desperately for the waiter to not screw up our order, for my grandfather's steak to be a true medium-rare, for the cooks to be swift in the performance of their duty.

Again I asked, "Are you okay?"

"Yes," Marilyn hissed and withdrew her hand. She took another sip from her glass, then put it on the table roughly. My own eyes got teary. I'd just been trying to help.

Our food came. I didn't feel much like eating. My grandfather tucked a napkin into his collar and draped it over his chest. He cut into his steak with gusto, then threw the pink plastic "rare" marker onto his plate.

"Goddamned steak is overcooked." He pulled off the napkin and looked around for our waiter, who'd chosen that exact moment to go missing.

"Waiter!" my grandfather shouted in his best Royal Navy–officer voice. When no one appeared immediately, he began again, repeating, "Waiter! Waiter!" as if he were an air-raid siren.

Dining in the restaurant had come to a standstill; everyone stared. A woman swiveled on her bar stool to get a better view. The amorous couple raised their eyebrows and smirked. A manager dressed in a double-breasted suit, not much older than our waiter, rushed up to quiet my grandfather. He seemed slightly afraid of us; restaurant managers were almost always slightly afraid of us. I didn't really blame them.

"Can I help you, sir?" he asked.

"Yes, you can fucking help me. This bloody steak is overcooked." My grandfather flicked a hand toward the plate. The manager whisked it away.

I stared at the napkin in my lap, feeling everybody's eyes on me. I contemplated running out of the restaurant, but I knew my grandfather would chase after me, dig his fingers into my shoulder, and pull me back. Once during a restaurant scene, I had left the table for an extended dawdle in the restroom and was soundly chastised upon my return, which had drawn even more stares. What I really wanted to do was crawl under the table.

Life at the Hungry Tiger slowly got back to normal. There was the gentle clink of silverware on plates, murmured conversations.

"Well, you two, eat!" my grandfather insisted. "Don't wait for mine. Yours will be cold."

I looked up. Marilyn sat in stony silence, her plate untouched, the sad red snapper turning mushy. A tear welled slowly up and over her lower eyelid, rolling down her creamy cheek until she wiped it away with the back of her hand.

"Why aren't you excited about the boat, Mommy?" I asked Marilyn. We were driving, me eating the trail mix we'd just bought at the store. Melted goo from the white-yogurt-covered raisins coated my fingers.

She didn't say anything for a second, but when she did, she sounded tired, wary. "I don't know, honey. I'm just…concerned."

"About what?"

We stopped at a light. She turned and looked at me, her sunglasses hiding her eyes. "You know about Daddy's first boat."

I nodded my head. In our living room, by the front door, on the wall above the liquor table, hung a framed and matted photograph of my grandfather's first boat. She was a decommissioned U.S. Navy patrol craft, a two-hundred-foot subchaser from World War II that he'd bought used from someone else. Ships and boats were always changing hands in the LA Harbor in more-or-less shady deals. Her postservice name was the *Sirocco*, and my grandfather had kept that name because Errol Flynn had owned a sailing yacht named the *Sirocco*, after the Mediterranean wind.

The *Sirocco*, Marilyn said, had started the same way as our new boat, only she didn't know what she was getting into then. At first, she'd liked the idea of owning a yacht; it sounded glamorous and fun. But the *Sirocco* was a wreck, and as my grandfather began the expensive task of renovating her, he spent so much money that he and Marilyn couldn't afford the rent on their house in Benedict Canyon. They moved on board to save money before the ship was even close to being finished. For a few years, they lived with the sounds of hammering and welding, the inconveniences of an unfinished kitchen, unreliable plumbing, a leaking hull, and a leaking deck. They moved their belongings from room to room and deck to deck to make way for the construction. But they still couldn't pay their bills; sometimes welders would come knocking on Marilyn's bedroom door to ask for their pay. She couldn't keep jewelry because it kept disappearing. At the end of those few years, the ship was still unfinished, and when they finally sold it, they were practically bankrupt.

"Anyway," she said. "I just don't want to go through that again. And here we are, with another boat."

"Maybe this time it'll be different," I said, trying to cheer her up. But perhaps in the back of my mind, I was a little worried too. I didn't really know what bankruptcy meant, but I knew it was really, really bad. Adults spoke of bankruptcy the way they spoke of death; it was the thing that made people homeless.

We stopped at another light.

"Well, it *is* a smaller boat," she said, as if she were trying to believe me. She looked at me and smiled, then noticed my hands. "You're always such a mess, Kelly. Here," she said, handing me a Wet One from the stash she kept behind her seat.

8

I^T WAS ON ONE OF MARILYN'S TEACHING NIGHTS THAT FALL, when we were alone, that my grandfather finally told me the truth about my mother's death. We sat at the dining room table, our empty plates and glasses still before us. I don't remember what we were talking about or how we got to it, but suddenly there it was, the truth, sitting between us like a round, hard stone.

"...the man who killed your mother."

"I thought she died in a car crash," I said. I thought maybe he was talking about a drunk driver who'd killed my mother or some teenager who drove too fast. Marilyn was always complaining about teenagers who drove too fast.

"No, she was murdered."

I remember how my mind leapt from question to question.

"How?" I started.

"She was strangled."

The answer was brutal; it removed all ambiguity. My mother had been murdered. I'd always known that my mother had been killed when I was three weeks old, and I'd always wondered, but never asked, why I wasn't in the car with her. Now it made sense; there had been no car.

"What about my father? I thought he was killed in the crash

too." The truth was, until that moment, I'd never thought to ask about my father.

"We don't know who your father is."

I pulled my legs up underneath me and fidgeted with Marilyn's orange vinyl place mat.

"Who killed her?"

"We don't know."

"You mean—they'll never go to jail?" It didn't seem fair. How could a murderer not go to jail?

"The detectives on your mother's case thought that maybe she might have been killed by the Hillside Stranglers, but there wasn't enough evidence."

"Who were the Hillside Stranglers?"

"No one you need to worry about. They were serial killers, but they're in jail now. Besides, it was just a guess."

I knew what serial killers were. They were like Jack the Ripper, who'd killed a lot of women in the age of Sherlock Holmes but of whom no one seemed especially scared. They whisper-hissed his name—*Rhiiiperr*—like he was Darth Vader or Lex Luther, a bad guy who was not really real.

That night, as I fell asleep, I thought about how, suddenly, every-thing seemed different. The whole story of where I came from had changed. My mother had died when I was three weeks old. Before, it had been an accident; now it was a murder. She might have been murdered by a famous person. I was special now. They were always doing stories on the evening news about special kids. To be a special child, you couldn't just make all As or excel in sports; you had to do it while fighting cancer or having a parent die. Sometimes I'd been a little jealous of those kids and the love and admiration I was sure they were receiving from the whole city. A secret part of me had always wanted to be special. Now I was, and I couldn't decide if it felt good or not.

And yet nothing really was different. I would still live with my grandfather and Marilyn. We still had two dogs and a cat. We'd still live in our house in Palos Verdes. Try as I might, I couldn't make myself sad about Michele's death. I didn't even know what she looked like. What had changed was something that had happened a long time ago, before I could even remember.

That night, I watched for the headlights from Marilyn's car, the flash and arc of them against my bedroom wall. I pretended to be asleep when she came in to kiss me good night, her face cool from the night outside, her hair smelling of fall, of chimney smoke and wet leaves.

The next day, my grandfather asked me if I wanted to have lunch with the detective who'd worked on my mother's case. I said yes.

A few weeks—or perhaps it was only days—after the brunch with Detective Varney, I asked my grandfather about my father. Before my grandfather had told me about my mother's murder, my father hadn't existed. But when I'd asked, "What about my father?" I'd called him into being: a faceless shadow, someone who did not even have, as far as I knew, a name.

"His name was Archibald," my grandfather told me. We were driving up Crenshaw Boulevard, where it climbs up the steep side of the peninsula, and the diesel engine on the dirty-tooth-colored Mercedes strained with the effort. Maybe it was after school or maybe we were just running errands, but what I remember most is the sound of the engine; the peculiar leather-and-diesel smell that often made me nauseous; the tall, brown grass at the roadside; the sandstone cliffs where the road was cut, the sun making them gold.

"Archibald" had been my legal last name when I first came to live with my grandfather and Marilyn, but I'd always used "Grey" at school. Archibald. I'd known my father's last name the whole time; I just hadn't realized it.

"What was his first name?" I asked.

"I don't remember," my grandfather said. We drove along in silence for a bit. "He was an asshole. An absolute motherfucker. He was in jail when Michele died. When he found out she was gone, he tried to use you to get out of jail. He said he needed to get out to look after you, but he didn't give a shit about you." My grandfather's voice had a growl to it. "If he could, he would have taken you away from Marilyn and me."

I couldn't imagine anything worse than being taken away from my home, from Marilyn and my grandfather. Suddenly, I felt as if I'd betrayed their love just by asking about my father, as if I were asking to be taken away.

"I'm glad he didn't take me away," I said.

"Well, we put a stop to that. I knew someone who knew someone, and I paid to have the living shit beaten out of him in prison. Never heard another word out of him. Cowardly bastard. Besides, he probably wasn't really your father anyway. She probably just put his name down on the birth certificate."

I felt safer when he said the part about beating him up.

"A lot of people wanted to take you away from me," my grandfather continued as we crested the hill. "Spence's relatives tried to steal you after she died. Her sister and her mother. Absolute cunts. They would have taken you to Mexico, and I'd never have seen you again. That's why I had to go up to Dee's in the mountains to get you right away, after we pulled the plug on Spence. They were on *their* way too."

I wanted to know what "cunt" meant; I hadn't heard that

word before. But it didn't seem like the right time to ask. Instead I said, "I love you and Mommy. I don't want to live with anyone else. I don't even want to know them, those other people."

I felt as if I needed to reassure him, to let him know I wouldn't leave. He reached his rough hand from the wheel and held mine until the next curve of the road. I squeezed it tightly.

Although I'm sure I must have, I don't remember ever asking about my father again.

9

WHEN MY GRANDFATHER TOOK ME AWAY FROM DEE AFTER Spence died, back when I was four, he promised her that she would see me again. He kept his word. Every few months after Spence's death and before Dee left LA, I'd been sent to visit Dee for the weekend in Wrightwood. Marilyn and I would meet her at a Denny's in Pomona, halfway between the peninsula and the mountains. And when she came through the doors, she'd crouch down, and I'd run to her and give her a big hug. She'd lift me with a grunt.

"You're getting so big, Kelly!" she'd say, and I'd feel her soft cheek brush against mine.

I'd watch Marilyn and Dee drink coffee and talk—Dee on my side of the table and Marilyn on the other—their lipstick staining the chunky, white mugs, Dee's just a little brighter than Marilyn's. Marilyn would update her on my progress in school; Dee would talk a little bit about work, the mountains. If we could have stayed at that table, me with the two women I loved most in the world, I would have been happy. But always too soon, it was time to say goodbye to Marilyn. I always cried when she left, and I hated it when she drove off and her car got small and became just another set of brake lights. But then it would be time to leave with Dee, and I would forget all about Marilyn.

I'd watch the mountains slowly get closer, watch as we left the city behind us. When I saw the Mormon Rocks in the Cajon Pass, as big as buildings and the color of sand, I knew we were getting close. We passed yucca, their long stems crowned with a flame of pale flowers. Soon the yucca turned to pine and oak, and with that change, I knew we were there.

"I'm glad you could make the visit, dear," she'd say with a smile as the road began to curve and climb the hillside. "Sinbad and Sam miss you, and so do I."

"Me too," I said. It was true, but in a funny way. I missed Dee most when I was with her, as if I only then realized what I had been lacking. I reached my hand into hers and kept my watch out the window until I spotted her green house among the trees. We'd cross the same threshold where Spence had died, but I never thought of it that way; I never felt anything but happy as I walked through that door.

In the evening, Dee would take me over to visit her friends Rita and Virgil, who'd also been Spence's friends. They'd all been probation officers together, except for Rita, who was a regular cop. Virgil had skin the color of fine leather and a silver five o'clock shadow. He always smelled of Coors, and so did his dog, whom he'd trained to suck on the empties. When I was very little, Virgil taught me to do both the Mexican hat dance and the chicken dance and to count to a hundred in Spanish and to say *por favor*, *gracias*, and "right on, homeboy!" All the newspapers and magazines in Rita and Virgil's house had holes in them because whenever there was a picture of President Reagan, Virgil cut his head out and burned it in the fire. Virgil thought the two most important things in life were love and being creative, and he'd spray-painted red hearts all over the house that he was building for Rita in the neighboring lot. Sometimes he would take me down the hill to the new house, blast mariachi music on his eight-track, and, together, we'd do crafts. We made mice out of halves of walnut shells, with pink felt tails and ears and green sequins for the eyes; turkeys and Christmas trees out of pine cones; a Yule-log candleholder for Marilyn. When we were done, Rita and Dee would "ooh" and "aah" over our creations; then we'd all go up the hill to eat Rita's cooking—green bean casserole or baked beans and maybe pork chops cooked in Lipton soup. I couldn't remember much about Spence, but on those nights, as I fell asleep in Rita's lap while the adults talked, I thought how this must have been what it was like before, when she was still alive.

After Dee and I went back home, we'd have a snack together and then get ready for bed. Dee let me sleep with her. We'd watch *MASH* and Johnny Carson, and I felt safe and happy, curled by her warm side in the big bed, glowing in the blue light of her TV, listening to people laugh at old Johnny. I always fell asleep before the screen went dark.

After she retired from the probation department, when I was seven, Dee moved to Anniston, Alabama. And so my grandfather, true to his word, sent me on my own to visit her the summer I was eight.

————————————

The Jetway in Atlanta was humid, the hot air thick with water. I had never felt air like that before, although Marilyn had warned me about it.

"It's gonna be hot and muggy down there," she'd said as she carefully packed my suitcase that July with neatly folded tank tops and shorts. I hadn't understood "muggy" until the moment I'd gotten off the plane.

My right hand held the flight attendant's slender fingers, soft and cool from the plane's air conditioning; my left hand gripped two Delta pilot wings, their sharp tips digging into my palm. I had two more wing pins, plus two Delta buttons, three packs of peanuts, and a deck of Delta playing cards in my backpack—all the result of my being too shy to answer the various flight attendants when they asked, "Are you traveling alone? Do you have one of these yet?"

At the end of the Jetway where it opened into the terminal, I scanned the waiting area for Dee, looking left and right at businessmen and other people's families, until I realized she was right in front of me. My hand slipped from the flight attendant's, and I ran to her.

Even now, I remember Dee in her lavender pantsuit, how she crouched her big body down to give me a hug. Her hug was warm after the cold plane, and she smelled like baby powder and White Shoulders perfume. Her hair was short and curly, maybe a little grayer than the last time I'd seen her, but I wouldn't have noticed when I was eight. I remember the thin line of her scarlet lipstick and how her eyes narrowed and shone when she smiled. Even now, whenever I fly alone—no matter the city, no matter how long she's been dead—I still look for Dee as I exit the Jetway. It always surprises me: the flash of anticipation, the pang of disappointment when she isn't there.

Dee had been raised in an orphanage in Philadelphia, her mother dying young and her father hardly around before he, too, died. When World War II came along, Dee joined the Women's Army Corps. She served in North Africa and as part of the occupying forces in Berlin. She found a family in the service—women who, like herself, were down-to-earth and independent, who didn't really want husbands when most girls did. She did things women of her generation never dreamed they could do. She drove jeeps and ran an office and played softball with the WAC exhibition team, traveling all over Europe after the war. When she was discharged, she attended college on the GI Bill, graduating with her BA in social work. She found a job with the LA County Probation Department, where she met my grandmother, Spence.

Anniston's Fort McClellan had been the Women's Army Corps' headquarters and was then home to the Women's Army Corps Museum. Many of the old WACs had settled there. Now, in Anniston, Dee had found a new life with her old friends from the corps, one that revolved around cookouts and pool parties, fishing ponds, the Legion Hall, and the WAC museum, and that was how we spent our two weeks together.

I loved the WAC Museum. It had a jeep you could touch and a dozen dioramas with glamorous WAC mannequins in various uniforms: winter, summer, dress. The dress uniform featured a lovely navy cape with a white lining—so different from what Major Houlihan wore on *MASH*. They also had a life-sized statue of Pallas Athena, who, besides being my favorite Greek goddess, was the WAC mascot. Dee bought me a Pallas Athena pendant in the WAC Museum's gift shop. I wore it for years.

That summer when I was eight, I wanted with all my heart to be an astronaut. Marilyn had gotten me a subscription to *Odyssey,* a space magazine for children, but my grandfather had told me I wouldn't be good enough at math. Dee and her friends took me to the U.S. Space and Rocket Center in Huntsville. Every time I met a new WAC, she'd say to me, "I hear you want to be an astronaut! That's great! You can be whatever you want to be!" I wonder now if they said it because they themselves had overcome so much to be what they wanted to be.

One afternoon toward the end of my trip, Dee and I stayed home instead of going swimming or fishing. She sat me down in the kitchen. The bright light filtered in through the filmy, white curtains, making everything white. She brought some cardboard boxes out of the spare bedroom and placed them on the table, opening them and carefully unwrapping a set of square ceramic flour and sugar canisters. They were glazed in bright colors, lime greens and grape purples. Then she unwrapped round, white porcelain pots with gold-enameled fruits on top of their lids. She gave one to me to hold, and I wrapped both of my hands around the smooth sphere.

"These are to hold jam," she explained, touching the slender porcelain spoon that sat inside, its dainty handle emerging from a small hole near the fruit. "Spence made these. She was an artist—really creative, just like you. Aren't they beautiful?"

Dee picked up another jam pot in her big, soft hands and turned it over to where my grandmother had inscribed her initials. I touched the letters. YKS.

"One day these will be yours, but I'm not going to give them to you now. I don't want them to get broken in your luggage, and you probably don't have a place to put them yet. But when you're all grown up and you have your own house, you can put these on your counter and have something of your grandmother's."

It occurred to me then that I did not have anything of my grandmother's. A few snapshots, buried in a drawer somewhere. The only thing I really had from when I lived with Spence was my orange teddy bear, Applesauce, who had a blue bib with a red apple on it and a squeaker in his bottom. Sometimes I still slept with him.

"But you can have this now," Dee said, setting a gold pendant on the table, a small sheepdog with emeralds for eyes. "That belonged to Spence too. That's solid gold. Don't lose it." It was heavier than I thought it would be.

Then she set down a gold-painted bear wearing a belt with the Olympic rings on it. "And this is a pin from the 1980 Olympics in the Soviet Union. They're really rare because we boycotted them. I don't know how Spence got it. She was always getting unusual things like that."

I held the pin in wonder. The Cold War was waged every night on the news. Something from the Soviet Union seemed as exotic as a rock from Mars.

We spent the afternoon looking at pictures of Dee and Spence together, fishing at Pismo Beach and laughing at parties, then of pictures of Spence on her own in Hawaii.

"I sent her to Hawaii for a present once. I thought she needed to go see the place where her family came from. The people there are so lovely, so happy, just like she was. Just like you are!" She smiled. "You know your grandmother really loved you, right? You were really important to her."

I smiled back. I liked to hear about Spence. Then suddenly it occurred to me that Dee might have known Michele.

"What was my mom like?" I asked.

Dee stopped smiling and looked down. We'd been sitting together, side by side, at the table. "I didn't really know your mother, dear. I just wasn't around her much."

"She was murdered," I said.

"Yes, I know. I don't know anything about that either, really."

I was quiet.

Finally, she said, "I'm sorry."

"It's okay," I said.

That night after dinner—sandwiches, because Dee couldn't

cook—she gave me Spence's badge from the probation department. She'd dug it out of a cubby in her rolltop desk.

"Spence would have wanted you to have this too. It meant a
lot to her."

I traced my finger along the scrollwork in its brass, the county
seal set in its middle like a stone. A tiny brass plaque beneath it read
"Yvonne K. Spencer, Los Angeles County Probation Department,
Retired."

"See, I still have mine." Dee opened her wallet and held it
next to the badge in my hand. Her badge, identical to Spence's,
sat next to her driver's license. "I keep it with my license because
sometimes it gets me out of traffic tickets." She winked, the skin
around her eyes crinkling in merriment.

"You know, I was thinking about your mom," she said. "You
don't know a lot about where you come from. Has your grandfather ever mentioned Spence's family? Your grandmother had a
sister. Yvette. Yvette...well, her maiden name would have been
Spencer, like your grandmother. I don't remember her married
name." She thought for a second.

My grandmother's real first name had been Yvonne. All I could
think of was how silly it was to name two sisters *Yvette* and *Yvonne*.
If that had happened to me, I would have gone by "Spence" too.

"She married some Italian man," Dee continued. "It was an
Italian name. Genoa? Giordano? Anyway, I think she's still alive in
Riverside somewhere. She and your grandmother didn't get along.
Personally, I couldn't stand the woman. But maybe one day you'll
want to find her."

I didn't really want to find her; I was scared of her. She was the
person my grandfather said had wanted to take me away.

When I went to bed that night, I slipped my grandmother's
badge under my pillow, then put my hand on its cold metal. I

carried it around in my pocket for weeks afterward, fingering its ridges, smoothing my thumb over the raised seal.

———————————

Dee and I left for Atlanta the day before my early morning flight back home. It was a rainy, gray day, and the water poured like sheets over our windshield. As we drove out of Anniston, I felt a pain I wasn't expecting. It was the same pang of sadness and panic I'd felt when I was five and Marilyn drove off from Denny's without me. We were quiet the whole trip. The pain didn't go away, and with every mile that we got closer to Atlanta, I felt the ache in me grow.

"I don't want to go home," I finally said from the passenger seat.

Dee didn't say anything, but reached her hand over to mine. I knew that she didn't want me to leave either.

I cried that night at the hotel after we went to bed, hiding my tears in the dark, stifling my sobs in my pillow. I tried so hard not to cry at the airport, but Dee must have felt me shaking as I hugged her goodbye.

On the plane, I tried to hide my tears from the strangers all around me. I remember looking out the window of the airplane at the ground below, everything blurry from the height and my wet eyes. I was convinced I'd never be happy again without Dee near me. I worried I'd never see her again. What if something happened to her? What if she died before I could visit her again? And even if she didn't die, how could I stand not to be near her? The only thought that comforted me was thinking of Marilyn. I imagined how she'd be waiting at the airport for me in her soft fake-fur coat even though it was July. It would be just her and me, and I would run into her arms and hide in the coat's softness. She'd hug me and kiss my head and hold me and tell me it was okay. Marilyn always held me when I cried; she always told me it would be okay. I thought of that the whole flight home, how I would just collapse in her arms and cry all I wanted to, and she would make it all better.

But when I got out of the Jetway, instead of just Marilyn, there was also my grandfather and Beatrix, my friend from Le Lycée. I couldn't collapse and cry and hide in Marilyn's fake-fur coat (which, of course, she wasn't wearing in the summer). I couldn't cry in front of my grandfather and Beatrix. I had to be brave and hold back my tears.

I remember how they tried to make my homecoming special. When we got home, I'd see how Marilyn had redecorated my room with frilly Cabbage Patch curtains and a lacy Cabbage Patch comforter and a cute table to do homework on. And when they picked me up from the airport, they took me to the restaurant in the spiderlike Theme Building at LAX, a place I'd always wanted to go. But we all sat around the table in silence. I couldn't trust my voice to speak, afraid I'd cry at any minute, and they'd all know something was wrong. Finally I couldn't hold it anymore, and the sobs came pouring out of me and into the fancy cloth napkins. I knew I shouldn't be crying, but I couldn't stop. All I could do to explain was periodically bleat, "I want Dee. I miss Dee."

After a few minutes my grandfather had had enough and stormed up from the table. "Well, goddamn it, let's call her," he growled.

I felt everyone in the restaurant's eyes on me as we walked toward the pay phone, his hand gripping me tightly around the wrist. I felt like a traitor. He dialed and handed the phone to me. When Dee finally answered, I started sobbing even more loudly. "I love you," I kept telling her, "I miss you."

I don't remember what she said or what happened next or how

it all got better. All I remember is that dim phone booth—its ivory wood, the pink cushions on the seat, the cool plastic of the phone held hard against my ear. All I remember is gripping its curled cord tightly between my hands and pulling it, as if I thought somehow I could pull Dee back to me.

That night, I created an elaborate system of keeping the people I loved alive. Every night before I fell asleep, on the wall by my bed, I drew a series of concentric circles with my finger. The middle dot was me; the next was my grandfather, then Marilyn, then Dee, then my friends. I arranged the circles in order of the person's impor- tance to me, but if I hadn't thought it somehow wrong, I would have put Dee before my grandfather, maybe even before Marilyn. I prayed for each circle three times, "Dear Lord, please keep Daddy safe tonight. Please keep him safe tomorrow. Please keep him safe tomorrow night. Please keep Mommy safe… Please keep Dee safe." Once I got through the list, I stopped worrying long enough to fall asleep. I trusted God to keep everyone safe until I prayed for them again. I prayed that way every night for years.

The next morning while I ate breakfast, my grandfather sat in his dressing gown at the end of the table to put his contact lenses in, as was his habit. He spread a napkin before him, then lined up his lens case, wetting solution, and a bowl of water. He cleaned and rinsed each lens, then placed the left one, prying his eyelids open to do so. He blinked twice, staring across the room at the *Sirocco*.

"You know, your mother hated Dee."

"Michele?" I put down my spoon.

"Yes, Michele. Couldn't stand her." He put in the right lens.

I didn't understand. Why would she hate Dee? I loved Dee.

Dee was nice. Dee loved me. I crossed my legs beneath me and folded my hands in my lap.

My grandfather blinked the second lens into place, then looked at me. "When she was a teenager, she walked in on Spence and Dee in bed together."

I waited for him to go on.

"You know, screwing?" my grandfather said, growing impatient with my silence. He seemed angry at something. "You know…making love. Fucking! A couple of dykes."

I still said nothing.

"*Lesbians*," he hissed, leaning over the edge of the table.

"What's a lesbian?" I asked.

He sighed impatiently. "A lesbian's a woman who has sex with other women. Who loves women instead of men."

"Okay." I picked at my shoe.

"Well!?"

I didn't know what he wanted me to say.

"Well, just bloody remember that about Dee. She isn't as wonderful as you think. She's damn lucky I let you visit her."

"I'll still get to see her, though, right?" I was suddenly worried.

"Goddamn it. Yes, you'll bloody get to see her!"

10

THAT NOVEMBER, FOR MY NINTH BIRTHDAY, MARILYN GAVE me a picture of Michele. She had spent days looking for it in the garage and my grandfather's closet and had put it in a red-lacquered frame. When I first unwrapped it, I didn't understand.

"Who is this?" I asked.

"It's Michele," she said.

It was the first time I'd ever seen my mother's face. I didn't know what to say. I spent a long time looking at the picture before I moved on to my next present.

Michele sat in a straight-backed chair by an empty fireplace, holding her hands out as if she were talking. Even though she was the only person in the photograph, she was far off to its right. A red-and-blue cloisonné plate hung above the mantel; there was a fluffy, white rug by her feet. My mother looked straight into the camera, her tired eyes narrowed a little from the flash. She wasn't pretty, exactly, but sturdy, clean. Her flared jeans seemed new and were held up by a thick, leather belt; her shirt was navy blue and snug. She had long, brown hair, thick arms, and thick eyebrows, like mine. She wore a quiet half smile that said *I don't really want to have my picture taken.* I knew because I smiled like that too.

I touched the side of her face, gently, my finger grazing the cool glass. I smiled a half smile too, but for different reasons.

"Thank you," I said to Marilyn. I knew the present meant something to her as well as to me, and as she stood by my chair, I leaned into her, my arms circling her hips.

Later that day, we put Michele's picture up on my dresser, along with an old snapshot of Spence, and her badge, the one Dee had given me. Marilyn found some lace to cover the dresser beneath the pictures. I found a dusty glass bud vase under the bathroom sink and an old sprig of artificial flowers in my closet. I rummaged through the junk drawer in the kitchen and found two candles: one was an emergency candle, white and unused; the other was the melted-down blue stub of a taper, its black wick broken off short against the wax. I propped them in two shot glasses and put them on top of my dresser. I lit them, one for my mother, Michele, and one for my grandmother, Spence.

It was raining on my birthday, a Southern California storm: dark clouds and a steady downpour that lasted all day. My room was dim; I sat on my bed, across from the dresser, and stared at the pictures behind the two bright flames. I watched their faces flicker in the candlelight and thought the shifting light made them beautiful. Long after I'd blown the candles out, when I closed my eyes for sleep, I could still see the flames on the back of my eyelids, as if they'd burnt themselves there.

The next day Marilyn took me to the grocery store to buy new candles. She bought me the big, Mexican kind—white pillar candles in glass vases painted with brightly colored saints that they sold in the ethnic-food aisle—because that was what I wanted.

Soon I added another picture to my dresser.

"What am I doing there?" Marilyn asked when she saw it. "I'm not dead."

"I know," I said. "But you're my mother too." I didn't want

her to feel left out. I thought, too, that having her picture there might keep her safe, as if she could somehow be protected by the candles' glow.

———————————————

That year, I became obsessed with the idea that the people I loved would die. It didn't help that my grandfather kept talking about how he was going to "kick the bucket" soon, probably of a heart attack, he thought, but maybe a stroke or the "big C." As long as they were with me, I figured they were safe; but whenever my grandfather or Marilyn left the house, I half expected them not to return. I hated going to sleepovers or parties. I couldn't rest until I'd told them I loved them three times and made them promise to stay safe. I thought the promise was what kept them alive. Marilyn eventually got annoyed with me, but my grandfather seemed to understand. Perhaps it was because he, too, worried.

My grandfather almost always screamed at us for being late, screamed at us for all the horrible deaths he'd imagined for us while we were gone. Hours later, he'd apologize. "I'm sorry," he'd say. "I was just worried about you."

I suppose my grandfather had a reason to worry. The night my mother, Michele, was taken from the streets, murdered, and her body dumped in an empty lot, he was reading a book or watching TV or sleeping. He never called the police to report his daughter missing because he didn't know she was missing. I now know that by the time she died, he'd stopped talking to her. She hadn't called in months. I imagine he assumed his daughter would be all right because she always had been. He'd stopped worrying because he'd decided there was nothing he could do to make her go back home or stop taking drugs or change her ways. My grandfather never called the police to report his daughter missing, and then one awful day, the police called him to report that she had been found.

"You know, Little Toad," he said one night when I was nine, the year I'd started being scared. "I'm getting older. I'll probably die before you grow up. But if something should happen to me, I'll tell you what's going to happen. I'll come back and haunt you."

"Just like *The Ghost Goes West*?"

"Yes, exactly."

"You'll shake your chains?"

"Yes. And anytime you miss me, if you're lying in bed, all you have to say is 'Daddy, come here, you old bastard!' and I'll shake your bed and rattle my chains."

"And howl?"

"And howl."

"And if anyone wants to hurt me, you'll scare them away."

"I'll scare the motherfucking bastards shitless."

"You promise?"

"Yes, I promise."

I went to him and gave him a hug. My grandfather gave the best hugs—the kind that tall, fat people can give, that shelter your whole body and make you feel safe and loved. Every once in a while, I'd remind my grandfather of his promise, for years afterward, even after he'd long forgotten the conversation.

11

LISA AND I WAITED PATIENTLY IN MY GRANDFATHER'S MERCEDES in the parking lot of the Hostess outlet store on Gaffey Street in San Pedro. I'd opened the windows against the heat of the spring afternoon, and the sweet, yeasty smell of fresh Wonder Bread from the factory wafted through the open windows, setting both of our stomachs gurgling. It was after school, and I was hungry anyway. Finally, my grandfather pushed through the frosted glass door, his arms loaded with two large cardboard boxes of two hundred small cookies each. Lisa whined from the back and put her snout on my shoulder. Her wagging tail thumped against the seat. Oatmeal was her favorite.

We headed down Gaffey, then turned left on Channel Street, went under the 110 Freeway, then took John. S. Gibson Boulevard to the entrance of the American President Lines terminal, but instead of entering the yard, we veered off to the small dusty road that led to Donahue's. We waved at Gray, APL's security guard, as we passed. We drove by the red barge crane that was so seldom used that tall, green weeds grew on its wooden deck. We drove by the pack of rusty, black barges chained to their rusty metal pilings, all of them frosted with bird poop. Then came our boat at its end tie, then the rest of the marina, until we bounced into the dirt parking lot.

My grandfather carried the boxes of cookies, and I held Lisa's leash. Lisa peed all over the sidewalk outside the marina office, the amber flood carving a path through the dust. While we waited, my grandfather sent a friendly wave to Chuck, who sat in the marina's dark office.

"Sir Richard! Hey!" he called, but did not come out from behind the desk.

We walked down the ramp to the dock. A woman passed us wearing a belt with a Mercedes emblem as a buckle. I looked at it carefully as she passed, the emblem to my grandfather's car having been broken off and stolen at the marina only the week before. Hers was gold plated; it wasn't ours.

When we got on board the boat, I took Lisa and the cookies to the front cabin while my grandfather went upstairs. The doorknob to the cabin's plywood door was a hole with a string pulled through and latched to a nail. Inside, there was a cheap twin bed, a couple of rickety chairs, and windows shaded with faded Ronald McDonald sheets. It was the only room so far that had windows, huge ones custom made to my grandfather's specifications at Gandy Glass in Wilmington and delivered in special crates.

My grandfather had named our boat the *Intrepid,* not the *Athena.* Just after he'd bought her, he'd had her entire cabin torn down and the lower decks gutted. He paid a marine architect—a slight man with bad breath and a collection of pens in his shirt pocket—to design a new two-story cabin with a galley, dining salon, and living quarters on the main deck and a chartroom and pilothouse on the upper. He only came to dinner at our house once. When he wouldn't make the cabin's ceilings as high as my grandfather wanted them to be, my grandfather fired him, took the plans, and simply wrote new heights for the cabins. The result was a boat that looked something like a three-tiered wedding cake, whose tall superstructure would catch the wind like a wooden sail, making her difficult to maneuver or dock.

Upstairs, a saw whined, then grated against wood. I could hear the end piece fall to the floor above me. Then I heard my grandfather's heavy steps, and the saw turned off.

My grandfather had hired Guillermo, a fifty-something Argentine carpenter with a perpetually bad back and delicate stomach, along with a revolving assortment of other laborers, to build the boat's new cabin and interior. By now, he'd built the cabin's main deck and was working on the top. Guillermo lived in his own tiny boat perched on top of a cradle in a small boatyard in Wilmington. He became a regular at dinner. Sometimes he brought his friend Mexican Jack, who also lived in the boatyard. Jack was in his seventies, tall and thin, with silver hair, dark brown skin, and eyes that always glinted with some kind of friendly mischief. Guillermo was his straight man, and together they'd keep me laughing with silly joke after joke. Jack worked with Guillermo on our boat sometimes, lifting heavy loads and moving swiftly from woodpile to saw to scrap heap. Sometimes they'd bring me gifts carefully chosen at the Goodwill or Pic 'N' Sav: multicolored sweaters, a used silver chain, a framed print of an Indian princess and her canoe. The Indian princess sat on my shelf for years, and I'd daydream myself into that lush, moonlit forest, piloting that sturdy dugout down the silent, silver stream.

Guillermo was a slow, careful worker, and a nervous one as well, inclined to ulcers and diarrhea when stressed. It was stressful to work for my grandfather, who visited the boat every week. If Guillermo had made enough progress to satisfy him, all would be well: We'd all sit in the front cabin, my grandfather and I drinking tea made on a hot plate and served in perpetually dirty mugs, Guillermo sipping mate from a silver straw stuck into a silver cup.

We'd eat cookies, scooping them straight out of the box, and watch boats go by.

Just as often, however, something was wrong. As it was this day.

"What the fuck are you playing at?!" I heard my grandfather scream upstairs, and I knew there'd be no tea and cookies. My stomach tightened. Soon I heard footsteps ranging over the boat, my grandfather shouting as he took Guillermo on a tour, showing him what he hadn't done or what he'd done wrong. Once in a while Guillermo would try to get a word in edgewise.

"But Mr. Richard," I'd hear him start, his words drowned out by the stomping of my grandfather's feet and more shouting.

Lisa lay on the floor, whining softly. She looked up at me with her brown eyes.

After a while, Jack knocked on the door to the cabin and sat down on a chair across from me. His skinny brown ankles stuck out between the hem of his dirty jeans and dusty, black orthopedic shoes. His eyes were wide behind his big glasses.

"I hate it when he gets like this, you know?" he said. "No offense."

"It's okay," I agreed. "I hate it too."

"He shout at you like that?"

"Sometimes," I shrugged. It wasn't *that* often.

I felt ashamed of my grandfather, the way he raged at people for no reason. It made me nervous too; my stomach, a little like Guillermo's, tied itself into knots and twists. Together, Jack and I waited for the storm to subside, watching the empty channel through a gap in the sheets. When it was over, my grandfather opened the door to the cabin and called in.

"Come on. We're leaving."

The way he screamed at the people who worked for him made no sense and neither did their loyalty to him, except that he was also a very generous employer. He supplemented paychecks with cash under the table, paid doctor and hospital bills, made interest-free loans, cooked dinner, and poured drinks. When somebody was sick or had to go home to visit family for extended stays, he held their job for them until they returned.

Guillermo would disappear for a week at a time after these episodes, then come back when he and Jack were running low on money. He'd apologize, my grandfather would apologize, and for a few weeks, all would be well. Work on the boat was very slow.

That evening, after dinner, I spread a picture of Bob Dylan over the coffee table and lined up my pencils: 3H, 2H, 2B, 6B. I didn't really know the difference between them, but lining them up with the tortillon, art gum, kneaded eraser, and silver-tone pencil sharpener made me feel like a real artist—though I didn't feel like a very good one at that particular moment. One of Bob Dylan's nostrils was too big, and I was trying to erase it without ripping the newsprint or erasing any more of his nose than I had to. Our fourth-grade art teacher, Mrs. Mole, had shown us how to draw enlargements. You took a small photograph or a drawing and drew a grid of squares over it. Then you drew a grid with the same number of bigger squares on a much larger sheet of paper. You reproduced each small square in the larger square, drawing the same lines, filling in the same shadow. At the end, the squares combined to make a larger version of the picture you started out with. It was painstaking, required a sort of mindless focus, and took a very long time—the kind of meticulous art project I liked best. Drawing was my favorite thing to do after reading; when you drew, it was like you walled yourself off from the world around you while you created a better world all your own. But because procrastinating was maybe my third-favorite thing to do, I'd left too much of the project until the night before it was due, and my heart was beating a little too fast in my chest. What would happen if I didn't finish? I always turned my homework in. Always. And now Bob Dylan's nostril was too big.

Of the many black-and-white photographs she'd brought for us to pick from, I'd chosen a torn-out *Life* portrait of Bob Dylan. Beautiful, supercool Mrs. Mole, in her black denim skirt and Chucks, had nodded approvingly. "*Dylaaan*," she'd said, in a way that suggested we shared some significant knowledge, which, in fact, we did not. I had no idea who Bob Dylan was.

For days, I'd colored each small square with an artist pencil, evening out the pencil strokes with the tortillon and carefully erasing stray marks. That night, as I worked on my picture, kneeling at the coffee table, Marilyn sat on the couch behind me, watching the news. My grandfather still sat at the dining room table behind us. Bowls containing the dregs of beef stew were strewn across the table, a half-eaten baguette sat in its own crumbs. Peter Jennings was busy telling us what was wrong with the world, and I'd just fixed the nose, when Marilyn jerked forward and threw up on the coffee table.

"I'm sorry, I'm sorry," she said, softly, wiping her mouth with the back of her hand.

I'd never seen Marilyn sick like that before. "Are you okay? What's the matter?" I asked.

"What's going on?" my grandfather hollered from behind us.

I went to grab a glass of water for her and some towels to clean up. When I came back, he was telling her she only had herself to blame: "That's what you get when you drink on an empty stomach." She hung her head like a scolded child.

"Are you okay?" I asked again as I helped her clean up. I didn't understand the worry I felt; I knew I shouldn't be so scared.

"It's okay, honey, I just don't feel good." She let me wipe her freckled legs, the spatters on the table.

"She drank too much," my grandfather said, still seated at the table, spraddle-legged. "You drink too much on an empty stomach, then eat too much rich food, that's what happens."

"It wasn't that, Richard," Marilyn said with a sigh and got up to wash her face and brush her teeth.

For as long as I could remember, Marilyn had had a cocktail or two while making dinner. She usually drank rum and Cokes—a drink we called an "Engineer's Special" after some naval engineer my grandfather knew. Sometimes she drank sherry, the Dry Sack my grandfather kept among several bottles on the small table by the door. The rum and the sherry were among the few that needed to be replaced regularly. The others were the Beefeater Gin and the Johnnie Walker Scotch that our across-the-street neighbors drank when they came to visit. I'd never thought twice about Engineer's Specials or sherries; they were just a treat for the person who cooked.

That night, I was worried that Marilyn was sick, but I was mad at her too. The portrait was splattered with reddish-brown vomit; it had soaked through beneath a curl of Bob Dylan's hair. I dabbed it with a wet towel and got most of it off, though the paper was now stained with brown dots. I stayed up late to finish, moving to the table in my room, shading squares as hastily as I dared. An argument began in the living room.

"We've got to get income *up*!" I heard my grandfather say. "We're spending more than we're taking in. Any fool can see that."

"Well, maybe we should spend less money on the boat," Marilyn offered.

"It's not the fucking boat."

"Well, what the hell is it then, Richard? We can't magically make more money out of thin air."

Soon there were sounds of shouting and cabinet doors slamming, chairs being shoved into the table, Marilyn stomping into the kitchen, my grandfather stomping after her. I hated hearing them fight.

Nothing really bad happened when my parents fought. No one was beaten; few things were broken. It always started as a rumble, usually at dinner. Perhaps Marilyn, who'd started working more and more on the business, had been delayed running errands and made dinner too late for my grandfather's liking. Perhaps the food wasn't prepared quite the way he thought it should be. And so the fight would start with a one-sided dissection of the meal gone wrong:

"Yes, you've got to be careful with fish. It gets overcooked so easily. Of course, this fish wasn't so great to begin with. You've got to get fish at Bristol Farms, not Hughes or Ralphs. I've told you that."

"Okay," she'd say, looking down at her lap.

"Now, the potatoes are quite good. If you'd put just a touch less salt in them, I think they'd be very good indeed. The brussels sprouts, I'm not sure what you were thinking. You've overwhelmed them with all this crap."

The brussels sprouts, as it happened, had been a hit with him two weeks before. They were smothered in tomatoes, onions, and bacon—even *I* liked them.

"I thought you liked them," Marilyn would say, lifting her chin. "You liked them last time."

"No, no. I've never eaten these before. The thing is, when you cook them this way, they get bitter."

"I like them," I'd pipe in.

"No one asked you."

And things would progress from there to the store, the boat, money.

That night, I closed the door to my bedroom to muffle the voices and went into my closet. I'd put the step stool I'd used as a little girl to reach the sink into the far end of the closet for just such occasions. I sat on my stool in the dark, breathing in the smell of my clean clothes and Marilyn's dry-cleaned coats and dresses in their plastic sleeves.

Lisa nosed her way into my bedroom and shoved her head into the closet, wagging her tail wanly. I got up and closed the bedroom door again, pushed aside some clothes to make room for her. Together we waited it out.

Dear God, I thought, please don't let them get a divorce. I was scared of divorce the way I was scared of nuclear war, another Great Depression, the "big one" on the San Andreas Fault. I knew if they got divorced, I'd have to go to live with my grandfather and that Marilyn, unrelated to me by blood and not my legally adopted mother, would have no rights to see me. My grandfather had told me as much after one of their arguments.

"And I wouldn't give her any, either," he'd said. "If she leaves me, she loses you, as far as I'm concerned."

That particular fight was a memory so hazy even then, as I sat in the closet at nine years old, I think it must have happened when I was much younger, before we started looking for boats. It might have been the summer I explored every inch of our house, narrating my adventures in pseudo-documentary style, like the National Geographic specials we watched on TV; the summer I'd climbed up the shelves of our pantry like the side of a mountain and found old, battered tins of Lapsang Souchong and Coleman Mustard Powder, mysterious artifacts of a time before Twinings tea bags and Grey Poupon in glass jars. It was the summer I'd first spotted

Michele's ashes in the garage, the summer I'd found Marilyn's collection of bath salts and tiny, beautifully wrapped, rose-scented soaps piled beneath the sink—years of gifts from ESL students. And next to the bath salts, Marilyn's diaphragm, nestled in a box that looked like a cosmetic case, which is why I'd opened it.

When I asked her what it was, she'd calmly explained that it stopped her from having babies. This made me profoundly sad because I'd wanted a little sister; I'd even asked her for one. Perhaps she saw my crestfallen look because, almost as an afterthought, she added, "Not with Daddy. With someone I wasn't married to."

That evening, she let me use the bath salts and little soaps. She sat on the closed toilet while I washed, patiently opening each one and letting me smell so I could pick the right scent.

The fight during that summer of exploration hadn't been especially loud, and so I hadn't heard what it was about. What was different was what happened the next day. The morning after, Marilyn had refused to get out of bed. My grandfather shooed me away when I knocked on her door. Around lunchtime, she left the house without taking a shower and without saying goodbye.

"Mommy's gone for a drive," he told me.

"Why?" Marilyn never just went for a drive.

"She's had a nervous breakdown."

A breakdown, I thought; she broke. Something had been too hard for her to bear, like the donkey and the straw. That was a breakdown.

"Women have them sometimes," he explained.

I thought he meant a drive around the peninsula, something short, but I waited hours for her to come back. My grandfather was preoccupied, too busy to play or watch a movie. We ate TV dinners.

"She'll either come back or she won't," he said when I asked. I think I must have panicked when I heard this, but I don't remember reacting at all.

Finally, I lay on her bed in her quiet, clean room, and breathed in her smell from the sheets. I watched the sun set against her silver, bamboo-patterned wallpaper, making it shine orange and gold, then watched it fade into smoky shadow. I fell asleep.

She woke me in the dark, scooping me up and cradling me tightly against her chest.

"I thought you were gone," I mumbled.

"Oh, honey," she sighed into my shoulder and rubbed small circles on my back. "I wouldn't leave you."

Afterward, she seemed sad for days.

I turned in my picture of Bob Dylan the next morning. When Mrs. Mole gave it back to me, she circled the throw-up spots with her red pencil. *Don't drink or eat while you're working on your art,* she wrote in the margins, *MESSY.* I felt ashamed that Mrs. Mole thought I was a pig, and another shame that stopped me from explaining what had really happened.

12

ONE SATURDAY MORNING, MY GRANDFATHER TOOK ME ALONG to drop some tapes off at the store. While I waited, I spied on the customers. Cars came and left, a BMW and an old Chevy Caprice, a couple of Hondas. A Toyota pickup pulled into the slot next to me. A fat white man in sweats got out and waved his hand at me. Not knowing what else to do, I waved back shyly. A black man in jeans and a clean, white shirt walked purposefully down the sidewalk on Century as if he were going to keep going, but at the last minute, he swerved into the store's entrance. Another white man, this one bald and skinny, walked out with a brown paper bag.

My grandfather had tried to explain to me what porn was and why it wasn't that bad. His main argument was that if a man needed to have sex, wouldn't it be better if he went to our video store instead of raping someone? So I'd thought the men who frequented my grandfather's store were probably those too ugly to get a date and rapists, although I still wasn't entirely sure what rape was. I imagined the men having greasy jowls and handlebar mustaches—that they'd be fat men with receding hairlines, freckled men with yellow teeth. But the men who parked in our parking lot always looked like normal men.

A yellow cab pulled into the lot, stopping behind me. A Japanese man in a suit got out and asked the cab to wait. He walked out a few minutes later with a full bag, my grandfather walking beside him. When they got to the cab, he opened the door for the Japanese man, shook his hand, then waved as the cab drove off.

"Good man," my grandfather said as he got in the car. "Hard stuff to get in Japan, I suppose."

So many different kinds of men came to our store, I thought every man must look at porn once in a while.

"And thank goodness they do, too," Marilyn would sometimes say with a roll of her eyes. "Our little gold mine."

Everything we had, my grandfather would often remind me, came from that store, and we had more than many families I knew. It was why Marilyn and I could buy new clothes at stores like Buffums and Bullock's and take trips, why we could own a boat, and why I had toys, a playhouse in the backyard, books, videos.

"That store," he'd say, "is the reason you're so fucking spoiled."

That day, as we pulled out of the parking lot, my grandfather asked, "Shall we get some lunch? Let's go to the old Chinaman's. You'd like that, wouldn't you?" I nodded happily.

He took me to the Flower Drum, the Chinese restaurant that was a few blocks west of our store on Century Boulevard. I loved going to the restaurant we called the Flower Drum Song, after the movie, the way you walked by the red-lacquered columns and stone lions of its entry into a dark room paneled with wood intaglio, then were seated at a round table.

"I've been coming here for years," my grandfather said, sighing as we entered.

"How's the old man?" he asked the waitress who came to our table, as he always did. He knew the owner and the owner's father.

Then he ordered hot tea for himself, a virgin piña colada for me, cashew chicken and kung pao beef, pork fried rice, and wor wonton soup. Wor wonton was my favorite. It was what we ate instead of chicken noodle soup when someone in our family had a cold.

As we ate our soup, with its cloudy dumplings and soft bok choy sitting in the steaming broth, an old Chinese man walked slowly to our table. He'd come downstairs from the apartment above and looked sleepy, as if he'd just woken up, but his white undershirt was tucked neatly into his brown pants. He smiled at my grandfather and then at me. After they talked a bit, about business and the neighborhood, he pointed at my drink, then shuffled away again. There was the sound of the blender. A few minutes later, he returned with a new virgin colada, then left once more.

After we finished eating, my grandfather sighed a little, then crumpled a napkin on the table with his clawed hand.

"The boat's almost ready for us to move on board," he said. I was busy picking the tiniest crumbs of fortune cookie off of my place mat with a wet finger. "Marilyn doesn't want to move, so you be the tiebreaker. It's all up to you. You'd like to live on board, wouldn't you?"

I tucked the fortune into my pocket so that it would come true. I hadn't realized that we were going to move on to the boat, or at least I hadn't thought about how that would mean we'd have to leave our rental house. I thought of what Marilyn had said about the *Sirocco*. I glanced at the bar where one of the waiters sat bored in the middle of a slow afternoon. I thought about our house, the yard with the coral tree, my bedroom with its many shelves of toys. I looked back at my place mat, its zodiac animals arranged neatly in a circle. I thought about the boat, how it smelled of fresh sawdust and paint thinner. It always held some new adventure—a new tool, a new joke from Jack or Guillermo, a new laborer with a new set of tattoos to peruse. I thought of whale watching and seeing dolphins. I thought of Marilyn, who had seemed a little sad recently. I knew she didn't want to move on to the boat. But Marilyn often seemed sad and had as far back as I could remember. And then I looked up at my grandfather, who stared at me across the table, eager and prompting and hopeful. I knew that he wanted to move on to that boat, maybe more than he wanted anything in the world.

"Yes," I said. "I want to live on the boat."

He seemed proud of himself on the drive home, as if he'd won an argument. His estimate of the boat's level of completion was optimistic. It would be two more years before we moved on to the boat, and even then, it still wasn't finished.

13

THE DAY WE MOVED ON BOARD SEEMED LIKE A SMALL-TOWN
Fourth of July at Donahue's Marina, and we were the
parade. Weathered, suspicious men and women poked their heads
out of portholes and hatches to check on our progress. Some
people pulled up lawn chairs and coolers of beer to watch us as we
went by wheeling boxes on hand trucks, carrying trash bags stuffed
with clothes, furniture, small appliances, and heavy boxes of books
down the 150-yard dock. Two very large and friendly dogs, Lisa
and Charlie, led the way, merrily peeing on dock boxes and piles of
rope. Ugly had finally died, and her box of ashes had joined everyone else's in the closet. She'd been replaced by Charlie, a Great
Dane mix my friend Beatrix and I had found shivering on the side
of the road. Of course my grandfather let us keep him.

As we went by, the guy who lived on the *Hump or Jump*—a
disheveled brigantine with a statue of the Hamburglar strapped to
its foremast, a boat which would later be renamed the *Sin or Swim*,
complete with the outline of two pairs of feet facing each other—
let out a large belch.

"It's like a floating trailer park," Marilyn muttered under her
breath.

We had enough possessions to sink any one of the boats we
passed; the people who lived on them must have wondered how

we would possibly find room for it all. Indeed, we'd gotten rid of our dining room table, which was too long for the dining salon; we'd sold and stored many of my grandfather's books; we'd given away most of my toys. Marilyn had given up her leather steamer trunk of memorabilia and notebooks.

Some people offered to help us, but we already had help. My grandfather had that morning gone to the gas station at the corner of Gaffey and Channel Streets, where Latino men gathered to be picked up for odd jobs. Construction trucks and vans would pull up, their drivers haggling to get the most workers for the lowest wages, waving cash around to make the offer more tempting. The men never knew where they'd end up or what kind of dangerous work they'd be getting themselves into. If they got hurt, there was no worker's comp, no help. My grandfather hired three guys to help with the heavy boxes, while Guillermo, Jack, Marilyn, and I carried the lighter things. At the end of the day, after dozens of trips up and down the dock and back and forth to our house, we were finally settled in our new home. I still have a picture of myself that first night on the boat, lounging in my top bunk, grinning from ear to ear at the adventure of it all.

When everything went wrong—when debts mounted up and the work on the boat never seemed to end—I thought it was all my fault. It was my fault because I'd told my grandfather yes when he'd asked that day at the Flower Drum. It was my fault we'd kept the boat, my fault we'd moved on board, my fault Marilyn was miserable. I'd be in my thirties before I'd realize that nothing I could have said would have stopped him.

When he was a little boy, my grandfather, like many English boys before him, dreamed of going to sea. He dreamt of foredeck and mast, sextant and chart, the Adriatic, the Aegean, the Baltic. He dreamed of voyages on the *Golden Hinde* or the *Endeavour,* adventures with Sir Francis Drake or Captain Cook. He dreamed of Admiral Lord Nelson, so beloved by his men that they carried his dead body home with them from Trafalgar, preserved in a cask of rum. I imagine that my grandfather, who was orphaned as a baby, also dreamed of being loved. After his parents died, he'd floated from relative to relative, to school after school, all over England—always moving, always alone. When he left England after the war, it was forever. He never returned for a visit, never wrote or received letters, never phoned anyone. He turned his back on his country, but the United States was never his home either. He spent most of his forty years here on an expired visa—refusing, even during the period of amnesty—to become a citizen.

My grandfather told me once that he wanted to live on a boat so that he'd be able to take his home with him wherever he went. If he'd learned anything as a child, it was always to be prepared for the next move.

II

When We Lived on a Boat

14

THE AFTERNOON BREEZE PUSHED OUR BOAT GENTLY UP AGAINST the dock, then released it, then pushed it up again. It wasn't a rocking, exactly, but a rhythmic glide and sway, followed by the gentle clunk of our rub rails and fenders against the dock, the creak of rope and wood. I was pretty sure my grandfather was taking a nap upstairs in his cabin. Marilyn was out running errands. It was hot outside, but it was pleasant in Marilyn's cabin in the cavelike hull, with her big portholes open so the breeze could blow through, carrying with it the sound of sheets hitting metal masts and the cries of gulls. But now I went around the room and closed each window, then drew each set of custom-made blinds. I wasn't sure if someone standing outside on the dock would be able to bend down and see through them, and I didn't want to take a chance.

I lifted the first heavy box from the stack lining the cabin wall and heaved it onto Marilyn's bed, then climbed onto the bed and knelt beside it. My heart was beating a little quicker than usual, although I'd done this before. I pulled open the thick flaps of cardboard and looked inside, careful not to touch the video boxes themselves. Brand new as they were, straight from the warehouse, their glossy surfaces were perfectly shiny—shinier than normal video boxes—as if pornography manufacturers thought their product needed an extra dose of slick. I didn't want to leave finger-prints. Marilyn would know what I'd done.

On a blue box, two young men in fake police uniforms and gun belts touched each other behind a set of fake black bars, their pants around their ankles: this was "gay action." The only penises I'd seen in real life were Peter Gererra's small, curled one in the second grade—he'd decided to flash the whole class after Mrs. Vaux told him to go to the principal's office—and my grandfather's uncut, wrinkled, hairy one, which hung out every time his dressing gown flapped open. But penises on porn boxes were huge, veined things, hard like metal flashlights or clubs, more like weapons than anything else. They were called "dongs" and "cocks." I'd known these words before I'd started looking at the boxes, though; my grandfather used them all the time. But I couldn't imagine a penis inside me the way these were jammed into the glistening vaginas, anuses, and mouths on the boxes. The prospect scared me. I was twelve.

Since we'd moved on to the boat from our house, Marilyn had taken to storing the big cardboard boxes in her office and bedroom, which were right next to each other, on the other side of the bathroom from my cabin. The heavy boxes lined one entire wall of the rooms, two or three high, sometimes blocking the portholes. Even though I wasn't supposed to, I looked inside them every once in a while. Sometimes I also looked in Marilyn's office, which was littered with junk from the store. There were months' worth of tape rental contracts and receipts; decrepit parts from coin accep-tors; the occasional forgotten, defective toy hidden under Marilyn's desk: inflatable dolls with round mouths and badly drawn pubic hair, a forlorn vibrator in its opened box, colorful plastic things called "butt plugs."

I was trying to understand something.

The year before, Le Lycée had gone boy and girl crazy, but I hadn't. The girls wanted to talk about French-kissing, and the boys wanted to talk about "second base." My friend Pauline wanted to tell me how far she'd gone with my classmate Benito, but I didn't want to think about that. I could still remember the time Benny peed his pants in first grade. I thought I liked guys fine, and I imagined that kissing one would be nice, especially if it were Gregory Peck. No one in seventh grade was like Gregory Peck. And I was nothing like the girls on whom the boys had crushes. I was fat, round in the wrong places, and flat in the others. My hair hung limply against a shiny face. I still had traces of a mustache, even after Marilyn had taken me for expensive electrolysis treatments, and my eyebrows bore a striking resemblance to Bert's from *Sesame Street*. I was tired of how everyone at school kept talking about boys and girls and sex, including me in the conversation because I happened to be standing there, but not because they thought I was kissable or cute. I thought if I looked at enough video boxes, I'd understand what they were so excited about.

On the back of a red box—the deep red of velvet theater curtains—a woman ran her pink tongue along a man's penis, her mouth glistening. On another box, a man lay spraddle-legged on a bed, gripping his penis in his hand while two ponytailed blonds knelt in front of him, kissing each other and caressing each other's impossibly big breasts.

Breasts, I'd learned, were called "knockers." Two girls kissing was "girl-on-girl;" if you added a guy, it was a "threesome;" if you added a bunch of other guys, it was a "gang bang;" if you added guys *and* girls, it was an "orgy." Vaginas were "pussies" and "cunts." I hated the word "pussy;" it made me think of the soft, furry back of a cat—one of our cats—which meant it was filthy with the dust of the marina. "Pussy" was the word boys called each other when what they meant was "chicken." I hated the word "cunt" too; when I whispered it to myself, it made me cower a little, as if I were about to be hit.

I left the box and went to my cabin to look in my mirror. First I made sure no one on the dock was looking through the portholes. Then I covered the pictures of Michele and Spence on my bookshelf with a towel. (My little shrine had moved with me on to the boat, although my grandfather forbade me from lighting the candles in case of fire. I sometimes did anyway.) Covering the pictures with the towel didn't really help; I was pretty sure they could see me from heaven. I was pretty sure they were ashamed of me, but I couldn't stop myself.

In front of the mirror, I tried, but failed, to form a porn star's sexy pout, her alluring lick of the lips. When *I* did it, I looked like a self-conscious fish. When I licked my lips seductively, it just looked like I needed Chapstick.

I pulled up my T-shirt. Beneath it I wore the bra, not yet underwire, that Marilyn had taken me to buy. I pulled it up too. My breasts were not knockers; there was nothing "knockout" about them. They weren't round like melons, which was another word the boxes used. My nipples were not a rosy pink or a dark chocolate, but something boring in between. They didn't stand out pertly but were soft and limp, the nipple tips blending in with the areola. More than anything, they looked like the breasts of fat boys—my friends Ernesto and Mike from Le Lycée in their swim trunks at the beach. I turned to the side and while still holding up my shirt, pulled down my shorts to my knees. My thighs were mottled with cellulite, and my butt was fat and white. I tried to arch my back a little, the way porn stars did, to accent my curves. Still no good; you couldn't have curves when your middle was thick. I pulled my panties down and moved my hand toward the spot that was still only sparsely haired. And then I heard three thuds on the

escape hatch just above my head. I pulled my shorts up quickly.
Did my grandfather know what I was doing?

If I were ever caught in my cabin during a maritime disaster
and the watertight door to the bow were sealed, I was supposed to
use the escape hatch in my ceiling to climb up to the main deck.
But no one had thought to put a ladder in my room. Instead, the
hatch's more practical purpose was as a communication device
between my grandfather's cabin on the main deck and mine on
the lower one. It worked much better than the expensive inter-
com system he'd had installed. We'd discovered this use one night
when he collapsed and thought he was having a stroke. He'd
crawled to the hatch to thump on it to wake me up to call the
paramedics. When I got up there, my grandfather was dry heaving;
the floor was covered in vomit. He was too dizzy to stand. I
thought he was going to die, like Spence. I called 911 and didn't
cry until after the paramedics had gotten there. After a couple of
days at the hospital, he turned out to be fine, but now he stomped
his foot on the hatch whenever he wanted me, which was several
times a day. As I rushed to close the box of tapes and put it back
on the stack, I heard him stomp again. The noise always made my
heart leap in my chest.

"I can't find Stormcloud," my grandfather said when I reached
the top of the stairs. Like many of his statements of fact—"The
dishes are dirty," "This tea is cold"—it was not an indicative
sentence, but an imperative: "Go look for Stormcloud." Of our
six cats, Stormcloud, the charcoal one with the white tummy and
paws, was his favorite. She often went missing.

"Where have you looked?" I asked.

"Everywhere. She isn't with you, is she?"

I went back to look downstairs in Marilyn's office and her
cabin. I checked the towel shelves tucked behind the RV toilet in

the bathroom. Koko was asleep on my top bunk; Blackie Girl was asleep under Marilyn's bedspread. But Stormcloud was not.

I went upstairs to the top deck, looking beneath the chart table and in the boxes of papers and books we stored up there. I looked in the pilothouse under the navigation console. I looked outside on the top deck, in case she'd gotten out and couldn't get back in again. I thought I heard a faint meow and stopped to listen. It was just a seagull, high in the air.

I went downstairs and looked all over the main deck, in my grandfather's cabin, his tiny office, his closet, his bathroom with its Jacuzzi tub. I looked in the cabinets under the galley counter, where the cats often got themselves trapped among the cereal and water pipes. I looked outside on the main deck, where I found two cats snoozing in the sun and one of the tabbies sitting on the rail, chattering at a pelican, hind legs and tail twitching as if to pounce.

"In your dreams, Big Eyes," I muttered.

I cast an eye on the sailboat next door, where the cats sometimes ventured. Nothing. I looked in the room we called the "quiet room," where we kept a couch no one used. I went down to the aft lower deck. I looked in the laundry room behind the freezers. I peered into the lazarette back at the stern, which, like many things on the boat, was still unfinished. It was completely dark. There was no floor, only open bilges divided by the massive rods of the boat's twin propellers. If you cast a flashlight toward its low ceiling, you'd see the glint of hundreds of nail points that held down the deck above, like the inside of an iron maiden.

"Stormcloud," I called into the void. "Kitty, kitty!"

Again I thought I heard the faint meow, only this time, behind me. Could she have gotten into the engine room?

The generator was off. I could barely lift the lever of the massive, watertight door that sealed the engine room off from the rest of the ship. When I did, the door's rubber seals gave a tired sigh.

The engine room was its own shadowed world, and because of the noise of the generators and its dirt, I hardly ever went inside. When the *Intrepid* was a working boat, this room had been its heart, but now it was quiet and cool. It smelled of bilgewater, diesel, the nutmeg scent of dry rot—a combination of smells that for some reason I loved.

"Stormcloud?" I called and began to search. I peered under the three generators—Northern Lights 8kW, 12kW, and 20kW—then moved to the engines. Only two of her four original GM engines remained. My grandfather had had the other two Jimmies stripped and cannibalized for parts, their heavy, bare skeletons removed by crane through hatches in the dining room's floor and ceiling.

The *Intrepid*'s serial number and building date were stamped on a center beam above her empty engine mounts, like the date on a building's cornerstone. Standing in the engine room, I felt closest to the boat's soul. It was the only place you could tell how old she was, where you had a sense of the years she'd weathered. None of us knew it at the time, but our boat had served at the Normandy invasion, one of fifty-four Coast Guard ships that rescued wounded men. Now, sloppy piles of loose parts covered every flat surface; stacks of ceiling tiles, insulation, and tools were crammed into corners.

"Kitty, kitty?"

The engine room was Pete's domain. A urinal bottle stained with black grease sat on top of one of the engine mounts. A plaid shirt and a pair of work pants hung neatly on a hook by the tank room door. My grandfather called Pete our "engineer," but he also did electrical and woodwork. I never saw him without his leather dress boots, no matter how messy a job was, the left boot wedged into a clinking, metal brace; his leg had been injured in a plane crash, back when he ranched sheep on Santa Cruz Island. He'd been trapped for a whole day in the wreckage on a remote hillside, and if you asked nicely, he would show you the long scar running up his calf. Pete called me "peanut" and "half pint," and for a week—when I'd cut my leg open ice-skating—"gimp," as in, "You're gimpy now, just like me." This was why he needed the urinal: the nearest bathroom was a long, clumping walk up the steep stairs.

"Stormcloud?" I called again. "Kitty, kitty!" I peered into the tank room, whose bilges had only recently been floored over by Pete. No cat.

I, too, was getting worried. Cats falling overboard had been an occasional occurrence. Usually they pulled themselves up out of the water and appeared at our door soaking wet. We hadn't lost one. Yet.

Another meow. I moved to the starboard side of the engine room and listened. It was definitely a cat, and it was coming from outside, at water level.

Outside on the dock, I kneeled and peered through a gap between worn planks. I could just make her out, sitting on one of the Styrofoam floats, trapped.

"What is it? Have you found her?" my grandfather wanted to know.

"Yes," I said. "I'm going to have to go get her."

I changed into my swimsuit and waited for the breeze to push the boat farther from the dock. I stuck my feet into the cold, shadowed water between them; it made my skin crawl to touch it. Every night we pumped our holding tanks of raw sewage into the water, the smell wafting back to us through our open portholes. The toilets behind the marina office also flushed straight into the harbor. A smelly slick of diesel floated on the water's surface. But the cat was crying, and my grandfather was telling me to hurry, and, also, I wanted very badly to be a hero. I lowered myself carefully into the water, resisting the urge to gag, then held my breath and dove under to swim beneath the dock.

When I came up, I was beneath it. I treaded water madly because there was nothing to hold on to. The salt stung my eyes. It was a shadowy world, the water lapping against the Styrofoam floats and wood and onto my lips, the only light coming through the gaps between the dock's planks. Mossy fronds of algae and slick sea cucumbers tickled my shoulders and back. Stormcloud crouched on a float, meowing, her ears flat against her head.

"Come here, kitty," I called. She didn't budge. I tried to grab her, but I couldn't tread water without my hands. I sank; I came up again. That cat wasn't going to move from the one dry perch she'd found. I'd have to grab her, then dive underwater toward the boat. I hoped she'd know to hold her breath.

"Can you see her?" I heard my grandfather call.

"Yes! Just a second." I didn't know if he'd heard me.

I gave one hard kick, grabbed the cat, squeezed her close to my chest, then dove back under the dock again. I popped up between the boat and the dock and hurled her over my head and onto the dock. She made a mad scramble onto the boat. My grandfather followed her inside. I tried to pull myself onto the dock, but my arms weren't strong enough. The top of the dock was two feet above my head, and there was nothing for my feet to push off of. I tried again. I was alone in the shadow between the boat and the dock. The boat drifted slowly toward me. Finally, I heaved myself onto the dock. My chest and arms were bleeding from cat scratches. I was alone and breathless, left to feel heroic on my own.

When Marilyn got home, she wondered why I'd closed all the portholes on such a hot day. In all the excitement, I'd forgotten to reopen them.

"You did what?!" Pete asked the next morning as we all drank tea together and I boasted about rescuing the cat. "Richard, you let her do that?"

"What do you mean? If she hadn't done that, the cat might have drowned. She's a hero."

Pete straightened the crease in his street pants. "Yeah, but *she* might have drowned. If the boat had swung to and she was between it and the dock, she would have been crushed."

"Well, I knew which way the wind was blowing," my grandfather muttered.

Pete turned back to me and spoke gently; his blue eyes were serious. "Don't you ever do that again, pumpkin. I don't care what for. Don't put yourself between a boat and something else." He smiled again, perfect teeth white against his full beard, then flicked my knee with an oil-stained finger. "Wouldn't want you to get smushed."

15

Y OU HAD TO HIT THE TENNIS BALL JUST RIGHT AGAINST THE wall of the yellow shack that housed the marina office, careful to avoid the cracked plate glass windows and their rough, blue frames. The empty lot that surrounded the shack was dirt—a fine dust, really—sprinkled with bits of chalky shells, sun-bleached clams, and whelks. If the ball landed in the dust, it sank instead of bouncing, and you couldn't hit it. But there was an old finger of dock placed against the shack that served as a sidewalk to the two bathrooms and showers at the back, and if you hit the ball just right against the wall, it bounced onto the dock and back onto your racquet. It took a lot of patience to achieve a rhythm, but when you did, it was like breathing: the steady beat of your heart, the bounce of the ball, and the swing of the racquet. The practice did not make me better at tennis, but I didn't much mind. I only ever played with Le Lyçée's PE teacher, Mlle Cussaguet, who gave lessons after school. I liked how playing tennis felt, even if I didn't care about being good, so I had spent many of my seventh-grade lunches hitting a ball against a cinder block wall in the far corner of the playground and my after-schools and weekends and vacations hitting against the wall of the marina's office.

Into my tennis practice that day walked Perry on his way to a shower, wearing only his jeans and flip-flops, the only kind of shoes that still fit his bloated, calloused feet. The edges of the thongs were buried deep in his flesh, threatening to cut the skin. Perry was big but frail at the same time, sick with something like emphysema, although no one was sure what was wrong with him, exactly; he wouldn't say. He was tall and his legs were thin, but his belly was inflated, stretched round and tight as if close to bursting—different from my grandfather's stomach and different from the beer bellies at the marina. He stared at the ground in front of him as he walked, careful not to trip, leaning back a little to counteract the pull of his dog's leash. It was only because of Suzy Q's pinch collar that she did not pull him over trying to get to me. I stopped hitting the ball as they passed.

"You want me to look after Suzy Q while you're in the shower?" I asked.

"Yes, sweetheart. That'd be wonderful," Perry sighed as much as said, rubbing a hand over a week's growth of silver whiskers. He let go of the leash, which unfurled from his fist like fishing line off its spool, and Suzy Q came bounding toward me, her white paws still too big for her body, her head coming up to my shoulder when she jumped. We already had two dogs on our boat, Lisa and Charlie, but I wasn't loyal; when I was twelve, I loved any dog, hard. Suzy and I played tug-of-war outside the shower door with the increasingly slithery tennis ball, Suzy's claws scratching my legs and arms. Behind the wooden door, a toilet flushed and then the shower came on.

Perry lived on a tiny cruiser in the first slip of the marina, right next to the ramp, across the finger from the *Hump or Jump*. His boat was not much bigger than the yellow, 1960s Econoline van he drove; it might have been smaller. He spent most of his days sitting shirtless on its stern with Suzy Q, either smoking or taking his oxygen or hacking up huge wads of phlegm and spitting them into the water. We'd lived at Donahue's for a little over a year, and Perry was the only person there I really liked. Every day after school, when I came walking down the ramp, he was there to greet me, and while Marilyn or my grandfather walked ahead, I usually stayed to talk to him and pet Suzy Q. Before I'd leave, I'd give him a hug; it was the only time I saw him smile. But Perry was getting sicker and sicker, we could all tell. Everyone at the marina seemed to think it wouldn't be long now. No one said what would happen to Suzy Q if he died.

When Perry came out of the shower, his skin was still damp and he smelled like Irish Spring. Different people came out of the showers smelling like different soaps, but most of them went in smelling the same way, the way sweat smells when a person drinks a lot of beer. It was something you noticed if you played tennis outside of the marina showers. My family, ensconced on our big boat at the far end tie, didn't drink much beer—Marilyn preferred wine—and we didn't use the marina's communal showers. These were only two of the things that made us different from everyone else.

"Thanks, darling," he said as he took a seat beside me on the dock sidewalk. He pulled out a cigarette, the generic kind, and lit up.

"I wish you wouldn't do that," I said. "You know you're not supposed to do that."

Perry took it from me because I was a girl, but he didn't put the cigarette out. I knew that if anyone else had said it, he would have told them to fuck off. I'd even seen him tell Annie to fuck off, and she cooked his meals for him, and sometimes, when he was nice to her, gave him a shave. Annie, who lived with her husband on a white trawler three slips over from Perry, said that when he was young, Perry was a real SOB. But he wasn't now, or at least he wasn't to me.

We sat a while together, side by side. A ship had come in at the

APL terminal, and the longshoremen were unloading it. Waiting semis lined the road that led from our marina to the terminal's entrance. Across the water at Todd's Shipyard, the green metal cranes rumbled along the tracks built into the dock; white pickups rushed along the water's edge.

"They're getting ready...to close Todd's," Perry said. "You know, in the War. That place built a ship a week. Now what?" He stopped to breathe. "Well, all those people are losing their jobs. That's what."

I didn't say anything; I didn't want Todd's to close either. Sometimes Navy frigates or empty cruise ships tied up across the water from us, casting a shadow over our marina, and I'd watch the crews scramble over their towering decks, looking like so many ants.

"Maybe they won't close after all," was all I could offer. Perry snorted.

When he was done with his cigarette, he smashed the butt beneath the rubber sole of his flip-flop. He got up and walked down the dock sidewalk, then slowly down the steep ramp to the dock, leaning back as Suzy Q pulled.

My tennis ball was too soggy with drool to play with anymore, but I didn't go home right away. I kept my seat on the dock sidewalk and watched the harbor instead, the seagulls wheeling in the blue sky, the crews loading a tanker at the oil farm next door. The breeze coming from the shadows of the eucalyptus trees smelled of must and menthol. Jerry's chickens foraged in the weeds by his RV. Out at the other end of the channel, beyond the reeds, the traffic hummed along the 110 on its way to the Vincent Thomas Bridge.

Compared to other marinas in the harbor, Donahue's was tiny, nestled in the Southwest Slip of the West Basin, at Berth 117. The Southwest Slip opened into the harbor's Main Channel, the waterway that leads to the Outer Harbor, then to the breakwater, and then out to the Pacific. The other end of the slip dead-ended into a small, saltwater marsh. Two hundred years before, most of the LA Harbor was like that marsh: wetland and mudflats edged by a shallow bay. It was the home of the Gabrielino Indians, and later, Juan Capistrano Sepúlveda's adobe home. But these were gone without a trace, not even a historical marker, obliterated by busy roads and strip malls, freight yards and oil refineries. The marsh at the end of the Southwest Slip was one of the last remnants of that original wetland. Birds haunted the reeds—white egrets and night herons and great blue herons—ghosts against the rustling green. Sometimes the birds landed on the schooner next to our boat, standing one-legged on its railing, waiting for fish.

The eucalyptus trees were the only plants in the marina's lot, except for a few anemic weeds. When the mudflats had been dredged to build the port, the salty mud was piled up on the newly formed shore. Eventually, most of the harborside was paved over or landscaped with grass. But nobody had ever thought to pave the part of the West Basin where we lived, and the mud had long since dried to a fine, beige dust that couldn't support life. With the right wind, or when the APL trucks used our parking lot to turn around, the dust blew in waves off the shore, shrouding everything in a pale cloud.

But it wasn't just the dust from shore that made the marina such a dirty place. All the exterior surfaces of our boat were flecked with particles of metal—iridescent reds, greens, and blues. These came from the scrap-metal terminal half a mile away on the Cerritos Channel, where cars were shredded and the metal loaded on to ships bound for Japan. More mysterious was the oily soot that clung to every smooth surface of our boat, covering it in a thin, black film. It made gray the white doors of our refrigerator and washer and dryer, the glass of our mirrors. We weren't sure whether the film came from the exhaust of ships and trucks or from the black smoke of our own diesel generators, which drifted back through our doors and portholes.

Sometimes I think that if you cut me open, my insides would still be black as soot, that they'd sparkle with a thousand flecks of steel. Maybe home is what you carry inside you, the way a place makes itself part of you, for good or for ill.

———————————

I put my racquet back in its case. I left the tennis ball on the ground for Suzy Q or some other lucky dog and headed home. Coming up the ramp from the dock was a young black woman followed by the Old White Man. I didn't like the Old White Man. He lived on a little, brown boat in the middle of the marina and always wore a khaki uniform with his name embroidered on the pocket above his heart, a silver pen inside the pocket. White, curly hair made a halo around his bald head, and a large nose sat stuck on his face like a lemon. In fact, he always looked like he'd just eaten a lemon, his face an angry pucker, his elbows frozen at sharp angles to his body. He never smiled, not once, no matter how many times I smiled at him or said hello. Every week, he had a different girlfriend.

I'd watch him bring his girlfriends up to the parking lot to wait for a ride. They were always much younger than he was and always black—some with short, straightened hair, some with braids, some short and curvy, some tall and lean—almost all with incredibly short shorts and tank tops that showed their cleavage. I hated him for how he always left them in the parking lot alone to wait for their rides, usually a cab or a friend with a car. I hated how he wouldn't even call the cab for them, but stuffed money into their hands or back pockets, and then, without so much as a goodbye, left them to call on the pay phone that was bolted to an old stub of a telephone pole in front of the shack. Sometimes the women didn't have quarters, and they'd ask softly to borrow some from me; but I never had any either, so I'd always shrug and say, "Sorry."

I smiled now at his girlfriend as she squeezed by me on the ramp. I wondered if she knew he'd break up with her soon. She smiled back shyly, as if she were embarrassed. The girlfriends always smiled back, and that was how you could tell they were nice— much too nice for him.

As I passed Perry's boat, I could hear the sound of his TV coming through the porthole—*Wheel of Fortune*—and his hacking cough. Two boats down, Stinky, the black-and-white cat, came trotting up to me, meowing furiously and rubbing against my legs. No one owned Stinky, but Wade, who lived in a two-story house-boat squeezed between the dock and the shore, fed her on a more or less permanent basis. Mostly she lived on his patio, among the potted plants and propane grill. I looked up at Wade's houseboat as I petted her; I could see him through the screen of his patio door, sitting on the couch, a can of Bud in his hand, the TV flickering blue light off his glasses.

"Hey, sweetheart," he called, waving.

I waved halfheartedly and walked on. I didn't much like Wade. His beer belly protruded from his too-small T-shirts as if he were eight months pregnant, and he always wore a cap with fake bird poop on the bill that said "Shit Happens." His hat especially bothered me. He had kids and a wife, but they weren't around very much. He was on disability, but Annie said there wasn't anything wrong with him except that he started drinking at eight in the morning.

I walked past the small, blue boat that belonged to the Pentecostal woman and skirted the broken plank where you could see through to the water. I passed the Chris-Craft where Davy and his two sons lived. Once, in a misguided attempt at philanthropy, I'd tried to teach the little one to read, but the magazine he'd brought from belowdecks was an old issue of *Hustler*. I passed by Gunner's sailboat and the retired tug *Ready*, as well as a dozen other ramshackle sailboats. I scurried past the boat with the high school boy who made fun of me, wolf whistling or calling, "*Hola, señorita*," then guffawing. I didn't understand why he did this, but I assumed it had something to do with my school uniform or our big, fancy boat or the way everyone at the marina called my grandfather "Sir Richard." I hated when the boy made fun of me, but I also understood it. In another set of circumstances, I would have hated us too.

All that lay between me and home was the small boat docked just behind ours where the tattooed woman lived. People said she had sex with men for drugs, but all I knew for sure was that something was wrong with her. Her brown hair was always greasy. Her shorts hung off her hips, exposing the sharp bones of her pelvis, the curl of her navel. Every inch of her skin, except her face, was covered in angry tattoos—dark blues and greens, deep reds, crosses and swastikas, all swirled and melted together. When she first moved to the marina, I lingered as I passed between her boat and mine, staring at her from the corners of my eyes. But I was scared of her now, and unfortunately for me, she was standing on the back of her boat as I passed.

"Hey! Hey, you!" she screamed.

Against my better judgment, I stopped; I didn't want to be rude.

"Hey, you tell your father he's an asshole, okay?" she swayed as she shouted. "I know what he's doing! I know what they're doing in there!"

I started walking again and turned down our wobbly finger of dock.

"Hey, hey! I'm not done, you little bitch, come back here!"

I didn't take her screaming personally. She screamed at anyone who passed; she screamed all the time. But she still scared me. Once, late at night, she'd come on board, trying to open the locked doors and knocking on our windows, like Catherine Earnshaw's wraith in *Wuthering Heights*. "Let me in! I want to come home!" she'd called at our sealed doors until, finally, she'd wandered away.

And then I was home, climbing up the creaky plywood stairs Guillermo had built, opening the gate of our bulwarks, and sliding open the door to the deckhouse. Crybaby, the light gray tabby, slinked in quickly, as if he, too, were alarmed by the screaming woman.

She would disappear a few months later, vanish overnight. Her boat was still there, but she was gone. Donahue's was like that. People came and went. Sometimes they'd come to live on a boat that was already there; sometimes they'd bring a new boat. Sometimes they left with a different boat; sometimes they left with nothing more than the clothes on their backs.

16

I HADN'T BEEN HOME LONG WHEN I HEARD TRACY KNOCK; I WAS never home long before she knocked. Even before she began calling my name, I knew it was her. "Kelly, Kelly!" she yelled.

I hid downstairs in Marilyn's office, away from portholes where Tracy, peering in, might see me. She was the only other child on the dock close to my age. She lived on board a small Chris-Craft with her mother, Sharon, and sometimes her stepfather—or father, I was never sure which—named Al. I was twelve and she was eleven, but she looked fourteen. She wore short shorts and swung her hips when she walked. When she'd come over to play, she'd manage to snap her bra strap at least once to let me know that she was wearing one. And she lied. All the time. About everything. I hated playing with her. Soon I heard her pacing along the dock as she called my name, over and over again. Whenever I didn't answer her summons, she'd walk along the dock, yelling and staring in all the portholes to make sure I really wasn't home. Sometimes, if we'd left the door unlocked, she'd just come in and poke around. But if my grandfather or Marilyn were home, they'd *always* let her in. Which was exactly what Marilyn did now.

"Kelly, Tracy's here!" she called.

I stood at the bottom of the dark staircase that led from the main deck to Marilyn's rooms and mine. Tracy was standing at the top of the stairs in her Daisy Dukes, her dirty-blond hair teased just so, her bangs crunchy with hair spray.

"We need a milk shake," she said, instead of hello.

For a while, my grandfather had been buying frozen milk shakes that you microwaved for twenty seconds to thaw. Even when I was twelve, I recognized that they were ridiculous. But they were Tracy's number one favorite treat. We had to have one before she could do anything else. If I told her we were out, she'd march over to the fridge near the galley and check to make sure I was telling the truth. If there weren't any, she'd go downstairs to look in the big freezers in the laundry room, where my grandfather hoarded frozen food.

"You need to get more," she'd tell me if we were, indeed, out.

I heated up two milk shakes in the microwave. It took a few minutes because our generator wasn't on, and there was barely enough shore power to make the microwave go. Donahue's electricity arrived on a thin, weathered cord that was strung up on a series of mini telephone poles that ran from the marina office, along the length of the dock, to our boat at the end tie. Every boat was connected to the same wire, and the already-anemic current became progressively weaker as it advanced down the dock. There was usually enough electricity to turn a television on, but only enough for a picture the size of a matchbook and sound that rose and wavered at odd intervals. There was enough electricity to operate a toaster very slowly, but usually not enough to run the microwave. Hundred-watt bulbs emitted a dim, yellow light that became dimmer when someone two boats away turned their heater on. Fluorescent lights gagged and sputtered and finally died. Sometimes there wasn't any electricity at all.

A few people at Donahue's could afford to buy a small, red Honda generator to run when the power went out or shrank to a useless trickle. Some people would share their electricity with the neighbors they liked. My grandfather decided that the small Honda wasn't good enough for us. The first generator he bought was a Northern Lights 12kW diesel marine generator. It weighed eight hundred pounds, and its installation required a trip across the water to Todd's, where we paid to have it lowered by crane through our dining room and into the engine room beneath. After a year, my grandfather decided that the 12kW generator wasn't enough; we needed an 8kW as well. He said we would run the 8kW at night when we were at anchor on sea voyages, when we didn't need as much electricity as the 12kW made. Two years later, my grandfather would decide that we needed a bigger generator than the 12kW, and so he bought a 20kW. He also never shared with our neighbors. "Let them get their own fucking generator," he'd say.

Once Tracy and I were settled in my teak-paneled cabin, sitting cross-legged on its narrow floor and leaning against the sloping walls of the hull, she started the story of the day.

"My great-great-great-great-grandmother was Pocahontas," she said, slurping from her milk shake and staring at me across the cup.

"I don't think that's enough greats."

"Well, maybe it was more than that. But that means I'm really an Indian princess. If we lived back then, you'd have to worship me. Also, on my mother's side, I'm Chinese. That's how come I know how to play Chinese checkers so good."

Tracy and her mother were white, or at least Tracy was. Sharon *was* a shade darker than Tracy, but her hair was red and her round eyes blue.

"That Chinese must have been way back," I suggested, picking at the carpet.

"Well, if you don't believe me, you should see the tea set I inherited. It's real Chinese. From China. It belonged to the Empress. Even my mom says so."

A few days later, she would show me the china set, an ordinary, doll-sized white porcelain tea service with English roses painted on it. It sat in the ledge of a porthole, gathering dust.

She took another drink from her milk shake, uncrossed her legs, and stretched them out so that I had to move to avoid her feet.

"I'm going to be a fashion model," she said, flexing and unflexing her red-painted toes.

"Really?"

"Yeah. I already have contracts."

"How?"

"I auditioned for DeVry."

"I thought they taught people electronics."

"They do fashion modeling too." With her long legs and delicate face, Tracy could very well have become a model. Now she drew her legs up beneath her butt and puffed her chest out a little. "My mom was a model. She was really famous."

"Really? The other day you said she was a maid."

A few weeks before I'd told Tracy I had to do chores instead of playing, but Tracy had volunteered to help. We were cleaning the windows in the dining room with Windex and paper towels.

"Here," I'd said, "Start from the top and work your way down. That way the spray doesn't drip over what you've just cleaned."

"That's not how you do it. You're supposed to do it from the bottom to the top."

"That doesn't make sense."

"Well, it's the right way," she said. "That's the way my mother taught me."

"Well, she's wrong."

"She can't be. She was a maid in a hotel. She knows all about cleaning."

I couldn't really argue with that. It was possible that Sharon had been a maid in a hotel. No one in my family was a maid in a hotel. Tracy would have known that. I felt rich and stupid, living on our big boat. We cleaned the windows her way, leaving drips of dirt on the glass. Marilyn made me do them over again later, the right way. As I cleaned, I remembered that Marilyn *had* once been a maid in a hotel, long before she met my grandfather. That was why I knew how to make beds with hospital corners. But Tracy also knew that we had a cleaning lady who came to the boat once a week and that there was no real reason for me to be cleaning windows anyway, except that I was looking for something to do.

"Do you want to play Chinese checkers?" I asked once we'd finished our milk shakes. It was something to do. "We have time for one game, and then I think I have to help make dinner."

"Okay. We'll play best of three."

I got the board out from the cabinet beneath my upper bunk. As I set the board up between us, the floor and walls rumbled and shook. The black cat asleep on my lower bunk woke with a start.

"It's okay, Blackie Girl," I said. "It's just the generator."

We were on the second game when Tracy asked, "Have you had sex yet?"

"No!"

"Have you kissed a boy yet?"

"No."

An empty glass started to vibrate as it sat on the bookshelf; the generator made everything on the boat buzz. Wine glasses that hung from a rack sang high pitches, dishes rattled together, any wood paneling that was loose buzzed. It made your very bones hum, the muscles in your shoulders tense. I moved the glass so that it rested quietly on a book. No, I hadn't kissed a boy. This was not a conversation I wanted to have.

Tracy's eyes followed the motion of my arm. It felt as if she were touching me. "Well, I have," she said. "Lots." After a pause, she asked, "Have you gotten your period yet?"

"No."

"Well, I have."

"Okay."

"It doesn't hurt."

I changed the subject. I worried that Tracy might actually know a thing or two about sex, and I didn't want to talk about it—not with her, not with anyone. I thought of the big cardboard boxes sitting in Marilyn's room, fresh from the Valley, filled with shiny new tapes.

We finished the game, and finally, she went home.

"Just ignore it when she lies," my grandfather said that night at dinner, wiping his face with a napkin. "People who lie like that usually have a reason."

"But she lies *all the time*," I protested. "And she's a mooch. And she's boring." I left out the sex part.

"She hasn't had the advantages you have," my grandfather said, spooning out another helping of bubble and squeak.

"It's just a nice thing for you to do," Marilyn said, patting my hand. "Just play with her, sweetheart. It doesn't cost you anything."

It *did* cost me something, I wanted to protest. It cost me painful, dig-my-heart-out-with-a-spoon *boredom and annoyance*. But I didn't say anything; not wanting to play with her made me feel heartless now. Noblesse oblige and all that.

That night, before I fell asleep in my upper bunk—one cat curled on my feet and another on my pillow—I watched the welders working on the nuclear submarine down at the other end of the basin, by the marsh. It was a pleasant night, and my portholes were open. The generator was off. The loud clangs of the metal workers carried down the channel, but by the time they got to me, they were soft, almost musical. The breeze flowed across my cabin, bringing with it the fresh smell of the evening, but also, underneath, something vaguely unpleasant—the nutty-sweet smell of the sewage tank we'd pumped out earlier that night, dead fish, the muck on the shore. I didn't mind the smell; it had begun to smell like home.

I wondered for a moment why I was supposed to be nice to Tracy, why my parents—who looked down on everyone else at the marina—should care about her. The blue-and-orange light of the welding torches flashed and sparked.

At first, we hadn't known what they were building on the flat barge, which they'd covered with a skirt of black metal panels, but one day Wade stopped his car as he drove by and asked one of the workers. They were building a set for *The Hunt for the Red October,* a fake submarine to be used for exterior shots. Now, the conning tower loomed menacingly over the water. Sometimes a welder would step in front of a spotlight, and his shadow would be thrown up against the tower's wall—giant, heroic, like some Soviet propaganda poster.

17

ONE AFTERNOON THAT SUMMER, I SMELLED SMOKE. I WAS reading on Marilyn's bed. Perhaps it was only a bilge pump overheating. I checked the pump switches in the bathroom she and I shared, as well as the one for the sewage-holding tank. They were all off. I went upstairs, then aft below to check the pumps there. The smell was stronger. I cranked open the heavy engine-room door. Acrid black smoke drifted out. My eyes stung, and I could taste something bitter and metallic. A flame flared up on the port wall, then died. I knew I should go try to put it out. I knew where the fire extinguisher was. But I couldn't move toward the flame. I was too scared. I ran upstairs to get my grandfather from his cabin.

"There's a fire in the engine room. There's a lot of smoke." I could hear the panic in my voice.

"Let's go see." His voice was calm. Usually when something went wrong, his voice took a panicked, angry edge to it. But not now. He walked quickly and grabbed the fire extinguisher from its bracket by the stairs. He handed it to me. "You carry this," he said. Then he clumped his way down the stairs, gripping the banister on one side and the ledge on the other.

I was scared of the fire, scared he might have a heart attack from the excitement. My own heart was beating a mile a minute. I didn't want him to go into the engine room, but if he didn't, who would put the fire out? I followed him.

In the engine room, he took the fire extinguisher from me and sprayed down the flame with the white powder.

"Get out," he said, but I wouldn't leave. Instead, I cowered by the starboard engine, across the room from the flames.

It seemed to take forever, emptying the entire extinguisher canister until it sprayed no more. We were both coughing, but he managed to say, "It's out," before pushing us both out the engine room door. As we left, he turned on the two massive fans to vent the room.

"Electrical fire," he said, when we'd gotten back upstairs and caught our breaths. "It's what smells so bad." He patted me on the back. "It's okay, Little Toad. You did well." I was still shaking.

We were both covered in gray and black soot; even my spit was black. I felt as if I'd never cough out all the smoke.

That night, the boat didn't seem as safe anymore. By then, I was used to its swaying and jerking in storms, the shrieks of rubbing wood as it pulled against its lines. The fact that its hull leaked a little didn't bother me too much—that's what pumps were for. But the idea that a fire could erupt at any moment from the electrical wiring frightened me. What if it had happened when we were asleep? What if he hadn't been able to put the fire out? And if the wires in the engine room could spark, why not the ones behind the teak paneling of my cabin or Marilyn's?

———————————

My grandfather wasn't the kind of person who let the grass grow under his feet or bad wiring sit in place. He sought a professional electrician. By the next evening, he'd hired our neighbor Bill to rewire our boat.

Bill lived on a homemade sailboat called *Le Pirate,* one slip over, with his own three cats and a much younger woman. He'd hand-built *Le Pirate* to look like a pirate ship, complete with faux square-rigged masts, a lantern on the stern, and a figurehead on the bow. I was impressed, but as Pete pointed out to me one morning over tea, you could tell it was an amateur job.

"You see how all the ends of the planks in the hull meet up in the center?" He pointed through the window and drew his finger down the glass. "How there's this one seam that runs down the middle like a zipper?"

"Yeah."

"Well, something were to hit that, that's exactly what it would do, open like a zipper—rip a big hole in the hull—and the boat would go down fast. If you look at other boats, you'll see the ends of the planks are staggered, so there's never a row of joined wood like that. It makes the hull stronger."

Later that day I looked at the side of our boat. Sure enough, the planks were staggered.

Bill was an electrician at a candy factory somewhere in LA. For the next couple of months, he worked in the evenings to replace our boat's electrical system—a confused web of 1940s wiring and years of haphazard patchwork. He cut up piles of orange extension cords and used the cable to replace the old wires, connecting them to a new electrical box and carefully labeling the breakers. Pete observed the progress skeptically.

Until he started to work for us, we did not know that the woman Bill lived with was his daughter, Catherine; we'd assumed she was his much-younger wife. Her long, brown hair reached down to an enormous backside encased in grapefruit-pink shorts. We'd called her Squeaky because she spoke with a high, squeaky voice—higher-pitched than even the shrill cries of gulls. In fact, when we first heard her speak through our open portholes, we thought she *was* a bird, the words she spoke so shrill and fast, they sounded inhuman.

I understood how a girl could grow up to be someone like Squeaky if her father was someone as odd as Bill (because, of course, our family was a paragon of normalcy). Bill was about five foot five and ageless in the sense that he looked much older than he probably was. His weathered face and arms seemed tanned, but when you got closer, you realized it was just dirt. It was as if he'd stood outside for years, like the figurehead on his boat, and been begrimed with the metallic grit and greasy soot of the harbor. At first we thought it was dirt from his job at the candy factory, but it became apparent after a few visits that Bill just didn't bathe very often. He didn't stink, exactly, but he had a definite, distinctive odor, a little bit like sweat, but more like an electrical fire or a bin of metal parts in a hardware store. His smell was something you got used to; he just smelled like Bill, the way a ferret just smells like ferret. No matter the season, he wore baggy Hawaiian shirts and brown utility shorts. The top of his head was almost completely bald, but tufts of his mousy, brown hair stuck out from beneath one of two porkpie hats he wore—baby blue or eggshell. They'd been worn so many times that their creases were gray with dirt. Smaller, coarser tufts of hair shot out from his ears; a few wires of hair peeked out from his nose. His cheeks and chin were usually covered by two days' growth of beard. His eyes were sheltered by bushy eyebrows, the brown, tangled growth streaked through with gray.

Every evening after he'd finished working, Bill would sit with my grandfather at the dining room table. They'd drink fancy liqueurs and talk about various and sundry things, and I'd perch on the pilot-house stairs to listen.

"Well, of course, the Incan pyramids were built by the

Egyptians. They discovered celestial navigation before anyone," Bill would proffer.

"Then there was Leif Erickson," my grandfather would rejoin. "No seamen like those Norse. Except the English. Of course, they're half Norse themselves."

"What?"

"All those Viking raids. Dark ages. Rape and plunder, you know."

"Oh. I've often wondered if the Egyptians weren't extraterrestrial in origin," Bill would begin again, at which point my grandfather would offer him another drink.

Although he seemed to enjoy Bill's company, my grandfather still had plenty to say about him behind his back. "There's something wrong when a man lives with his grown daughter like that. In such a small space. He's fucking her, or she wants him to or something. I mean, why else would she stay? She should be seeing men, keeping her own place, getting on with her life."

Or he had other theories. "Perhaps she just doesn't like men," he'd say. Or, he wondered, perhaps she just didn't like penises. "It's like that joke, you know."

I didn't know, so my grandfather explained. "Well, so the young aristocrat comes into the bedroom on his wedding night, and his bride's wearing a long, white glove, right up to her elbow. 'Why're you wearing that glove, love?' he asks. And she replies, 'Mummy said I'd have to touch the thing!' See, maybe she's just frigid."

Frigid, I thought. Cold, frozen. Someone who didn't want to touch a penis.

Ever since I could remember, my grandfather had been telling me jokes about sex—stories whose punch lines I couldn't really understand. Jokes like, "So the young man takes his girl back home, and of course, he can't go inside with her because her parents are home. So he puts her against the front door, hikes up her skirt, and starts going at her, and right when he's about there, the father opens the door and they both go falling inside the house." When I first heard it, I didn't understand why they fell inside. Even now, at twelve, when I understood the mechanics of sex, I didn't understand why it was funny.

Sometimes I watched Bill and Squeaky through the galley window while I washed dishes. They'd be cleaning the decks or playing with their cats or swinging in twin bosun chairs as they sanded the wooden masts. It did seem strange to me that they would still be living together. Perhaps my grandfather was right.

Bill and Catherine went on vacation that summer—something they hadn't been able to afford for a while. They asked me to catsit for them. You could tell it was a big responsibility they were entrusting to me; they loved their three cats like children, carrying on whole conversations with them on deck. Since we had six cats, they felt we were exactly the kind of people who could be trusted with theirs.

Of course, it was entirely my fault we had the six cats. A month or so after we'd moved on board, an old minesweeper had docked at the end tie next to our slip. The man who lived on her was scrawny, almost starved, often wearing jeans and nothing else except a bushy, ginger beard and long, ginger hair. He climbed up and down the sweeper's round flanks on a rope ladder, a cigarette in his mouth and a six-pack dangling in one hand. He kept a cat who'd just had kittens. I heard about it from Tracy, who'd been promised one. I was a little jealous.

But one day after school, as I was walking up the finger to get on our boat, the bearded man jumped off the sweeper, making the dock lurch. I cast my eyes down and tried to avoid him, but he walked right up to me. He had something in his hand and pushed it into my chest.

"Here," he said. "Have a kitten."

He was gone before I could say anything. I held the furry ball against the white blouse of my school uniform, felt its tiny claws dig into the fabric and, so very faintly, into my skin. A flea crawled along between her blue eyes, and I fell in love.

My grandfather let me keep her. "It'll keep the rats down," he told Marilyn, although we'd yet to see a rat at the marina. I named her Koko. She grew up to be a sleek, long-haired cat, white with a silver face and tail, and those startling blue eyes. I begged Marilyn to let Koko have kittens before we got her fixed, following her around the boat to beg like a three-year-old. I just wanted to see something being born, I argued. I'd find them all homes, I promised. They would be such beautiful cats, I said, just look at their mother.

Koko had six kittens. There were three tabbies, whom we named Crybaby, Sunshine, and Big Eyes; two black ones, Blackie Boy and Blackie Girl; and Stormcloud. Once they were weaned, we fed them all on a single plate, Marilyn calling them to eat by singing, "Kitty, kit-tyyy, kitty, kit-tyyy" to the tune of Yale's *Boola, Boola* song.

We only gave one of them away. My grandfather hated seeing her leave so much that he forbade us to give away the rest.

And so that summer, it was agreed by my grandfather on my behalf that, for five dollars a day, I'd go over to feed and water Bill and Catherine's cats, pet them, and change their litter boxes. But I had other motives for saying yes to the job: I was certain that, once I was alone in their boat, I'd be able to tell what was going on between them. Surely there would be telltale signs of the perversion of which my grandfather so often spoke.

That first day, I opened the hatch to their pirate boat and climbed down the steep ladder into their home. It was small and dark but neat as a pin and cool like a cave. Weak beams of light passed through the tiny, square portholes. Just past the galley, there was a piece of stained glass that served as a window to the bathroom. It was a picture of a pirate, someone who looked like Edward Teach, leaning down on a table, squinting at a pile of coins. Bill had told us about it one night. Catherine had made it when they were building the ship. He was so proud of that stained glass and so proud of his daughter, how she had made it herself, how she'd found the pieces of glass for his beard, his hat, and, finally, the perfect milky-blue circle for the pirate's eye. The window was, indeed, impressive, and I wondered why someone who could make something like that lived with her dad in a tiny, dark space that rocked with every step she took.

But as much as I'd planned to, I didn't poke around their home. Something stopped me. Maybe it was the cats watching me—two from the shadows, one entwined about my feet. But I think it might also have been the quiet of the little boat as it gently rocked. It was a safe, calm place—and it was Bill and Catherine's safe, calm place. Maybe, I thought, it was the only place in the world where they could feel at home. I understood then that it was something special, something private that should not be violated. My grandfather and I had thought there must be something seriously wrong with a daughter who still lived with her dad at thirty, something seriously wrong with a father who let her. It hadn't occurred to me until just then, as I stood in the blue light of the portholes, beneath the yellow gaze of the cats and the benevolent squint of Edward Teach, that perhaps, just perhaps, Bill and Catherine lived together simply because it made them happy. I fed the cats and left.

18

Y AGENT IS GOING TO GET ME A PART ON THAT MOVIE,"
Tracy said. We were sitting in the tiny kitchen-slash-living-room on her Chris-Craft. It was warm and stuffy in the cabin and smelled of bilges and urine, but it was clean. The only dust was in the ledges of the portholes, and even though the ashtray on the kitchen counter was full, the dishes were put away; there was no clutter on the floor. Her mother, Sharon, was sunbathing on the deck. I could see her long, tanned legs through the cabin door, her short denim shorts tight on her thighs, a sprinkle of cellulite just by the hem, a heart and blue thorns melted into the freckles above her ankle.

I wanted to say something like, "Yeah, right," or "Don't you think they already have the actors picked out?" but I didn't. More than anything, I just wanted to go home. I hadn't been able to get out of playing with her. I was bored.

We were talking about *The Hunt for the Red October*. The submarine was now completed. It was the Russian sub, the star of the show, a red hammer and sickle having been painted on the side of the conning tower. Every morning that week, she'd been towed out of the basin by a tug for filming, and every night she returned. When she went by, people gathered on the dock or stuck their heads out of hatches to watch. It was the closest any of us had gotten to Hollywood, except, of course, my grandfather, who had pointedly ignored the proceedings.

"You see that deep fat fryer?" Tracy pointed to the galley counter. "My mom got it for her birthday. It's really expensive. It makes french fries."

"Cool," I said. "We have one too." We used it almost every night.

There was a thump, and the boat rocked suddenly; someone was coming on board. Our boat didn't move as much when people came on board because it was big.

"Nice ass," a booming voice said. Sharon shushed it. "Oh, sorry. Pardon my French."

Al came into the cabin. He wasn't wearing a shirt, and his skin glinted. Tattoos ran all along his muscled chest, and a faint line of curly, gray hair plunged down his tight stomach to the waist of his jeans. Tracy got up as he came in and swished her long hair back behind her shoulder. She kissed him on his stubbly cheek.

"Hey, sweetheart," he said and slapped her butt. I jumped a little at the sound. His hand rested on the embroidery of her back pocket. I watched as his fingers pressed a little harder, testing something. Tracy swayed away from his hand, leading with her hips, as if they'd been dancing.

That's when I saw it, when I understood why my parents wanted me to be nice to her. Tracy's long legs and tight shorts, her halter tops; her mother's even tighter shorts and lower-cut tops, as if she were competing; the way this man's hand rested on her ass; all of them together, stuck on that tiny, stuffy boat that smelled vaguely of pee.

And then the moment was over. Al grabbed beers for Sharon and himself. In a second, their laughter carried from the deck into the cabin.

"You wanna go fish?" Tracy asked.

"Sure."

When we were done playing cards, I walked slowly back to our boat, trying to make sense of the kiss, the hand, the way she swayed away from him. In the evening, my grandfather wanted to watch a war movie, but I didn't feel like it. Besides, he often cried during war movies—great sobs that demanded attention but which he refused to explain. I sat on the dock instead, facing the west end of the basin, the boat behind me, and watched the sun set behind the marsh and the peninsula in the distance. One by one, the lights in San Pedro and Palos Verdes twinkled on. The dip and rise of the reeds in the wind made the marsh seem like a breathing creature. The evening star appeared, the only star we could see at night.

Sometimes in the evenings, I folded paper boats and set them loose to see how far they'd go. Or I'd make sailing ships from empty milk cartons and plastic bags. Sometimes I tried to catch fish with a piece of twine and a bent paper clip. But that evening, I dangled my feet over the edge of the dock, careful not to let my toes touch the dirty surface, and crumpled two heels of bread into the water.

First the minnows came, as I knew they would, darting just beneath the surface, glistening silver and copper beneath the water. They nosed the bread, spinning it around as they took tiny bites. Then a big fish raced up from below, his body tracing a smooth arc to the surface. He was the advance scout for the school, because just after he vanished, hundreds of his kind swarmed around the bread. The water quickened with their shadowy movements, their dark bodies squirming beneath the green surface, the glints of their silver scales like shooting stars. I was mesmerized by their movement, still staring at the water long after they were gone. I heard the whir of a bilge pump coming on, then the trickle of water into water.

The marina was an ugly place, but it was also the first place

I'd really noticed beauty: The glint of swarming minnows, the way a full moon hung suspended in a cargo crane, a great blue heron standing like a ghost outside our kitchen window, his yellow eye staring through me. The way the sickly brown of a red tide could be beautiful at night, when fish darted through the water, setting off phosphorescent arcs and trails through the dark.

That year on Tracy's birthday, in September, I willingly went to her party: cake and punch in the marina's dim office, streamers hanging limply from the ceiling, very few friends. I bought her her own set of Chinese checkers and made her a card. I'd bound it with a pink ribbon, and on its cover, I'd carefully drawn a graceful ballerina because that summer she'd told me how much she loved ballet and how badly she wished she could take lessons and didn't once brag to me about how well she could dance.

———————————

Perry was right; Todd's did close that summer. The *Red October's* services also were no longer needed, and she sat abandoned at the crane barge, weeping orange rust through flat, black paint. An eerie quiet descended over the West Basin, the only noises now coming from the APL terminal behind us, the faint roar from the 110.

Summer faded into fall. The beginning of eighth grade was uneventful, except that my class at Le Lycée had gotten smaller; almost everyone had moved on to other schools. There were only three boys and me, and I was only friends with Ernesto. The other two weren't mean, exactly; they just preferred talking to the seventh-grade girls, who were cute and who, during recess, hiked up their uniform skirts and rolled down their knee socks. I, on the other hand, spent most lunches hitting a tennis ball into a wall or reading or staring at the ocean from the playground, watching for whales.

It wasn't just my lack of interest in boys that made me not fit in at school. I didn't really understand the world I was supposed to belong to, the world of people my own age, my schoolmates and friends. We never listened to music at home, except for the occasional "lite classics" CD or the easy listening Marilyn put on late at night. Not only did I not know the music my classmates had grown up with—Madonna, Prince, Michael Jackson—I didn't know generations of music before them. I didn't really know who the Beatles were, except that they had appeared on the *Ed Sullivan Show,* or anything about Sonny and Cher or The Doors or Sting. I'd heard of Janis Joplin because Marilyn told me that Michele had liked Janis Joplin, that she was "really into her." She said it in a disapproving way that made it seem as if Michele had gotten into trouble *because* of Janis Joplin—that somehow, Janis Joplin was responsible for Michele being dead. I decided I didn't ever want to listen to Janis Joplin.

I didn't watch very many new movies, either. Most of the new movies I watched were at the occasional sleepover: *Pretty in Pink, Dirty Dancing, The Princess Bride.* Instead, I was more familiar with old radio shows from the '30s, '40s, and '50s, shows made before some of my friends' parents were born. I listened to them on KNX 1070 at nine every night while I washed dishes, staring out the galley's window. My favorites were mysteries and thrillers like *Dragnet, Suspense,* and *The Green Hornet,* but I also liked Jack Benny, *The Lone Ranger,* and *Sergeant Preston of the Yukon.* I liked them better than TV—the way a voice told you a story in the dark of your imagination, how your mind brought the characters to life. I imagined that Sergeant Preston looked something like Nelson Eddy. I could see his crisp, red coat and dashing hat, hear King's galloping footfalls in the snow. At night, while I rinsed cups and plates, I stared out the window at *Le Pirate* and the white schooner that had once won the Transpac Race and the tugboat *Ready*, but my mind's eye watched Detectives Friday and Romero walking quickly down the steps of city hall, off to break an important case. I felt an affinity for those shows, something I didn't feel for the sitcoms my schoolmates watched. Radio took me out of a world I didn't quite understand to one that was familiar and comforting: the world of old movies, a world of black and white and innumerable shades of gray.

That fall, I watched my first real sex scene. It wasn't porn, but Alfred Hitchcock's *Frenzy*, about a serial killer who rapes then strangles his victims in order to climax. I watched it on a Saturday in my room. The murderer, handsome in his 1970s corduroy sports jacket and brown pants, locks a business woman in her office, beats her, then forces himself on her. It turned me on—I knew that that was what I was feeling for the way it tingled from my nipples to between my legs, even the soles of my feet. It was the way he straddled her, the way her breast lolled from her bra, the way the camera seemed crammed in the small space between their bodies, the way it moved with his thrusts. It was the first time I'd seen a sex act in motion. I was aroused, but I was also scared—and I wasn't exactly sure where the line between the two was. The way he choked the very life out of her, the way she screamed and gasped and gurgled, the way her tongue extruded from her mouth. In the midst of everything, I remembered my strangled mother, and I was ashamed of my body, my desire. I thought I must be some kind of pervert. Her picture was right under the shelf that my TV was on. I thought I was dishonoring her memory, that she must be ashamed of me, wherever she was.

I still thought a lot about Michele. She was my own private mystery. I wanted badly to know more about her. I imagined myself the Sherlock Holmes, the Joe Friday, on our case—*our* case, because in finding out something about her, I believed I'd find something out about me.

Sometimes when Marilyn was out, I'd go to her office and open her oak filing cabinet. No one had said I couldn't go looking through the files, but I still clicked the tab gently, pulled the drawers out quietly.

Marilyn liked to keep files on almost everything—instruction manuals, articles from *Consumer Reports,* letters from friends, taxes filed and taxes pending, recipes from her past fad diets, interesting articles from back when we still took the *LA Times.* We'd stopped subscribing to the paper after we moved on to the boat because someone kept stealing our copy from the marina parking lot. There were four folders I liked to look through best, their labels typed neatly by Marilyn: Michele Grey, Richard Grey, Yvonne Spencer, Kelly.

In my grandfather's folder, there was a copy of his record of birth, November 19, 1917, in Marylebone, London. I remembered when he'd sent away for it to try to get a green card during the 1986 amnesty for illegal immigrants. In the end, he'd decided not to apply. It was one of the reasons he wanted to live on a boat; if he ever got caught and deported, he reasoned, he could take his home and family with him.

In my folder, there was my birth certificate, which listed my real name, Kelly Michelle Archibald, and listed my father as William Earle Archibald. It said he was from Pennsylvania.

In Spence's file, I found my grandmother's state-issued birth certificate, which spelled out her full name, Yvonne Kaia Spencer, and said she was born at the French Hospital in LA. Her father, James Spencer, was born in Honolulu, Hawaii. It listed his "race or color" as "white"—but the "w" was fuzzy, as if it was typed over some other letter. He was supposed to be my cliff-diving, Hawaiian great-grandfather, but when his daughter was born, he listed his occupation as "movie director."

In Michele's file, I found my mother's birth certificate and, finally, her death certificate: purple ink on shiny paper that listed her cause of death as "manual strangulation" in thick, bold caps. I read and reread her death certificate—looking for what, exactly, I didn't know. I just wanted to know more. Under "day of death" someone had typed "found," then "November 29, 1976." Her death certificate said she was found in an empty lot at 610 N. Hill Place. It said her last occupation had been as a student at Hollywood High, even though she was twenty-three when she died.

Something about those documents made me feel connected to myself, as if they held clues about the real me, the person I really was but didn't know. They were artifacts from some other country, the place where I'd come from but could not remember.

"Where you come from is important," my grandfather used to say. "It's who you are."

I still sometimes stared at my little altar, tucked into a corner of my bookshelves, safe behind the pin rail: that picture of Michele with her half smile, the picture of Spence and her badge, the picture of Marilyn. I'd light an illegal candle and watch as the light flickered over their faces. I'd wonder what my life would be like if they'd lived. If Spence had lived, would we still be living in the mountains with Dee? If Michele had lived, would I know my biological father? Would we live in a house? I had a strong imagination, but for the life of me, I couldn't imagine any other life than the one I had.

19

IT WAS AS IF I'D NEVER SEEN THE WORLD BEFORE. I SAT OUTSIDE Le Lyçée on a grassy hill overlooking the ocean, waiting to be picked up. It was very late, and the school was long empty, but I wasn't worried. The ocean blazed from the late afternoon sun. In its golden light, the white caps looked like shadows. Colors had never seemed so intense: the bougainvillea next to the wall, its blossoms dripping fuchsia, their tiny white flowers like bleached coral; the Palos Verdes Peninsula still covered in its rainy-season green; the palm trees' emerald and gold rustling in the spring breeze; the ocean's liquid fire.

Eventually, I heard my grandfather's Mercedes in the distance, the loud clutter of its diesel engine getting closer and closer until it pulled into the driveway. Marilyn and Richard were both in the car, and I wondered what it meant. They never picked me up together.

But nothing bad had happened; we were just going out to dinner. Marilyn was relaxed, and my grandfather was in a good mood. I stretched out in the back seat and leaned my head against the window.

It was the first time we'd gone to the Schezuan Chinese restaurant on the Pacific Coast Highway in Lomita, fifteen minutes from home. We parked in back and went in the rear entrance, passing ceiling-high fish tanks, each marked with the name of the fish in both Chinese and English—carp and bass and crappie—and what each cost to eat. We passed the empty banquet room and a chalkboard with specials written in Chinese characters, some of which had not been translated into English.

The food was good. Marilyn drank a mai tai, her old favorite from when we frequented the Flower Drum by the store. She'd gained weight since we moved on to the boat, but I still thought she was pretty—even though every six months she'd make doomed attempts at losing weight that only made her feel worse about herself. But tonight, her shoulders weren't hunched, her eyes weren't as sad. My grandfather didn't complain once, but instead cracked jokes with the waitress, who laughed politely. We talked about our days, and no one argued. We felt like a normal family—a happy family—just like the dish on the Chinese menu that we never ordered. We packed up our leftovers, and then we went home, full of good food and warm light.

The sun had set while we were at dinner, and by the time we'd driven down the dusty road to the marina, it was night. It never got completely dark at Donahue's because the huge mercury lights at the oil farm and container yards lit everything in an eerie, orange glow. You could never see the stars. It was a tricky light that lit the darkness but flattened everything out, made distances hard to judge.

We got out of the car. My grandfather walked a few yards ahead of me in the parking lot toward the ramp, toward one of the pilings the marina's management had scattered around the parking lot to stop cargo trucks from using it as a turnaround. But instead of walking around the piling, he seemed to try to walk through it; his body launched itself over the log. I reached out as if to catch him, but my hand closed on empty air. I heard the spray of gravel when he fell, face first, his yelp of surprise and pain. Then his entire body lay still. I dropped my backpack, the Chinese food. Marilyn and I ran toward him.

By the time we got there, he was trying to get up, but he couldn't lift himself. I bent over and reached around one arm while Marilyn reached around the other, but we couldn't lift him. He was too heavy.

"Goddamn it," my grandfather screamed, half his face muffled by the ground. "Get me up."

I couldn't make myself say anything. We were trying to help him, but we couldn't lift him. *I'm sorry, I'm sorry, I'm sorry*, raced a voice in my head, over and over, but it might have just been the blood rushing in my ears. He was too heavy. What to do? I wrapped my arms around myself and leaned against a nearby truck. *I'm sorry, I'm sorry, I'm sorry. Please don't die. Please be okay.* Why hadn't I caught him? I'd seen the log. Why hadn't I known he was going to trip over it? Why hadn't I stopped this from happening? I saw again my hand reaching out to catch him.

Marilyn ran to call the paramedics from the pay phone, then returned. A big man I'd never seen before helped us get him up. We leaned my grandfather against the truck. He was bleeding from the head, but he said he thought he was okay—except that he couldn't see out of his right eye. He thought maybe it was the blood getting into it; he thought maybe it was a piece of dirt. I held his hand. I still couldn't talk. *I'm sorry, I'm sorry. I'm scared. Please be okay.*

Soon I saw the fire trucks coming down the road, as if in slow motion. Because the marina was next to the oil farm, they always sent half a dozen engines for any call. One after the other, they roared down the street, each siren just a little bit off from the rest, as if they were singing mournful rounds. The trucks turned off their sirens, and we were left with the heavy hum of their engines, the slam of truck doors, questions that sounded like orders. Everything pulsed red. My grandfather sat on the truck bumper while the paramedics examined him.

My grandfather told me once that when he served in World War II, he saw horrible things and his mind's response was to stop seeing. The war wasn't just stringing piano wire across roads or blowing up bridges—my favorite stories as a child. When I was older, he told me how he and his secretary were caught behind enemy lines. He claimed he'd been fed false information by his superiors, possibly even betrayed by them, because they thought he would talk and give the Germans bad intelligence. He didn't talk, not even when he was tortured, not even when his secretary was tortured and killed in front of his eyes. Actually, he wasn't sure that he hadn't talked, but in the end, it didn't matter. He said he was sent to Buchenwald, where he was starved and beaten and saw others receive the same treatment. He said that by the end of the war, he was completely blind, even though there was nothing wrong with his eyes; he said it took a six-month stay in a mental hospital for him to regain his sight.

In the early 1970s, my grandfather was blind again, this time from cataracts. When I was a little girl, he'd talked of his cataract surgery and recovery as a miracle, a gift from God and science. He described how the surgeons cut his eyes open, making long arcs around the sphere, then teased the cataracts out. He described how once they'd taken the bandages off and he could see, he spent hours in the garden, staring at the veins of leaves, the hairs on the back of a blade of grass, the way water pooled at the base of a daffodil's stem. It was as if he'd never seen the world before. He told me, over and over, that sight was a miracle I should never take for granted.

When my grandfather fell that night in the marina, one of

those long arcs in his eyeball ruptured; the injury and the force with which he landed had detached his retina. The injured eye had been his best eye—without it, he could barely see. As we sat in the bright emergency room, I knew that our lives had changed, if not forever, for a good long while. The doctors said that, given his age and the condition of his eye, they probably wouldn't be able to fix the retina, but they would try.

If I'd only known to worry about my grandfather walking, I thought. I worried all the time. Worry could prevent calamity; it was my longest held belief. Why hadn't I been worried the one time I needed to be?

Although the doctors gave him slim odds, my grandfather was very hopeful—chipper almost—that with surgery, his eye would be saved.

"Don't worry, Little Toad," he said brightly from beneath the white bandage wrapped jauntily around his head. He patted the side of his hospital bed, a sign that I should come get a hug.

I recognized desperate hope when I saw it. I remembered the hope I'd clung to when I was nine, the night after the *Challenger* exploded, that somehow Christa McAuliffe would swim ashore and knock on my door for help—even though I saw the shuttle explode into bits, even though we were fifteen minutes away from the Pacific, and she had died over the Atlantic. On the way over to his bed, I decided to try to believe his hope anyway. I hugged him tightly and sniffed tears back. Blind was better than dead, I told myself. Blind was okay, right?

My grandfather's hope got us through that night, and it got us through weeks of treatments and doctors' visits and procedures. Each day of a doctor's appointment began in hope and ended in disappointment, with Marilyn or Pete updating me on what the doctors had said when they picked me up from school.

"It'll be okay, Peanut," Pete promised me with a wink. "We'll get him put back together again."

I was given the task of changing my grandfather's dressing and putting special drops in his eye. His eyelid still seemed swollen, its edge lined in goop and crust. When I could see the iris, it seemed like something congealed, clouded over. Sometimes the eye drops stung, and my grandfather would twist his head away from me so that I'd end up dripping them on his face.

"Clumsy idiot," he'd shout. "Don't waste them. They're bloody expensive."

Sometimes I'd jar his head accidently as I taped his bandage.

"Goddamn it, get away," he'd say, waving me off and screaming for Marilyn.

"He's not angry at you," Marilyn would tell me once she'd found me sulking in my room. She'd sit by me on my bunk and put an arm around me, rest her head gently on top of my head. "He's just angry and sad about losing his eye, and it comes out that way."

I tried to remember that. I tried to remember how, most of the time, he was pretty brave, all things considered. Marilyn was always good at explaining my grandfather. But sometimes knowing the reasons for things didn't make them hurt less.

One afternoon on our way home from school, I noticed Annie standing in mud by the marina office, her pants rolled up over her fleshy calves, her brassy, white hair falling out of her ponytail, her arms and large breasts jiggling as she dumped a bag full of garbage into a hole. I let Marilyn go ahead.

"What are you doing?" I asked, putting down my heavy backpack.

"Making me a garden," she said. She stopped to look at me and brushed a piece of hair from her eyes.

"How'd you get Chuck to let you have the land?"

She grinned. "Well, now, he just loves radishes and tomatoes. And I said he could have all the radishes and tomatoes he wanted if he let me make a garden."

I noticed then how the black toxic waste barrels had been moved out of the lot to under the eucalyptus trees; the earth had been tilled and was wet. She'd dug parallel trenches into it, and each was filled with trash: rotten fruit and potato peels, melon rinds and chicken bones, and all manner of organic things she must have been saving or scavenging for weeks.

"Why are you burying all that trash?" I asked.

"To make the soil better so it'll grow something." She waited a moment, then, seeing that I wasn't offering to help, returned to work. I watched as she covered the trash with dirt and soaked it all with water.

This was only the first step of Annie's soil-conditioning program. In the weeks to come, she mixed bags of potting soil and used cat litter into the mud. I knew this because I'd begun paying attention to the lot when we walked by—and also because Annie asked Marilyn for our used kitty litter. One of my chores became to deliver it to her in plastic bags, sifted clean of feces.

The next obstacle was the pay phone, which was bolted to a quarter bit of telephone pole at the front of the lot. Annie couldn't tear out the phone—half of the marina used it—so she had it beautified. Someone found a second-hand faux wishing well—the kind of yard art you might find in a day care's playground or your grandmother's garden—and Annie got Jerry to build the wishing well around the phone so that it sat in the middle, the receiver hidden by the miniature shingle roof and crank. Now she had her blank canvas: an empty, muddy lot sprinkled with chicken bones and watermelon rinds, with a wishing-well phone stuck in the middle.

I don't know if it was the cat litter or the trash or the potting soil, but that spring and summer, green things sprang from the earth. Along one fence, Annie planted morning glories that soon wove themselves between the fence chinks and blossomed with parasols of purple and pink and white. Against the fence that fronted the water, she planted butternut squash, whose vines swarmed up and over it and headed toward the sea. She planted tomato bushes around the wishing well. Then she planted a watermelon vine; an herb garden full of chives, rosemary, and basil; a tire full of mint; a tower of strawberry pots; hollyhocks, dahlias, and cosmos. Next to these she laid four squares of sod. Every garden, she said, should have a patch of lawn. And finally, she tended the ancient rose bushes that had grown by the dock's ramp since the marina had been built in the fifties. She was rewarded with a profusion of pink and peach and red blossoms, the likes of which none of us could remember having seen.

The last attempt to fix my grandfather's eye was outpatient laser surgery to reattach the retina. That day at the surgeon's, we were all nervous. The waiting room was the nicest waiting room I had ever seen. The wallpaper was deep green, burnt-out velvet against gold. The carpet was soft and green like moss. My grandfather and I sat in emerald wingback chairs; Marilyn leaned back on an overstuffed, gold velvet couch. The tables and lamps were made of dark, glossy wood. The magazines were *National Geographic* and *Architectural Digest*, not *Reader's Digest* and *Parenting*. The normal fluorescents were replaced with soft, warm light that came from brass wall sconces. I couldn't help thinking that this doctor must be very expensive, and I couldn't help noticing the other family that was also waiting, a tired Latina mother and her two small children. Their clothes were cheap, and she carried snacks in a crumpled Kmart bag. She looked as if she felt as out of place as I did. If all his clients were like us and that lady, I wondered, why did the doctor decorate his room this way? Of course, if all the patients were blind, why did the doctor bother to decorate his room at all? But then I stumbled on to a happy thought: maybe he wanted his newly sighted patients to see something nice when they got their bandages off. I had visions of my grandfather in one of those black-and-white movies where the handsome protagonist has his bandages removed with a flourish, and while the soundtrack swells, he blinks and finally *sees* the doctor's office and his loving, patient wife who has waited years for him to be cured. Suddenly I couldn't wait for my grandfather to be called in to the office.

A few minutes later a nurse came for him and Marilyn. I had to stay in the waiting room, so I sat cross-legged in the wingback chair. Ten minutes passed. The next time the door opened, the husband of the Latina woman came out, a white patch on his eye and a smile on his face. He was handsome in his crisp, white shirt with jeans and cowboy boots; his muscles were firm beneath his sleeves. His wife beamed when she saw him and took his hand, and together with their children, they all went home. Seeing them all together made me happy.

I was alone in the waiting room after that. It was very quiet. I waited and hoped that my grandfather was being healed. Then I heard it, first softly so I couldn't be sure it was him, then louder so that I had no doubt. I heard my grandfather growling and scream-ing in pain through the walls. Even the secretaries behind the frosted-glass partition paused their soft talking.

I heard him howling, and all I could think of was the way he sometimes howled when I gave him his insulin shots. He made such a fuss when I pushed the needle in—screaming like a child, slapping me away with his free hand, cursing me like he was being tortured—over a simple, two-second shot he'd had a thousand times before. All I could think about was how much he fussed when I gave him his eye drops or changed his bandages. In that plush chair, in that softly lit office, while he was being operated on, all I could think was, "For once in your life, grin and bear it. Shut up, or they won't be able to cure you. Weren't you supposed to be a war hero?"

When the screaming stopped, Marilyn came out and whispered to me, "They couldn't continue with the procedure. It was too painful."

That was it? I wanted to scream. Everything we had been through for weeks, everything I had been through, everything we had done for him? The very last chance for a cure, and he couldn't hold on for a few more minutes? I thought he was the biggest wuss in the world, and I hated him for it.

But when my grandfather came out a few minutes later, led gently by a nurse, a new white patch on his eye, he was a different person. He shuffled like he was wearing slippers. He held his hand out in front of him, no longer pretending that he could see just as well as before. His shoulders curved forward and his stomach and chin didn't stick out in that same proud way.

He didn't joke; he didn't talk. It was over. I reached out for his hand like the wife had a few minutes before. I held it all the way home.

20

A WEEK OR SO AFTER MY GRANDFATHER'S FINAL UNSUCCESSFUL eye surgery, on the first day of summer vacation, I received a summons from Annie. Bob delivered it at eight in the morning, while I still sat in my pajama pants, groggily drinking tea.

"Annie says for you to come help her in the garden," he reported, his hands stuck deep in the pocket of his Dickies, his gaze firmly on his dusty work boots.

Annie wasn't someone you really said no to, and besides, it sounded like fun. I'd never worked in a garden before. I took a shower and got into clean jeans, a new T-shirt, and my white sneakers. By the time I got up to the lot, Annie was almost done.

"Here," she handed me the hose, "water them tomatoes. No, not like that. Water their roots, like this."

I watered the tomatoes. At first I was dismayed at the way the muddy water splashed onto my jeans, the way the hose dragged dirt across my shirt. But then I noticed the orange beetles buzzing around the garden, a butterfly resting on the cosmos—small signs of life in what before had been a desert. And then I noticed the smell. I didn't know where it was coming from, but it smelled inexplicably green, and even though it seemed to be associated with the mud, it smelled perfectly clean.

"Okay," Annie said after ten minutes. "I'm done for the

day. Could you coil up that hose please? Just put it over by the spigot."

While I wrangled the stiff hose, Annie sat down on the dried-out dock that served as a sidewalk. She pulled a pack of Pall Malls out of her back pocket, pushed a stray bit of hair behind her ear, and sighed. When I was done, I went and sat down beside her.

"You be here every morning around seven thirty, okay, sweetheart?"

Seven thirty seemed like an impossibly early time, but I said yes. And I kept my promise all that summer, waking up at seven every morning, rolling out of bed into jeans stiff from mud and water, and making the long trek to the garden. Annie was always waiting for me, sitting on the dock sidewalk, a cigarette in her mouth and a stained mug of coffee in her hand. Every morning I noticed something different in the garden: the way the mist from our hose hung tiny beads of water on a spider's web, a baby watermelon growing quietly in the shade of a leaf. And then there was the hard work of gardening, a kind of physical labor I'd never done before. I liked the way my muscles were sore after a morning of digging or weeding or pulling out dead vines. It felt good to bend over in the sun, my back warm but my face cool from the shadowed, damp ground. It felt good to hear Annie say, "You were a big help today, sweetheart," or to hear her tell Jerry, "She's a good girl." It felt good to take a Folgers can of cherry tomatoes or a whole squash back home after a morning's work, to eat the food I'd grown, even if I wasn't entirely sure the soil wasn't toxic. I was proud of these small trophies. I finally understood why the expression was "the fruits of your labor."

Most mornings, Jerry, Bob, or Perry—or sometimes all three—came to watch Annie and me garden. They'd bring Annie coffee or smokes, and together they sat on the dock sidewalk, once in a while offering gardening tips, to which Annie snorted gently, "What the fuck you know about that?" And although they wouldn't let me drink coffee, they'd let me sit between them, and they'd tell me what was wrong with the world and President Bush, and who was dealing drugs in the marina, and what life on an oil tanker was like. For the first time, I felt like I really belonged in the marina, like I had friends.

Eventually the moment would come when the coffee ran out and the conversation slowed to a trickle, and we all stood to go home. I'd start the walk back, leaving the sunny garden for the dim interior of our boat, the sad quiet that filled it.

Before my grandfather was blinded, whenever I'd heard the phrase "a broken man," I'd thought of a pencil snapped clean through, but my grandfather wasn't like that. He was broken like an old upright piano with a clunking pedal and missing notes: He wasn't completely blind, but he couldn't drive anymore. He walked so slowly that it sometimes took him twenty minutes to walk down the dock. He didn't go out much that summer, but instead sat in his room or at the dining room table, sometimes reading, which he could still do with new glasses and a magnifying glass. More often than not, though, he wouldn't bother to dress or to turn on a light or open the curtains, instead brooding in the dark. The only thing that made him smile was his cat, Stormcloud. Since his accident, he'd become even more attached to the cats, especially to her.

The cats soon took over the boat, sleeping on the table and kitchen counters, covering everything with cat hair, and trailing cat litter behind them, peeing on dining room chairs, our beds, and even the stove. Marilyn and I couldn't keep up with the mess. The only times the boat felt really clean were on the Fridays the cleaning lady came. I still remember the relief of coming home those afternoons to the smell of Murphy's Oil Soap and Lysol. But it never lasted, and besides, there was only so much even she could do. When the cats peed on my grandfather's bed, he preferred to sleep in the soiled sheets rather than disturb a sleeping cat in order to change them. When I cleaned out my grandfather's room after he died, I found piles of mummified cat feces under his bed and in his closet, the wood stained with years' worth of urine.

For his accidental blinding, my grandfather received a settlement of ninety thousand dollars from the company that owned Donahue's. After they paid, the company put the marina up for sale. Gunner and Sonny, two men who lived at the marina, tried to get enough money together to buy it. That summer, they made the long trip down the dock to our boat to ask my grandfather if he'd like to invest. He said no.

"Why would I sink money into this shithole?" he asked.

They went away again.

"Maybe you shouldn't have been so mean," I ventured.

"Why? They won't be able to scrounge up enough to buy it."

"But if they don't buy it, who will? Pete says the marina will probably close if no one buys it. Where will everyone go?"

"So," he shrugged. "Why should I care? There are other marinas. Besides, we need to go into dry dock again soon. We'll spend the money on that."

But Gunner and Sonny did manage to buy the marina somehow. They repainted the shack white and put a new sign on its roof that said West Basin Marina, but everyone still called it Donahue's.

That summer, when Marilyn and my grandfather decided to send me to public high school, I was elated. I'd finally get to go to a school near where I lived. I wouldn't have to wear a uniform. When I walked down the dock, I wouldn't feel like a snobby rich bitch, but normal like everyone else. I couldn't wait to go to San Pedro High, which was the closest high school, only fifteen minutes away.

"You're not going to that hellhole," my grandfather snorted when I told him how I felt.

We were sitting around the dining room table. Outside the windows, cats prowled along the railings. I looked to Marilyn, confused.

"San Pedro High isn't a very good school," she said. "It's an LA district school. You don't want to go there."

"Yes, I do."

"Place is overrun by gangbangers and Mexicans. You wouldn't last three days," my grandfather said.

"But it's *our* high school. That's where I'm supposed to go."

"We'll find a way for you to go to school up in Palos Verdes. Mommy says Josette has volunteered to let you use her address," my grandfather said. "So we'll do that."

"But I don't want to go to school in P.V.," I said.

"I don't give a damn what you want. This is what's best for you!"

I looked to Marilyn, but she only smiled sadly. "Honey, it really is a good school. It's so much better than what you'd get here."

I knew that some people lied and said they lived up on the peninsula in order to go to school there. They used addresses of people who already lived up there, like Josette, to enroll in school. The peninsula was rich; their public schools were excellent. But I didn't want to be one of those people who lied, and I didn't want to be the kind of person who lived there—the manicured housewives at Bristol Farms, the suited men in their BMWs. I also didn't want to get caught and kicked out of school, either.

Josette lived with her husband, Tom, in a sprawling, single-story house that overlooked the Pacific. Josette was neither a manicured housewife nor a suited man in a BMW. Instead, she was a makeupless, thrifty Frenchwoman who listened fanatically to classical music and could not tolerate bullshit. She kept both their house and the books for Tom's medical practice; she also sewed clothes and did household carpentry, minor plumbing, electrical work, and landscaping. Josette took on projects—not just DIY or Halloween costumes—but people too. At any given time, she was assisting refugees, or helping the abused, or rehabilitating the recently unemployed or divorced—all with a smile, a good joke, and a limitless generosity of time and patience.

Together at her table, she and Marilyn had plotted my future: my parents would tell the Palos Verdes Peninsula Unified School District that they were going on a long ocean voyage and that Josette would be my legal guardian during that time. Josette went so far as to become a licensed foster parent, subjecting herself to interview after interview, her home to inspection after inspection.

"I hope you appreciate that I've had to lock up my gun, throw away the kiddie pool, and hide my prescription drugs," she told me later in her French accent, the skin around her gray eyes crinkling as she smiled. "You'd think you were a kindergartner, the way they act, instead of a big, scary high schooler. You do realize that you're scary, *non*? All teenagers are holy terrors."

We had lunch together that day, just her and me, eating homemade soup and crème brûlée. Then we hung clothes of mine in her grown daughter's old bedroom, pinned photos and notes to the bulletin board to make it look more real, and threw a coat over

the 1970s-era knobbed bedpost, just in case someone cared enough
to check out our story.

"This will be very good for you, Little Frog," she said as we
surveyed our handiwork. My grandfather had always called her the
"Old Frog," and she returned the favor, calling me "Little Frog,"
because I, too, spoke French. "*Tu verras*, it's really a good school.
Also, if you ever want to come stay here with Tom and me for
reals, you are always welcome. Maybe you'll want a change from
being on the water, eh?" She looked over her glasses at me. "Or
maybe you'll just want a change."

I didn't think I'd want to stay with Josette much; I liked being at
home mostly. Also, if I was at home, I could look after my grandfather.

Marilyn was a little more serious than Josette about the whole
thing: "You really can't tell anyone where you actually live, sweetheart. No matter how much you want to. Just tell them the same
story all the time so you don't get confused: Daddy and I are on a
cruise around the world; you live with Josette. It'll be fine."

I wasn't sure things were going to be fine; I was a horrible liar.
And how was I supposed to make friends if I had to lie to them?

Sometime in June, Suzy Q disappeared from Perry's boat. I hadn't
seen her leave, but suddenly I noticed she wasn't there.

"Where's Suzy Q?" I asked Perry as he sat at the back of his
boat one day, leaning on a chair beneath the blue plastic tarp.

"I gave her away," he wheezed. "She got to be too much for
me."

"Where is she?" I was afraid he'd taken her to the pound; I was
ready to go rescue her.

"Oh, I found a farm. Plenty of room there. For her to run.

Friend of mine owns it. Out in Missourah. Lots of squirrels to chase." He smiled halfheartedly.

"I'm sorry," I said. "I bet you miss her."

Perry wasn't someone who cried, but he passed a bloated hand over one eye. "It's okay, sweetheart," he said after a second.

I suppose I should have known what Suzy Q's disappearance meant, but I didn't. Perry died a couple of weeks later in the hospital. No family claimed the body; there was no money to pay for the funeral. They took a collection up at the marina. Even my grandfather donated.

One afternoon as Marilyn and I walked to the parking lot to go run errands, we passed Tracy and her mother dressed in black dresses and hose.

"Aren't you going to Perry's funeral?" Tracy asked. "Everybody's going."

I looked to Marilyn who shook her head. "No," I said. "I guess not. I didn't know it was today."

They drove off in their old, brown Buick, and I slid into Marilyn's minivan, sad not to be going with them.

Perry's little boat sat in its slip for a long time, covered up in the wrinkled, blue tarp. Someone sold his yellow Econoline. Eventually the little boat disappeared too.

21

I T WAS THE END OF JULY THAT SUMMER BEFORE MY FIRST YEAR OF high school, and I was sitting with Dee on a bench outside the Anderson Cottage at the Old Soldiers' Home in Washington, DC. She had moved there a few years before. I was visiting her for a week, staying in one of the home's guest apartments, where I had my own kitchen and a living room and a view of the Washington Monument. I felt like a grown-up.

We were sitting on the bench, waiting for the mess hall to open for lunch, and the DC heat was just beginning to ratchet up in the shade; the cicadas were starting to buzz. We didn't have cicadas in LA. The sound made me happy and gave me the chills all at once, as if I were in some primeval forest. Dee held her cane in one hand and my hand in her other. I was almost as tall as she was now. I looked at her gray, curly hair, her brown eyes as she watched the world go by, her lips lined with age but still scarlet with lipstick. I looked down at her arms, which—because she was fat and had avoided the sun—were smooth and buttery white against the navy of her slacks. I noted the gentle rolls of her stomach beneath her pink blouse.

Sometimes when I looked at Dee, I thought about how my grandfather said she was a lesbian. I tried to imagine her making love to another woman, something I'd learned to think was disgusting—unless it was on a porn box, when it became magically sexy. *Dyke.* It was a word people saved for ugly girls who didn't quite fit in or the ones who looked like boys. But as I looked at Dee, even thinking it might be true of her, even trying hard to judge her for it, I couldn't; I felt no disgust. She wasn't sexy. She wasn't gross. She was Dee, my Dee, and I loved her. We sat in silence, listening to the cicadas and the burble of conversations behind us. I leaned my head on her shoulder, smelling her White Shoulders perfume, the clean scent of her shirt.

"You see that tree," she said, pointing with her cane to a huge copper beech in front of the white cottage. "That's a pretty famous tree. Tad, President Lincoln's son, used to play underneath it. They say the president even climbed it once, playing with him."

I remembered reading about Lincoln's visits to the Old Soldiers' Home in a book. Lincoln had often stayed in the cottage on the home's grounds, back when the inmates still wore uniforms and raised their own food. That was *here.* I was filled with awe. The last Civil War veterans had died long before, but here was this tree that had known Lincoln.

"I have to go touch it!" I said and ran toward it.

I bent down to get under its lowest branches, which brushed the ground, but once I was inside, I could stand. Green and greenish-red surrounded me like a tent. I imagined that tall, sad, great man playing there with his son, his giant feet where my sandals now stood. I placed my palm against its trunk and imagined his gnarled hands gripping the bark to climb, the leather soles of his shoes slipping, then gaining purchase, his long legs wrapping around the wood. I took a deep breath, as if I could breathe in his ghost. I went back to Dee. My eyes dazzled in the bright sun.

"Neat, huh?" she said. "You're just like your grandmother,

you know. That's exactly what she would have done." She smiled and squeezed my hand.

We moved inside, standing by the imposing oak doors of the mess hall. Already the silver-haired troops were massing in the foyer.

"Just like a bunch of cattle waiting for the feedlot," Dee whispered in my ear. "Mooo!"

I laughed out loud, earning a stare from a bushy-browed man standing by a column, his WWII Vet cap crammed low on his forehead. I was the only young person in the room. Dee mooed louder. Audrey, Dee's wisecracking best friend at the home, joined in. Audrey had been a WAC, too, and a journalist for the *Stars and Stripes*.

After we'd gotten our food on drab plastic trays—our green beans steaming and our red Jell-Os wobbly beneath whipped topping—we sat at a round table.

"Audrey and I are going to break out of this joint soon," Dee said so only Audrey and I could hear, as if we were plotting an escape from jail.

"Yeah," Audrey agreed. "Too many old farts. I mean, we're old, but these people are absolutely *hopeless*."

Looking around at the people in the mess—mostly old men giving us suspicious glances or staring off into space—I had to agree. I was glad Dee was leaving.

Dee and Audrey would move later that year, back to Anniston, where they'd live together. A few years after that, Dee would move back to California, and then, finally, back to the Old Soldiers' Home, where she died in 2003. I kept in touch with her through all of it, visiting her every few years. The older I got, the better friends we became. I found out she'd died when the wedding invitation I sent to her was returned with "deceased" stamped all over it in black ink.

Dee and I always had trouble explaining our relationship to others.

"This is my good friend Kelly," she'd say to introduce me to friends and acquaintances.

"She's like an aunt to me," I'd say, shrugging when explaining our visits to friends, or "She was my grandma's friend." But no explanation seemed adequate.

The words we were looking for, of course, were "granddaughter" and "grandmother." Dee would never tell me that she and Spence were lovers, but in my heart of hearts, I believe they were. She always spoke of Spence with love. I hope they were partners; I want that for both of them.

Dee and Spence are buried in veterans' cemeteries on opposite coasts. I wonder, sometimes, what they would have thought of marriage equality, what would have happened if she and Spence could have married, how different our lives would have been.

When I got home from that trip to DC—the very evening I got back—my grandfather reminded me again that Dee was a lesbian. I was giving him his insulin while he sat on his bed. I clicked open the cold, white plastic box and took out the syringe, two bottles, and alcohol swabs and arranged them on the windowsill.

"Couple of dykes, you know, Spence and Dee. Michele always hated Dee. She walked in on them together in bed."

I grunted an acknowledgment, stuck the needle in the first bottle, and pulled the plunger back, drawing 10 units of clear liquid. Then I drew 10 units back from the other, cloudy bottle.

"You know, I didn't know your mother very well. When Spence got pregnant with Michele, she got a job at a gas station, pumping gas. Then the minute she gave birth and got me to pay for it, she ran off to Dee. She'd planned it the whole bloody time. I'm sure of it. She just wanted a baby."

I hadn't known that. I plunged the syringe into his flabby upper arm, just above the smallpox vaccine scars, then rubbed his skin with alcohol until it shined.

"All done? That was a good one. No, Spence didn't let me see Michele. Kept me from her. She said her mother didn't like me, that she'd cut Michele out of her will if I saw her. Utter bullshit, of course."

I sat down beside him on the bed. He looked out the window, and I looked at him. He'd shaved that day for my return; his shirt was stained from dinner.

My grandfather told me that Spence had lied to Michele, telling her that her father had run off before she was born. The times he did get to see her, he was introduced as a family friend.

"She called me 'Treat,'" he said, taking off his glasses and wiping them with the hem of his shirt. "Don't know why she called me that."

But he went along with the lie.

When she was a teenager, Michele figured out that the old family friend who looked so much like her was actually her father. "She hated *me* then—her own father. Wouldn't talk to me for months." He sounded hurt, as if he was just as much of a victim as she was.

I understood, then, why there were no other pictures of Michele in his desk, why still—no matter how often I searched the filing cabinets—there were only those two of her at her birthday party, the two of her back. I didn't know what else it explained, but I knew it had to explain a lot.

"But anyway, that's why she ran away from home. Well, then she got into drugs."

I hadn't known she'd run away from home. I thought of my mom in one of those teenage runaway PSAs, the ones for Boys Town. Running away had always seemed like the worst thing that could happen to someone, probably because I'd never had anything to run away from. I thought of Michele—something between the childhood photographs my grandfather had and the woman from the picture on my shelf—with shaggy hair and a tough expression on her face, sitting on a cold, dirty curb.

"She found Dee and Spence in bed together, fucking, and she ran away."

He was saying it was their fault she ran away? Was I supposed to be mad at Dee? Spence? Was he blaming them for her death too?

I got up and put the white plastic box back into the fridge. I was supposed to feel angry, but I didn't; I didn't feel angry at them or anyone. Mostly I just wished Michele hadn't run away. Mostly I felt bad that she hadn't had a dad, that people had lied to her, that she hadn't been happy at home. That she hadn't lived. Mostly I just wished I knew more about her. Even when my grandfather brought her up, I never felt comfortable asking him questions about Michele. Such conversations seemed to take us to his sadness, his loss—a place I didn't like going.

Mostly, I just missed being with Dee.

That night—and off and on again for the rest of my life—I imagined the scene of Michele walking in on Dee and Spence in bed: a teenager, not much older than I was, already hurt and lonely, discovering that her mother loved another person—feeling, probably, that her mother loved that other person more than she did her own daughter—and then discovering that this other person was a woman. I imagined Spence and Dee, too, at being discovered, how embarrassed or ashamed or shocked they must have been. I thought of Dee, who would never willingly hurt anyone, being on the receiving end of all that hate. I saw my mother and Spence and Dee, the triangle of them staring at each other, until Michele turned and walked out, never, never to come back home. I saw this scene in miniature, like the shoebox dioramas I'd made in grade school, and I wanted to reach my hand into that box—into the past that happened before I was even born—and stop her from walking out the door.

———————————

A few weeks later, Marilyn took me along with her to the video store. The parking lot on Century Boulevard was deserted. While she emptied the quarter slots and stocked merchandise, I sat in the car reading the sex scenes out of the yellowed and stiff Scott Turow novel she kept wedged beneath her van's cup holder so that her coffee cup—one of the small ones that fit on the end of the thermoses she carried everywhere—wouldn't fall through the hole. I read so I wouldn't have to meet anyone's eye.

That summer, I'd become painfully shy, mortified when I was noticed by a stranger, embarrassed about everything. I suddenly hated going to the store. I'd sit crouched in the car, every muscle tense, trying to will people away from me. What if, somehow, someone I knew were to see me in a porn store parking lot? What if one of the customers noticed me?

Fortunately, most of the men going to our store were like me; they didn't want to be seen in a porn store parking lot either. But some men getting out of their cars would give me knowing glances on their way inside, maybe a little wave of the hand. I wondered if they thought my father was inside watching a movie. Or maybe they were regulars and knew I was the owner's daughter. Their glances made me shrink into myself.

I always looked for the sex scenes from the book while I waited; I never bothered with the rest of it, which was boring, although its cover said it was a bestselling mystery. I turned a crinkly page. I was learning about pink areolas, and their apparent irresistibility to men, when someone knocked on the car window. I thought for a second it was Norm, the store clerk, but it was a stranger. I only caught a glimpse of him—his brown corduroy pants, the pink of his fingernails against his skin, his smooth cheek—before I ducked back down and looked at my lap.

"Hey, roll down the window, sweetheart," he said. "I'd love to talk to you."

I sat in my seat, too scared to move, stone-faced, staring at my lap, ignoring him the way I'd learned to ignore the people who taunted me at school. When I ignored *them* they usually stopped, but this man kept talking to me through the barely open window, asking me to open the door, asking me, "Please, please, won't you just look at me? Honey, just look."

Once when I was little and riding in Marilyn's minivan, a man in a sedan drove up next to us at a red light. He kept honking and honking at us. I looked over and saw his penis lying like a dead beige fish in his lap, his hand gently stroking it.

"Please, please," the man in the parking lot kept asking.

Once when I was eleven years old, I was at the beach with my class from Le Lycée; because it was across from the ocean, we often went there for PE. That day, I got out of the water before anyone else did and went to rinse off in the public restrooms, a cinder block building with slimy floors and open showers. It was dim inside, but I could see that someone else was there too. He was tall and skinny with black hair and pale, white skin. He wore one of those orange safety vests road workers wear and held a long wooden stick with a sharp metal point attached to it like a thick nail—the kind of stick janitors use to pick paper up off the ground. Only he wasn't picking up paper. He was staring at me in my red bathing suit.

"That's a pretty swimsuit," he said.

Suddenly he was behind me, his right hand gently pushing me farther inside the building. Then he was running his finger under my suit strap, saying, "Can you help me please? I just want to get a suit like that for my sister. What brand is it? I'm looking for the tag."

I knew he wasn't looking for the tag. But the big stick with its metal spike was hovering over me on my left. I knew he could kill me with it, and I was scared.

Then he was looking for the tag (but not really looking for the tag) between my legs, his fingers running along the inside of my suit and the outside of my labia, his arm holding me in place, that sharp point somewhere over me. He didn't need to hold me in place, though; I was frozen there anyway. "I don't think the tag is there," I whispered. Then we heard my classmates' voices approaching. He let me go.

In the porn store parking lot that afternoon, I knew not to look at the man at the window, no matter how many times he asked.

Now that I was getting older, sometimes when we were alone, my grandfather would tell me how Marilyn wouldn't sleep with him, had never slept with him, and how, even if she would sleep with him, he couldn't get an erection. He told me how frustrating it was to be a man and not get any sex, how frustrated he was that he didn't really *know* for a fact that he *couldn't* get hard because Marilyn wouldn't have sex with him.

"She says I don't turn her on. Like I'm a light bulb or something," he said, sighing angrily.

I felt like a grown-up when he told me these things, like I was his equal, someone worthy of his confidence. I didn't tell anyone what he said.

———————————————

At the end of that summer, a week before school started, Tracy, Sharon, and Al packed up the Chris-Craft and left Donahue's. Sharon returned on her own, a year or two later, to visit. Marilyn and I ran into her on the dock. Her face was pale, her lips were chapped, her eyes puffy; the afternoon sun made her squint. It took her a second to recognize us.

"How's Tracy?" I asked.

"Oh, she found an old man to live with," Sharon said. Even her voice was tired.

"You mean—?" Marilyn didn't finish her question.

"Yeah," Sharon said. "She says he buys her stuff. She'll be back, though, one day. I guess." And then she walked on.

III

A Normal Family

22

***

EVERY MORNING AT 7:20 SHARP, PETE WOULD PARK HIS FULL-sized '80s Ram van on the road just opposite our boat and honk. He'd keep honking until he saw me get off the boat with my backpack and start walking down the dock toward the parking lot. By the time I got up to the parking lot, he'd be waiting there, engine idling, the air blasting if it was hot, the heat if it was cold. Pete had been enlisted by my parents to take me to high school. Marilyn couldn't get up early enough to take me, and my grandfather couldn't drive. So Pete got the job. At first I hadn't liked riding with him because he tailgated other cars, bringing the snub nose of his van right up against people's bumpers or swerving suddenly to pass. I wasn't sure if he could hear the other cars honking at us; he was deaf from being around engines all his life. But after a few weeks, I'd gotten used to him and the van. I liked the way it smelled of Old Spice and engine grease, clean laundry, and just a hint of gasoline. What's more, Pete was always cheerful, even when his leg hurt or he hadn't slept well. He was steady. I didn't have to try to read his moods the way I did my grandfather's.

Every morning, almost like clockwork, he'd ask, "What'd you learn in school yesterday?" as if I were still in fifth grade. "D'you make any friends yet?"

"A few. I eat with them at lunch." There were only a very few.

"You got a boyfriend yet?"

"No."

"What's wrong with them boys?" He'd snort in disgust.

I thought it obvious that the problem was what was wrong with me, not them, but it made me feel better when Pete said things like that. Pete had a grown daughter; he knew how to take care of girls.

"Well, don't you worry. You're only a freshman."

It took forty minutes to get to school, driving through San Pedro and over the peninsula to Palos Verdes High School. The drive in Pete's van on my way to school became my favorite time of the day. Sometimes we took the coast road that wended around the peninsula's undeveloped coves and cliffs, and I looked at all the different colors the ocean made, white foam on bright green and blue, blue so dark it almost looked black, blue like sapphire, like steel. The empty land at Portuguese Bend stretched for miles, and the early morning dew made everything seem fresh. It reminded me of a fairy tale Marilyn had read me once, of a princess who tried to make a necklace with the morning dew, stringing the pearls of water with a thread and needle.

And I liked talking to Pete. He'd tell me stories from when he was young, chasing watermelon trucks to catch the falling fruit, or going to the Long Beach Pier as a teenager, or his days training for the Air Force in World War II, although the war ended just before he was deployed.

"I was all ready to go too, and they canceled the darn war on me. What the heck were they thinking?" he'd ask, winking to show the joke.

Then, suddenly, we'd be on the road that overlooked the high school. Pete dropped me off there because the main entrance was always choked with parents dropping their children off in shiny

Nissans and 'Benzes or with students driving their own cherry Mustangs and Miatas, gifts given for all As or sweet sixteens. I'd get out of the square van and sling my backpack over my shoulder.

"Have a good day, Pumpkin," Pete would call to my back. "Don't do anything I wouldn't do."

A set of one hundred stairs descended from the road to the school; they were a bridge from my world to everyone else's. At the top of the stairs I was carefree, happy to see the ocean stretched out beyond the peninsula, the sparkling swimming pool, the Spanish red-tile roofs of the school buildings, the seagulls circling above. By the time I reached the bottom of the stairs, my shoulders were tense and my eyes darted to the front and the side, waiting for the first cruel comment of the day. I wasn't lying when I told Pete I had friends at school, but I also didn't tell him how completely at sea I was.

The classes themselves were fine. In English, we'd read *To Kill a Mockingbird*, and I'd fallen in love with Scout and Harper Lee. Geometry homework was fun, the proofs like puzzles, although I slept through Mrs. Maas's transparencies. History was horrible, but that was mostly because burnt-out Mr. Miller spent each and every hour showing us slides of the animals he'd killed on his African safari. But like geometry, if you worked on your own and read ahead, history wasn't boring at all. If you read history, you could learn where the ideas you took for granted actually came from and, what I found oddly reassuring, that the world had absolutely always been a terrible mess.

What I dreaded about school was what happened between classes in the breezeways or in the shuffle and hum in the classroom just before the teacher started: The way guys asked to copy my homework before class, then called me a bitch when I refused. The way the pretty girls seated on either side of my desk carried on conversations over my head, without ever including me. The way someone in the back would make a gagging or sucking noise when I raised my hand to answer a question. The way my teachers heard them make fun of me and did nothing to stop them.

After eight years of school uniforms, I didn't know how to dress. I wore relaxed-fit Lee jeans with elastic waistbands while everyone else wore Levi 501s or Gap. I borrowed Marilyn's pumpkin and turquoise camp shirts—shirts that made me a target against the crowds of tight Billabong tees and cable-knits from J. Crew.

"Nice shirt," girls sniggered in the hall.

"Hey, I think my mom has those jeans," a boy would call from his locker.

It got worse the harder I tried. One day, I wore black leggings and a bright orange tunic, again borrowed from Marilyn, and a white cloth headband. I thought I looked trendy. Instead, even Mr. Miller joined in making fun of me before class.

Sometimes when I asked Marilyn for new clothes, she told me I was a "real clothes horse," even though her closet was twice the size of mine and she used the coat closet by the stairs to keep all the clothes that didn't fit her. But occasionally she'd take me to the mall to go shopping. We never went to the stores like Gap or United Colors of Benetton, where the popular girls bought their clothes. Instead we went to department stores or small boutiques that went out of business shortly after we shopped there. I always loved the clothes we chose together, colorful blue-plaid bodysuits and crinkly broomstick skirts or floral dresses. But no matter what we bought or how excited I was about it, when I wore it to school, I'd always realize the minute I got to the bottom of that long stairway that it was exactly the worst thing I could have picked.

After a few weeks, I'd almost started to get the hang of lockers and changing for PE, but I still felt self-conscious in my baggy shorts and Day-Glo tee. No one else wore Day-Glo anymore. As we waited for Coach Milosovic to make his appearance, I'd sidle up to Julia, the only girl in PE I spoke to. She wore clothes as inappropriate as mine: pleated khaki shorts and baggy tees with pictures of Jesus's bleeding hands and Bible verses. I avoided the other girls and would never meet their eyes.

I did this because of the way Chrissie and Meghan, two freshmen like me—only popular and pretty and already with upperclassmen boyfriends—looked at me in the PE locker room and smirked to each other. The school must have assigned the lockers alphabetically, because Chrissie's hall locker was next to mine too. She was the one I had asked on the first day of school for help with the lock, and she had helped—perfunctorily and silently, staring at me like I was the stupidest person on the planet—while Meghan and some boy looked on over her shoulder and laughed. My face burned as she speed-dialed my combination and loudly clunked the lock open; I barely managed a thank-you. I didn't know it then, but I'd asked for help with something everyone else had learned at the beginning of junior high; we'd never had lockers at Le Lycée. I was marked from that first day, and every PE class I changed under Chrissie's and Meghan's cold gaze, their sniggering at my clothes, my spray deodorant, my knee socks.

From Chrissie and Meghan and the rest of PV High, I learned a form of racial profiling: Pretty white girls were always mean. Ugly white girls, nerdy white girls, fat white girls, white girls with bad skin, pretty or ugly Japanese, Korean, Indian, or Chinese girls, as well as Latina and black girls, could be trusted, most of the time, to be decent human beings. I held this prejudice with me all through high school and college, scared of white, beautiful people and their narrow judgments. Sometimes I still feel the same way.

Everyone in high school looked through me as they passed me in the halls, unless it was to laugh at me, except for the few girls

I'd managed to make friends with. Our lunch group was composed of misfits like me: a drama nerd, a fat kid, a Latin geek, a granola-hippie, horsey girl. We spent whole lunch periods having fun and feeling safe—until the next apple core or half-empty soda can was thrown at us, accompanied by a gale of laughter. I was grateful for these friends, but still, I couldn't even tell them where I lived.

Sometimes I wondered what my mother had been like in high school. I thought about the way her death certificate said her last place of employment was Hollywood High. Was she popular? I supposed the answer all depended on how pretty she was and if she wore the right clothes or knew the latest bands. I wondered if she was smart, if she liked math or English or history. I wondered if she had a boyfriend or got asked to dances. But as hard as I tried, when I thought about my mother, I couldn't imagine the answers to my questions. That was how little I knew. There were thousands of possible answers. If my mother were a geometry problem, the sum of the things I knew about her would be zero. She would be the x in an algebra problem with too many unknowns to solve. When had she run away? Was it really because of Dee and Spence, or was it something else? Was it because she was miserable in high school too?

Boys, especially, looked through me, and most of the time, I looked away from them. So I was surprised when one day in PE, two were looking straight at me. One was tall, his shoulders too thick and sloped for the rest of his thin body, his long hair draped across them like a cape. The other boy was small and skinny, his faint mustache showing up black against his pale skin like the black soot on the white paint of our boat. They looked at me, then looked at each other, whispered, laughed. My shoulders tensed. I looked more firmly to the ground, waiting for the taunts and laughter that were surely going to follow.

Coach Milosovic blew his whistle, and as we gathered in a circle around him, I noticed the two boys looking at me again around his back. I inched closer to Julia. We moved together to the track to begin our jog, she to my right, both of us to the far edge of the outside lane so that the faster students could pass us.

I hated running. I hated how my shorts always bunched up between my legs, revealing more of my jiggling thighs. I was so embarrassed that I ran with my shoulders hunched up, my arms stiff alongside my hips, my eyes on the ground ahead of me. Back then, I thought it was a particular moral failing that I didn't like to run. If I would just learn to run, most of my problems would be solved—being fat, being ugly, being ungainly and awkward, being a dork. I sometimes set out to try to run at home. I'd lace up my sneakers and jog along the dusty road that led from the marina to the railroad tracks, dodging the APL trucks lined up along its side to wait for their loads. I'd be doing okay, perhaps just hitting my stride and finally feeling comfortable, when a semi driver would lean out of his cab and shout something about my ass. Or Wade or Bob would drive by, toot their horn, or slow down the car and say something to me—usually words of encouragement but sometimes hoots of appreciation. I'd wave at them and smile wanly, but I'd already tensed, my gait once more awkward. I stumbled, I slowed, I gave up and walked the rest of the way.

As Julia and I jogged slowly around the track, I heard heavier footfalls behind us, as if some particularly oafish wildebeest were pursuing us. They slowed as they came close; it was the boy with long hair. He loped beside me, his hair swaying back and forth as he ran.

"Hi," he said to me.

"Hi."

"What's up?"

"Um, nothing." I hated that question, "What's up?" People always asked it when it was completely obvious what was up. We were *running*, duh.

"Running sucks, man," he said.

"Yeah," I said, although I also knew that running was potentially less embarrassing than other sports: volleyball, basketball, softball, soccer.

"Hey, what kinda music you like?"

I'd already been asked this a few times since the beginning of the year, and I'd figured out that the true answer—nothing, really—was one that made people profoundly uncomfortable. *Everyone* listened to *some* kind of music, didn't they? The next year I would make a dedicated attempt to like new music like Morrissey, Stone Temple Pilots, Green Day, or at least to fake it. I'd fail miserably.

"All sorts of stuff," I answered, hoping he wouldn't ask me "like what?"

"Like what?"

"Just stuff."

"So, hey, what's your name?"

"Kelly," I said. "That's Julia."

Julia, whose arms were also stiff against her side as she jogged, bent her hand at the wrist, the tiniest wave.

"I'm Devin."

"Okay," I said.

"Oh, okay, well. I'll see you around later, maybe," he said and jogged on.

As he lurched on, I realized that nothing had happened. He hadn't made fun of me. He'd just talked to me. What was wrong with him? Julia and I jogged on without saying anything.

Later that day, after the bell that released us from the last class had rung, as we were all hurtling, like schooling fish, through the halls to our lockers, I heard my name ring across the hall. I turned and it was the guy from PE.

"Hey," he said as caught up to me, "can I have your number?"

"No!" I said, startled.

"What?"

"I mean, I don't know you."

"Oh. Okay. Well, can I have it anyway?"

I wrote it down, mostly to get rid of him so that I could get to my locker. That evening he called to ask me to the school luau on Friday night. I said yes, but not because I wanted to go anywhere with him; I didn't want to hurt his feelings.

"Great. I'll pick you up. Where do you live?"

"I'll just meet you there."

"No, seriously, I have a car. I'll give you a ride."

"No, it's okay. I'll just meet you there." There was no way he could come to the boat, and I didn't want to bother Josette.

The night of the luau I tore through all the drawers beneath my bunk, searching for something to wear. The only bathing suit I had was one designed to mimic a ladybug, which I'd bought at a swim shop that catered to "mature" women. I had no cutoffs or cute tank tops like the other girls would be wearing. I found a pair of Marilyn's baggy, white cotton shorts with a drawstring to put over my suit and a coral-colored bandana-print shirt of my own from REI.

When I got there, Devin said, "You look cute." I didn't believe him.

Music throbbed. Hundreds of high school students were splashing around in the pools, making out in swim trunks, tiny wet T-shirts, Daisy Dukes, bikinis with lots of cleavage. If you looked at the other girls, there was no way you could possibly call me "cute" and mean it.

After a few minutes of disastrous, stilted conversation, where it became clear that he liked death metal and I didn't, that I was "book smart" and he was barely passing class, he asked, "So what do your parents do?"

"Um," I said. "They have a meat market in the 'hood." (It just came out that way.)

"Oh. Okay. Hey, let's go swimming!"

I couldn't have been more relieved. At least there would be something to do besides talking. Unfortunately, the something Devin had in mind, once we got in the water, was to pull me close to him and stick a huge, probing tongue into my mouth. It felt like a slug with epilepsy, hell-bent on slithering down my throat. And it tasted bad. I'd never been kissed before. Although I knew tongues were involved, I had no idea they were *that* involved. I pushed him away, his soft arms slick in the water.

"Don't worry," Marilyn reassured me when she picked me up that night, after I'd told her the whole story—about the tongue, the stultifying conversation, the way I didn't fit in with anyone. "The boys get better in college. In high school they're all a bunch of idiots. And the girls pretty much are idiots too."

We drove down Channel Street from Western and rounded a bend. Suddenly the whole harbor was spread before us: the lights of shipyards and container yards, the Vincent Thomas Bridge.

"I thought it was just me," I said.

"No, honey, it's not you. It's them." But I knew it wasn't really *them*—the boys, the people who made fun of me—it was *me*.

That first year of high school, it became apparent that there were two kinds of families: the one I lived in and everyone else's. No one else lived on a boat with six cats who trailed cat litter, bits of feces, and tapeworm larvae onto the dining room table and kitchen counter. No one else had to pat down their sheets and blankets before they went to sleep to be sure a cat hadn't peed on the bed. No one else's father made half-hour phone calls to Omaha Steaks to order boxes of frozen steaks or chicken cordon bleu delivered to their boat or, in fact, had their own personal Omaha Steaks agent because they were such a good customer. No one else had to pull socks over their dad's calloused, elephantine feet. No one else had to watch their dad eat dinner with his testicles lying sloppily on the dining room chair, grease from the meal dribbling down his chin, and then give him a shot of insulin. No one else had to worry if their clothes smelled of cat urine, bilges, must, cigarette smoke, diesel. They didn't have to lie about what their parents did for a living. They didn't need to pretend not to see the boxes covered with penises inserted into women's asses as they walked through their mother's bedroom. They didn't have to lie to their friends about where they lived.

I didn't know then what I know now: that there are almost as many "weird" families as there are normal families; that "normal" isn't really normal; that we all have stories to tell about where we come from. And I didn't know then what I know now—that Marilyn really was right. It *was* them and their age, just as surely as it was me and mine.

23

ONE SATURDAY THAT FALL, WE ALL WENT TO THE LOS Angeles Boat Show. The show was one of the few things, besides his cats, that my grandfather had shown an interest in after his accident, and so we took him there. We loaded up his new electric scooter, but when we got to the convention hall in Marina Del Rey, he refused to use it. Instead he creaked down the long aisles, an eye patch perched on his bad eye, occasionally using his cane to point at things and people, sitting to rest on folding chairs begrudgingly lent from display tables. We passed by exhibit after exhibit of expensive marine equipment—EPIRBs, GPS, winches, sonar—insurance companies, maritime services, shiny, new speedboats, fishing equipment, even glittery spokes-models. He paused every few tables, chatting with salesmen and picking up glossy brochures that he deposited in the sack I carried behind him.

On a quiet aisle, he stopped at a booth for the U.S. Coast Guard Auxiliary. A trim, old woman sat behind the table, her silver hair topped by a white USCGA visor; to her right sat an older man wearing a white Izod shirt and khaki shorts. My grandfather placed his left fist on their white plastic table and leaned. The table creaked beneath his weight; I wondered if it might give way.

"Hello!" she chipperly greeted him.

"Greetings. Now, what does the Coast Guard Auxiliary do?"

"Well, we'd be glad to tell you," she said flirtatiously, flashing smokers' teeth through red lipstick.

The Coast Guard Auxiliary, we learned, was a civilian volunteer organization sponsored by the Coast Guard. They were mostly retirees and had uniforms and honorary ranks. On the weekends, they patrolled the harbor in their own private boats, reminding people to wear life jackets and reporting drunk boaters.

My grandfather turned on some of his old English charm, dropped Lord Mountbatten's name here and there, and described the glamorous yacht he lived on. He introduced Marilyn and me. Someone gladly pulled out a chair for him. The volunteers behind the table were smitten; after an hour, they were all the best of chums. Perry Mason and John Wayne were mentioned; so was Lady Jane Grey. Marilyn and I took turns going to the bathroom. At the end of the conversation, my grandfather gave the table his name and phone number. He promised to attend their monthly flotilla meetings.

"Yes, it's *Sir* Richard, actually, love," he corrected the woman as she wrote on a legal pad.

"Oh, *Sir* Richard, how wonderful!" she said, only too happy to make the correction.

I, however, was very ready for the audience with Sir Richard to be over. I wanted to go home. But after a much-needed trip to the bathroom himself, my grandfather had one more stop to make.

"Let's go back to that Calibogie booth," he told Marilyn. We trekked slowly to the back of the hall, where two fiberglass skiffs with outboard motors and center consoles were on display. Before long, we'd bought one. It cost ten thousand dollars.

"See this?" he pointed to his eye patch and told the slightly startled salesman. "I'll be paying with this eyeball!"

Marilyn was quiet, but I couldn't tell if she was upset or not. Maybe it was okay because he was using his settlement money. "Richard, are you sure?" was all she asked.

"We need a tender," he told Marilyn. "These are good boats, based on the old Hobies. Besides, Kelly will have fun running around the harbor in it."

I'd never thought about having a motorboat of my own before. My grandfather had bought me Chapman's *Piloting* and had tried to teach me knots; both experiences made boating seem complex, stressful. What I really wanted was a kayak, something quiet to explore the wetland at the end of the West Basin. Marilyn and I had rented kayaks on a trip once. I actually had money saved for one in a little cardboard box marked "kayak."

My reverie was interrupted by the sound of her calling to me. It was finally time to go.

Marilyn started driving my grandfather and me to the Auxiliary meetings, as my presence had been commanded. Once a month on Tuesday evenings, I was surrounded by white-haired men and women in navy polyester slacks and shirts who showed me infinitesimally different pictures of boat trips and grandchildren. When I was little, I would have eaten up all the attention, but I wasn't little anymore. They mistook my smiling patience for enthusiasm. They encouraged me to apply to the Coast Guard Academy, gave me USCG T-shirts, sweatshirts, pencils, and stickers.

"Don't you think she'd be great at the academy, Sir Richard?" the same woman invariably asked.

"It's a free education!" piped in her shorter, balder husband. "One of the best!"

"Of course," my grandfather boomed. "She'll be bloody great at anything she does."

During the social hour before the business meetings, my grandfather again told stories about writing for *Perry Mason*, living in the same building as Ava Gardner, his cousin Robert Donat, his exploits in the Navy and Special Operations.

"What an interesting life you've led, Sir Richard!" they exclaimed.

As for myself, I wasn't sure his life was that interesting. Not anymore. The thought had begun to float around my mind: How could all of his stories possibly be true? If he'd written for *Perry Mason*, how come I'd never seen his name on the credits, not even the summer I'd watched nothing but *Perry Mason* reruns? If he'd been in Buchenwald, how come he didn't have a tattoo? But I didn't stop believing him entirely. After all, if my grandfather's life wasn't that interesting, if he wasn't that special, what would that make me?

24

I STOOD ON THE CONCRETE POOL DECK OF THE HIGH SCHOOL. It was in the spring of my freshman year and still cool. I pulled my towel around my shoulders. Steam rose from the churning water where the upperclassmen were swimming a preseason workout. At the end of each set, the swimmers leaned against the pool ledges or pulled themselves out of the water to breathe the cool air. They waved at the freshmen waiting on deck—whom they already knew from club teams—male and female swimmers in their Speedos and imprinted latex caps, their upper bodies triangles of muscle perched atop narrow, sleek hips and iron thighs.

I tugged at my baggy suit so that it covered my bottom and pulled my towel more tightly around myself. That fall I'd learned how to swim the competitive strokes at the San Pedro YMCA. I'd swum lap after lap in my ladybug suit, which had faded until it was bronze and gray. After my hair had turned into straw from the chlorine, I bought an old lady's white rubber cap from the Y's front desk, complete with chinstrap and flower-imprint pattern. I hadn't bothered to buy a new suit for high-school tryouts; I wore my old lady cap. I had thought I could swim well enough to get on the team, but I knew better now as I watched the team practice. The swimmers in the pool could swim 150 yards in the time it took me to swim 50.

Once the team cleared the pool, it was our turn. The water was warm compared to the cold air. My toes and fingertips tingled as the blood rushed into them. Coach Terry blew her whistle, and the workout began.

I saw stars after each set of freestyle or butterfly. During each lap I was plunged into the chaos of the white wake of the swimmer in front of me, the clawing hands of the swimmer behind me. When I did backstroke, I drifted into the other swimmers. I was routinely lapped. I almost threw up after the sprints. At the end of the workout, I could barely lift myself from the pool. The tryouts would last a whole week.

Before I went back to the locker room that first day, I asked Coach Terry if she thought I even had a chance. She was shorter than I was, but thin, with spiked, silver hair and tanned skin. She appraised my dripping carcass and rubber cap.

"Well," she said. "I know if you quit tonight, you're definitely not going to make the team."

The next afternoon, Coach Terry wrote on the pool's chalkboard, "Pain is only temporary; pride is forever" in old-fashioned cursive. It became my mantra that week. I'd fallen in love with swimming, the way my body glided through the water, the way the world's sounds were muffled, the sunlight softened. I was hypnotized by the black lines at the bottom of the pool.

I even managed to ignore Chrissie and Meghan who, much to my chagrin, had also decided to try out for swim team, turning up on the second day. They were cute in their sporty bikinis, and I saw how the boys smiled whenever they came on deck. And I saw how they smiled at the boys smiling at them. They weren't much better swimmers than I was, but they were at least in shape. While I gasped for breath at the wall between swims, they giggled about pull buoys, the floats swimmers sometimes grip between their legs in order to strengthen their arms.

"It feels like a gigantic tampon," Chrissie smirked.

"No," Meghan said in a loud stage whisper. "It's like a foam dildo."

"I bet *she* likes it," Chrissie looked meaningfully in my direction.

Something magical had happened in the pool. While normally I would have cringed—maybe even cried, at what they said—in the pool, I just got mad. Being angry made me pull the water harder and kick faster, and by the time I was done with two laps, I'd forgotten they'd said anything at all.

I made the team. It didn't matter to me that Coach Terry had cut no one. It didn't matter that I was the slowest person on the team.

On long bus rides home from meets, I made friends. At meets, I cheered for everyone. I wasn't just *me* anymore; I was a swimmer. It was easier to walk those crowded halls with my swim parka on.

Swimming was the thing I loved to do best. I would do anything to be able to keep doing it—and the thing I'd have to do was get much faster. They were consolidating our high school with two others starting the next year, and there'd be three times as many people competing for the same spots. The day high school season ended, I started swimming with the San Pedro Y's team. I was so slow I had to train with the little kids, but I didn't mind at all. Little kids thought I was cool simply by virtue of being bigger than they were.

"Swimming is so good for you," Josette told me a few weeks before summer vacation, as we made crepes after school at her house, which was also supposed to be my house. "Here, the first one—*c'est toujours raté.*" She took the spatula from me and cleared the torn crêpe from the pan. "Yes, and you're getting skinny, too. Positively svelte." I smiled. "What else have you been up to?"

"My friends and I are starting a club next semester." We sprinkled powdered sugar over two of the pancakes—one for her, one for me. "We're going to call it Better Our World, so we can do whatever we want to do, like picking up trash at the beach or working at a homeless shelter."

"That's good. You should do more of these things because they will help you get into a good college," Josette said.

"You think I can go to college?"

"*Mais!*" She shut a cabinet door. "Yes, I think you can go to college, you little monster. It would be a *disaster* if you didn't go to college."

College had appeared on my horizon that first year of high school. My grandfather and Marilyn had probably always expected me to go to college, but I'd never really thought about it before. I still didn't know what I wanted to be when I grew up, but suddenly, everyone I knew was going to college. Suddenly, college was the place where adulthood started; it was the place you went when you left home.

I sat down at the table.

"Richard and Marilyn want you to go to college, right?" she called from the kitchen.

"Yes, I think so. Sometimes my dad says we can't afford it."

She brought our glasses of water to the table.

"He can afford it." She looked at me over her reading glasses, her gray eyes keeping my own from looking down. "You know, you're really very smart. I think you know that. But don't you dare forget it."

25

M Y FAMILY SPENT THE LAST WEEKS OF SCHOOL AND THE FIRST part of that summer high in a twenty-foot cradle at Wilmington Marine, the boatyard everyone called Dinko's after its Croatian owner, who had a reputation for dishonesty. "When you shake hands with Dinko," the harbor saying went, "count your fingers afterward." My grandfather, too, said this, but he didn't have much of a choice. A wood-hulled boat like ours needed to be hauled out fairly regularly for routine maintenance. It was one of the reasons many people preferred fiberglass hulls. Only two yards in the harbor could handle a wooden boat as big as ours— Dinko's or San Pedro Boat Works—and Dinko's terms were better. Besides, my grandfather had had a row with the manager at San Pedro the last time we were in dry dock.

I'm not sure that, technically, we were supposed to be living on board while our boat was up in the cradle, but we had nowhere else to go. So Dinko accommodatingly hooked us up to electricity and water. He turned a blind eye when our kitchen sink and dishwasher emptied out on to the ground, while we, in turn, used them only at night when no one was around but Bill, the white-haired night watchman. If my grandfather disliked Dinko because he charged people for his expensive services, he also respected him because he'd given Bill a job. Bill lived at Dinko's and, in the evenings, piloted the empty shopping cart he used as a walker around with his dog in the baby seat. He'd had a stroke a while ago. When you talked to him you could sometimes understand the answers, but more often than not, there was a burble, then a nod, and he walked on.

A thirty-foot, rickety metal staircase with open risers connected our main deck to the ground. As nervous as they made me, the stairs were much better than the steep wooden ladder Marilyn and I had used to climb on board our first night at the shipyard, my heavy backpack threatening to pull me backward with every rung. Dinko *had* been really nice about getting us the stairs, even when we hadn't asked for them, I liked to remind my grandfather.

"Don't think he won't find a way to put it on our bill, thieving Croat bastard," he grumbled.

But I thought the stairs were worth whatever he wanted to charge. We were living for a month on an 83-foot boat wedged into a high wooden cradle, secured with shims and good wishes, less than twenty-five yards from two jet-fuel storage tanks at the Ultramar Refinery. Stairs seemed like one of those little luxuries that make life bearable, like showers, which we didn't really have because we weren't able to pump our sewage tanks overboard whenever we wanted to, the way we could at Donahue's. Instead, Marilyn and I went up and down the big stairs and across the shipyard to the building where there was a little shower room. It wasn't that bad, especially on days I took a shower at the Y after swim practice.

My grandfather settled for sponge baths. During our time at Dinko's, he left the boat only once, his cane in one hand and his hand gripping the railing. I followed behind, willing him not to fall. He creaked down each stair slowly, making sure both feet were steady on each step before proceeding. When he was halfway down, his legs started shaking from fatigue, and he swayed forward.

I held my breath. He turned around and handed me his cane, then gripped the rail with two hands. He went down the rest of the stairs backward. I could hardly watch. No amount of coaxing or Milk Bones could convince Charlie or Lisa down the steps. Instead, Charlie would stand on his hind legs and lean against the boat's rail, whining as we came and went. When they needed to go to the bathroom, they just went on the deck.

Every morning at eight, workmen swarmed the yard, carrying their wood-handled tools in cloth buckets or in clunky belts slung about their waists. During the day, I wandered along the marked safety paths between the boats and the office where, theoretically, I wouldn't be brained by dropped belt sanders or run over by boats being pulled out of the water on train tracks. I watched the wooden ships high in their cradles, the dark-skinned workers agilely climbing up scaffolding or hanging in slings off towering hulls, hammering and chiseling and caulking, shouting entire conversations in Croatian and Spanish between boats. I did not know it, but I was watching the rare modern practice of an ancient art. As the LA commercial fishing fleet was decimated and fiberglass hulls became more and more popular, the art of maintaining wooden hulls was dying out.

When a boat first came in, its hull would be power hosed, then scraped by hand. Afterward the ground around it would be littered with glistening, green algae and clumps of dying barnacles, flakes of toxic, red paint, and spent zincs. Our own boat now sat high in her cradle, her hull having been hosed and scraped. Soon they'd begin caulking her with oakum and putty, chiseling hemp into the seams between the planks and then sealing them. Then they'd sand it and repaint it with antifouling paint, then attach new zincs.

All in all, except for the height and the shower situation, life in dry dock wasn't that bad. Away from our usual surroundings, it almost felt like a vacation, and my friend Jill came over for a sleepover on the Fourth of July. And being up so high wasn't that scary, especially if you stayed inside and away from windows, especially if you didn't spend too much time contemplating what might happen in an earthquake. I spent a significant amount of time contemplating what might happen in an earthquake. I imagined our boat landing on its side and collapsing under its own weight, the jet-fuel tanks next door exploding. But earthquakes didn't happen that often, I reminded myself. The last one I remembered had happened four years before.

The only other inconvenience was getting heavy things like big boxes of videotapes, sacks of quarters, and groceries from the car to the boat. From our years at Donahue's, Marilyn had perfected the art of transporting heavy things over long distances with a hand truck and sturdy cardboard boxes so that we only needed to make one or two trips down the dock. Here at Dinko's, the trip was similar, only through a boatyard where you had to follow a zigzagged path over rails, hoses, and power cords, then carry the load up the thirty feet of stairs. I was usually spared the task. Roger, a gentle Nicaraguan man who had been an agricultural agent in his own country but who now worked as a laborer for my grandfather, carried the really heavy items, like the boxes of videos. But if Marilyn got home after five, I'd get stuck moving the groceries from the car. And that's when I first noticed the wine.

One afternoon, I went to get the groceries out of Marilyn's minivan with the hand truck. I opened the red van's sliding door: there were four paper sacks crammed tight with groceries, dozens of cans of cat food, frozen dinners, cereal, meat, and chicken, then also sacks of dog and cat chow, and four bags of kitty litter from the dollar store. I loaded them into the boxes, then climbed inside to make sure I hadn't missed anything. Tucked behind the middle passenger seat, set away from all the other groceries, were two double-paper bags reinforced with plastic sacks and in each, two big bottles of red wine. They seemed twice as big as normal bottles; my hand couldn't wrap around them. Next to the wine, shoved under the seat, was a plastic sack with two cartons of Virginia Slims, menthol and regular. That was how I knew I wasn't supposed to see the bottles of wine. Marilyn tried hard to hide her cartons of cigarettes from me because I was always nagging her to quit.

I left the wine in the car, so that she could sneak it in later, and rolled the groceries home, turning backward to yank the hand truck over a train rail. The wine bothered me, even though I didn't really think Marilyn had a drinking problem. She never seemed drunk, really. But there was so much of it, and Marilyn was the only person in our family who drank. We hardly ever hosted dinner parties anymore, unless you counted Sunday lunches with Pete and our store's clerk, Norm, where no one drank. I wended my way around a forty-foot sailboat and weaved the hand truck wheels over hoses and cables. Why was she hiding it, unless she thought it was wrong; unless she thought she'd get in trouble?

———————————

"It's like there's no end in sight," Marilyn told my grandfather one night after dinner, shoving her napkin onto the table. "When is this going to stop?" They were talking about money. That day, Dinko's workmen had found dry rot in half a dozen planks and two ribs. It was going to be very expensive to replace them.

I didn't know if she meant there was no end in sight to the work at Dinko's or to work on the boat in general. Every time the boat seemed close to being finished, it ended up needing something else—an autopilot, navigation equipment, a mahogany rub rail, a tender.

"Well, we've got to fix them. If they're rotten, when we go out to sea, they might give way." Marilyn said nothing. "They're like the foundation of a house," he insisted.

"I thought with your eye money…I thought we'd be able to start getting out of debt. Or at least not add more," she sighed. She already sounded defeated.

Every month Marilyn juggled credit card payments, using cash advances from one credit card to make a payment on another, or using corporate lines of credit for the store to make payments at places like Dinko's and West Marine. At my grandfather's behest, she took cash from the arcades at the store and didn't deposit it into our corporate account at the bank or into our personal account—deposits that she would have needed to report as income for taxes. Instead, once a month, she took a paper grocery sack of money to the post office in San Pedro, walked past the homeless men who hung out on the steps, and waited in the long line beneath a Works Project–era mural of heroic, muscle-bound mailmen. When she finally got to the window, she'd buy money orders for the exact amount of bills we owed—$241.23 at Macy's, $129.45 at the dentist, my swim club dues—all from a list written neatly in cursive. She'd lay out the bricks of money beneath the old-timey brass teller's cage, then tilt her chin up strongly to meet the clerk's studied, neutral gaze. Money orders left no record.

I watched Marilyn do it all the time: make money out of thin air. We lived really well on thin air. But while my grandfather seemed perfectly happy with this system, Marilyn and I were waiting for the whole structure to collapse.

"Well, when I die," my grandfather continued, "I want you to be financially secure. I'm building this nice home for you, like a house. I want it to be in good working order for you, so you won't have anything to worry about."

Marilyn said nothing but got up to clear the table. I heard the squeak of a cork coming out of a wine bottle.

One morning toward the end of our stay in dry dock, I was lying in my bunk, awake, luxuriating in summer vacation. It was seven thirty, and the shift horn had already sounded through the boatyard. I knew I needed to get up because the likelihood of a stranger hanging suspended outside of my porthole, face-to-face with me in my bed, was growing every minute. But my sheets were cool and crisp against my skin, and it felt so good to stretch.

First there was a weird rumble, then the slowing down of time that allowed me to methodically eliminate several possibilities in a split-second: Was it our generator? We couldn't run them in dry dock. A large truck? There was no road close enough to us. A boat being pulled into the space next to ours? What was it? Then the trembling and shaking began, and I remembered: that sound, that's the way earthquakes sound just before the shaking starts.

I threw off my covers and jumped off the high bunk, not bothering to step on the lower one on the way down. I heard Marilyn say "shit" from her office; she didn't sound scared as much as dismayed and puzzled. Crybaby stood stunned on Marilyn's bed, then slinked off to hide. I stumbled to the doorway of my cabin and was bumped against its frame. Marilyn's makeup mirror fell over; knickknacks jumped around on their shelves but were stopped from falling off by pin rails. I waited for it to get worse, for everything to collapse, but it didn't. Then it was over. The boat was still on its cradle. The cats and dogs were spooked but fine. My grandfather and Marilyn, the workers outside, me—we were all absolutely fine.

26

AFTER WE LEFT DRY DOCK AND GOT BACK TO THE MARINA, I helped Annie in the garden again, planting and weeding, watering and harvesting.

One morning, as I came bounding up the ramp to the garden, I caught her leaning against the fence, squinting at Wade's houseboat with a hand cupped above her eyes. Annie and Wade hated each other. No one would tell me why.

"Whatcha doin', Annie?" I asked. My grammar and pronunciation changed when I worked in the garden, then changed back again when I went home.

"I'm waiting to see if I can catch that sonofabitch when he takes a shower!"

I didn't understand.

"Oh, he's been complaining to Gunner about the water I'm using. Says everyone else is paying for it. He says when I'm watering he don't get enough water pressure to run his shower. So I'm waiting for him to get in the shower so I can turn the hose on, just to piss that asshole off."

I looked at Wade's houseboat, at the tinted-glass window I knew belonged to his bedroom. I knew this because he had taken me up there one afternoon to see his pet iguana, Gomez. As we walked up the spiral staircase—Wade's pale, hairy legs a few steps in front of me—the hair on the back of my neck went up and my heart beat a little harder. Marilyn had always told me never to go with a man into his bedroom. I calculated how fast I could get back down the stairs. But still I followed because I didn't want to be rude.

He really did just want to show me his iguana.

"Ain't he handsome?" he'd asked, stroking the striped tail. Gomez did have a certain charm, at least compared to the psychotic, blue fish Wade kept in his kitchen. Oscar, who had a mouth full of tiny, white teeth, liked to charge the glass whenever you walked by. If Wade lifted the lid off the tank, the fish would launch himself out of the water onto the kitchen floor and thrash around angrily until Wade threw him back in the tank. One of Wade's favorite things to do was lift the lid off the tank.

"Annie, I can't see how you can see in there. He's got the windows tinted."

"Nah, I can see. Yep...yep. There!" and off she trotted, all arthritic knees and jiggly arms, to the faucet. She put the hose on full bore. "There! Sonofabitch. How'd you like that?"

A few minutes later, the window to Wade's bedroom slid open: "You bitch! You bitch! The hot water burned me!"

Annie bent over, cackling like a witch. How did she know? I wondered.

While Annie's hatred of Wade had increased since she built her garden, mine had decreased. I'd grown fond of Wade for the way he always waved at me when I walked by his houseboat, for Gomez and Oscar, and perhaps especially for his new car: a used hearse painted turquoise with rainbow racing stripes, and oversized fuzzy dice hanging from the mirror. But most of all, I liked Wade because he'd let me in on a secret.

The secret he didn't tell anyone but me was that he was once a professional chef. One afternoon as I walked by his boat, he called me inside. It was late in the day, and I was worried he'd be drunk already, but he was perfectly sober. He took me by the elbow and led me to his galley. And there in straight rows were dozens and dozens of perfectly made cannolis.

"Where'd you get those?" I asked.

"I made them."

"No way."

"Yes way," he said.

"You can't cook," I said.

"The fuck I can't—I'm a pastry chef."

"For reals?"

"Yeah, for reals. I couldn't buy these things. They'd be like three bucks a pop. That's like two hundred dollars."

I surveyed the lines of pastries. "Why'd you make so many?"

"Why waste time on small batches?" he said, pensively scratching his belly.

He made me eat one, and it was the most delicious thing I'd ever tasted. Everyone at Donahue's raved about what a good cook Annie was, but her potato bread was as heavy as a brick, and her fudge was sandy with sugar crystals. And here was Wade, whom nobody really liked, making fancy pastries.

"How come I didn't know you could do this?" I asked Wade.

"I never told anyone."

"Why not?"

"What'd be the point?" he said and packed some up for me to take home.

My grandfather was not impressed. He called Wade a "lazy shit" for drawing disability when he was perfectly healthy and even had a trade. But what my grandfather didn't know, and what none of us knew until later, was that Wade had another secret: he had

Lou Gehrig's disease. After I left for college, Wade sobered up. He started volunteering at a marine mammal rescue center; he reconciled with his ex-wife and kids. And not so long after that, he died.

27

I T WAS WITH A CERTAIN TREPIDATION THAT I LOOKED FORWARD
to the trip to Catalina my grandfather had planned for later in
the summer. It wouldn't be the first trip we'd taken on the boat.
Since Pete had finished repairing the remaining two engines and
installed fuel tanks, we'd gone on shakedown cruises around the
harbor, which my grandfather jokingly called "shake-up" cruises.
I didn't find the joke very funny; they certainly shook *me* up. Our
engines seemed, for instance, to have an unhappy habit of quitting
in the middle of the Main Channel—the busiest channel in one
of the busiest commercial ports in the world—leaving us stranded
without a captain until Pete could limp down from the pilothouse
to the engine room to restart them. Also, Pete and my grandfather seemed to have an unhappy habit of ignoring small obstacles
in our path: a field of lobster pots in the Outer Harbor, Jet Skis
crossing our bow, the odd Boston Whaler, a Coast Guard marker
as tall as our boat, which we smashed. As my grandfather liked to
say—adding to my terror—"Boats have no brakes." I was pretty
sure we'd smash something or be smashed by something on our
way to Catalina, possibly a 1,200-foot cargo ship (which also didn't
have brakes). Twenty years later, I still have nightmares about boats
with failed engines, boats crashing.

Preparations for our four-day trip took weeks. My grandfather made a reservation for us at a mooring in Avalon Harbor and called Omaha Steaks to order extra rations. He made a special trip with Roger to Bristol Farms in PV. He made a list of things we'd need to do before we departed and circulated it to Pete, Roger, and me. No one could read his writing. We checked radios and GPS, radar and sonar. We filled our water tanks and emptied our sewage tank. We loaded up on fuel.

Under normal circumstances, we kept four or five drums of diesel fuel on the foredeck. The constant running of our generators required a steady supply of fuel, for which my grandfather refused to pay full price. Early on in the renovations of the *Intrepid,* he had acquired a commercial fisherman's license, which exempts the bearer from paying sales tax on fuel, equipment, and supplies. He used it illegally to buy everything for the boat tax free. There was no way my grandfather could take our boat—three stories of white paint, varnished wood, and blue canvas—to a fueling station and pass it off as a fishing vessel; so he paid one of the fishermen at our marina to go get the specially dyed, tax-free diesel for him. The little boat returned to Donahue's laden with 55-gallon drums of fuel and tied off next to us. We sent a hose from our boat down to the drums on the fishing boat and pumped the diesel into the empty drums on our deck. Roger would usually do this, but often the transfer of the fuel from the drums to the tanks in the engine room fell to me. Roger and I shared this chore—along with cleaning up dog poop, hosing down the deck, and sweeping out the deck by the stern bulwark, where, due to misplaced scuppers, the water and dog pee accumulated into a small pond.

On fuel-transfer days, I'd set up the mobile pump on the deck amidships, connect it to a hose running to an open drum, then open the tank's cap, which was embedded in the deck. I'd send another hose down into the tank, not too deep, but deep enough so it wouldn't come flying out while the pump was running, spraying fuel all over the deck and dumping dozens, if not hundreds, of gallons before I could stop it. And then I'd plug in the noisy pump, squatting close by to make sure nothing happened. It was easy to spill fuel if you didn't pay attention. Even a small spill would make a wide, iridescent slick. I was adept at quickly soaking spilled diesel off the deck with special absorbent pads before it reached the scuppers, and Pete had taught me the old fisherman's trick of pouring diluted Joy around your boat to break up the slick so that the Coast Guard couldn't trace it back to your boat. Still, I dreaded pumping fuel for the almost inevitable spill. We couldn't travel on the open water to Catalina with the drums on our deck, so we had to transfer several drums' worth into our tanks, a process that took half a day.

My personal preparations for the voyage also included working hard on imagining the worst. I read the instructions on the life raft label over and over again, the instructions for the EPIRB. I planned how I would deploy the life raft, how I would get my grandfather and Marilyn into it, how I would get Charlie into it, how I would gather the cats up to put them into it. How would I keep us all safe on this trip? Marilyn could swim well enough to get on the raft, I thought, and so could I. Could Pete? Roger? Really, how *were* we going to get my grandfather on the life raft? I packed an overboard bag for us: some water and food, sunscreen and first aid, and the mirror I'd pried from Marilyn's old compact to signal search planes.

I asked Marilyn questions carefully designed to conceal my worry: "Do you know if sharks can smell people through life rafts, or is it just blood in the water they're attracted to, like in *Jaws?* I'm just wondering."

"Oh, honey. Don't be ridiculous. Nothing's going to happen."

"How much water does someone need to survive for a day?

I'm just wondering if I'm drinking enough, you know, because of swimming."

"For God's sakes, we're only going to Catalina!"

Catalina was only twenty-six miles away, across heavily travelled water, within short range of the Coast Guard. She was right. I still worried.

The morning of our departure, my grandfather was up early and thumping on my hatch. Not much later, Pete and Roger came to work, carrying backpacks and Walmart bags with their extra clothes. They'd be sleeping together in the lazarette, which had finally been renovated into crew quarters.

"You ready to go to Catalina?" Pete beamed. I mustered up a "sure" for him and an anemic smile.

"You no are happy," Roger whispered to me later, after he'd washed the deck and coiled up the hose.

"*Sí*. Not happy. *Tengo cerveza en mi cabeza*." I smiled tightly. It was a joke between us. *I have beer in my head*. He'd taught me the phrase once, but I'd long forgotten why. Now it was just something funny to say.

"Everything okay," he said gently. "You no worry. Have fun!"

"Your wife's okay that you're going to be gone. Your kids?"

"Yeah. Isokay." He waved his hand in a so-so motion, then shrugged his shoulders. I'd have to be sure Roger got into the life raft, I thought; he had kids.

I knew about Roger's wife and children because my grandfather had helped get Roger's wife moved up from Houston; he'd bought them a bassinet when their first baby came.

I went downstairs to make sure my portholes were closed. Once I'd left them open on a harbor cruise and seawater had splashed onto my desk. As I was walking back through Marilyn's cabin, the main engines fired up: first one, then the other, a loud rumble that shook everything, ten times louder than the generators. With the first rumble and sputter, two cats slunk under Marilyn's bedspread. They were quickly followed by the other four, who ran into the room with their bellies hunched close to the ground, then scrambled onto the bed and under the covers. I knew from previous voyages around the harbor that the shivering lumps would stay there until the engines had been turned off again.

"I'm sorry, guys. It's going to be a long trip," I told the lumps.

We cast off and sailed through the harbor without any problems. It was a beautiful day—sunny and warm, a gentle breeze spinning our wind indicator. The water was the same happy blue as the sky. I stood outside the pilothouse upstairs with Pete as he steered from the outside wheel. My grandfather was safely seated on a bench in the pilothouse. Charlie lay on the floor by my grandfather's feet, a concerned expression on his face. We passed by the United Fruit Company banana warehouse and the ornate passenger terminal from the '30s, its clock perpetually stopped, then sailed beneath the Vincent Thomas Bridge. We kept going down the Main Channel, past the *Lane Victory,* the Evergreen terminal, Ports O'Call, and the entrance to Fish Harbor, where the fishing fleet used to moor. The fish canning industry in LA was dying; it left the fishermen in San Pedro bereft, bitter, forced into taking jobs like ferrying fuel for my grandfather.

There wasn't much traffic as we moved from the Main Channel into the Outer Harbor, through Angel's Gate, then past the breakwater. Suddenly we were in the open sea of the Catalina Channel. Point Fermin was to starboard, its orange cliffs rising above the white surf and spray. It was too early to make out Catalina Island in front of us. Off to our port was a cargo ship, but its course was taking it into the harbor, away from us. The swells that run from north to south in the channel began hitting our bow; our boat bucked and swayed and rocked, as if it were a cork floating on the sea and not a ship plowing through it. It was hard to sense forward motion in all the lateral movement. Loud crashes came from belowdecks. I went down to see what was happening, clinging to the banister so I wouldn't be thrown down the stairs. I'd once thought all the grab rails my grandfather had installed all over the boat were excessive. I could now see he was right; the only problem was that most of them were too high for me to reach.

The noise of the engines downstairs was deafening, even after the expensive insulation my grandfather had installed in the engine room. I could only imagine what it sounded like *in* the engine room. The boat pitched and rolled. The dining room table hurled itself three feet across the dining salon and slammed into the wall with an angry crash; with the counter motion, it jumped back. The dining room chairs, which were on wheels, had all rolled into a pile in the corner. All the books my grandfather had carelessly stacked on top of the bookshelves, instead of placing them behind the pin rail, had flown on to the floor. I made my way through moving furniture and checked aft. The couch and desk in the quiet room were dancing. I moved forward again, fending off the table with two hands, worried it would hit me. Charlie's water by the galley was toppled over and dripping down the stairs. The refrigerator door swung open and shut, although, fortunately, its contents had yet to slide out. The plates in their racks hadn't fallen. In the small bathroom, where we also stored food, all the cereal boxes and cans of soup had flown off the shelf. Cans rolled round back and forth across the floor and bounced down the stairs. A can of Progresso was wedged into the bottom of the RV toilet, sitting in unflushed, undiluted urine. The hull creaked and groaned beneath the stress of the seas and motion. Everything was helter-skelter, and the world wouldn't stop lurching.

I realized suddenly how very sick I felt.

I cleaned up the water and fallen objects as best as I could, piling pots and pans and cans of food into the cabinets under the counter. I went downstairs and lay down on Marilyn's bed with the cats. The movement was less pronounced there, but I couldn't see where we were going. My worry grew because I could not anticipate what we might hit or what might hit us. I tried to sleep.

A cat threw up under the covers—the wretched honking and gagging sound, the smell. I pretended not to notice and went back upstairs without cleaning it up.

Marilyn was listening to talk radio in the galley and making sandwiches for everyone. A red plastic cup sweated on the counter. I couldn't understand how she could work with all the movement.

"Do you want anything, sweetheart?" she smiled.

I shook my head. "Do you need help?"

"No, no, I'm fine. I'm having fun listening to talk radio and puttering."

She did look relaxed, as if she thought we were on vacation. She patted my shoulder and went back to making sandwiches. Ham and cheese with lots of mayo, and peanut butter sandwiches with the bread lined with butter. I couldn't watch.

"What's the matter?" my grandfather demanded as I entered the pilothouse. "Where've you been hiding?"

"I don't feel good," I said. And I didn't, but that wasn't the only reason I was hiding. I was anxious, perhaps even vaguely terrified.

"Seasick! I wonder where you got that from? Not from me. Poor thing." He patted the bench he sat on with his paw. "Just sit here a while and rest. But try not to look so bloody miserable about it. At least for Pete you should pretend. He's working very hard to make sure you have a nice trip to Catalina."

I'd never asked to go to Catalina—not on our boat, anyway.

"When I was your age, I'd have given anything to take a trip like this."

"I'm glad you're enjoying it," I said. It had always been his dream, after all. It was the least I could say.

I stayed a while, then left to go outside on the upper deck. I wedged a chair against a bulkhead so it wouldn't move, then sat down in the sun. The cool wind and the warm sun helped, and I watched the ocean around me: the white, foamy swirl from our wake; the green, dark depths; the white caps. The peninsula was far away, beginning to be shrouded in mist the way Catalina Island was when viewed from the mainland. I'd recently read Richard Henry Dana's *Two Years Before the Mast*, and I imagined seeing the coast through his eyes. I imagined the peninsula without its houses, covered in grass and shrubs, spotted with cattle. I imagined a whaling station nestled in Portuguese Bend and two-masters entering the port at San Pedro. What must life have been like for those sailors, forever in this rocking, lurching motion? After months at sea, would the stillness of land have been just as disorienting? The peninsula shrank until I could barely see it.

"Honey." Marilyn leaned her head out the door. "Did you see the dolphins?"

I jumped up. They were all around us: in the foam at the stern, playing in our wake, up by our bow. She and I watched them together, leaning against the rail, their shadows just beneath the surface and then their arc through the glassy water—their sleek gray backs, the spout of white mist. I thought of how much life teemed beneath the silver surface, unfathomed and unseen, until it chose to show itself: red and orange starfish, purple sea urchins, lush sea grass and forests of kelp, velvety rays, burgundy sea slugs, orange garibaldi, vast clouds of anchovies and sardines, nurse sharks and sand sharks, tigers, makos, hammerheads. Whales. The dolphins arced and dove alongside. I gripped Marilyn's warm hand.

"We probably couldn't stop so I could swim with them?" I asked. I knew the answer.

"No, I don't think so, sweetheart." She patted my hand with hers.

My leg muscles twitched anyway, as if to jump over the rail. But then the pod was gone, on its way to something else. Marilyn went back downstairs. I went back to being sick.

Soon we were at Catalina. A pilot boat took us to our mooring. Pete set the anchor, and Roger set about securing lines to the floating steel ball. Marilyn and I helped with the ropes while Pete maneuvered the boat. Suddenly a breeze blew or Pete turned the wheel, and the boat lurched to port, away from the ball. Marilyn lunged and grabbed a line that was slipping. The rope pulled her hand through a scupper, crushing it between the taught rope and wood, fifty tons of ship and a stiff wind holding it there.

"Help! My hand." She made a hoarse moan, a sound of pain I'd never heard before. I panicked and ran toward her. She was kneeling on the deck, but pulled forward toward the bulwark, her left hand holding on to her right forearm. I couldn't get her hand out either; the rope held it tight. The skin was turning purple and blue and white. I tried to push the rope. I couldn't free her. I couldn't do anything.

"Move the boat!" I half screamed, half sobbed.

She groaned.

"Push back!" the man in the harbor boat shouted at Pete, and eventually he did. The rope slackened and Marilyn freed her hand. She gripped her arm and leaned back against the bulwark. She wasn't bleeding; I couldn't see anything obviously broken. She groaned. She'd been trapped less than a minute, but it felt like forever.

"Mommy, are you okay?" I asked over and over again, the

tears rolling down my cheeks. I couldn't stand to see her hurt, no matter how minor it was—a cut from a broken glass or her frequent tumbles down the stairs. When Marilyn got hurt, I lost my head. All I could feel was panic, the impulse to curl up and cry. Even in the middle of the red and dark of my panic, I knew I was overreacting. I couldn't help it.

"I'm okay," she said softly through gritted teeth. Roger and I took her into the dining room and helped her sit down. She cradled her hand against her chest. She was pale. I filled a bowl with ice water, my hands trembling so violently that it spilled. She set her hand gingerly in it.

"Are you okay? Are you okay? I love you. Are you okay?" I whispered.

"Is she all right?" my grandfather bellowed as he slowly stomped down the stairs.

"I'm okay," Marilyn said softly.

"Put some ice on it!" he ordered. "Do we need to take you ashore to hospital?"

"It hurts," she said. "I don't think it's broken."

"Are you okay?" I asked again. It was like I was a broken record, and I didn't know where the switch to turn me off was. In my head, a voice asked why I was so upset, and even in the middle of being so upset, I struggled to answer the question. Don't die, I thought to myself. Don't die.

"Don't die!" I said under my breath; I hadn't meant to speak.

"For God's sake, Kelly. I'm fine," Marilyn hissed. "It just fucking hurts."

I jumped back from her as if I'd been hit. I leaned back against the wall, letting my grandfather and Pete tend to her. Once I knew she was going to live, I went down to my cabin. I sat on the red carpet and leaned against the sloped wall of the hull, curling my knees against my chest. I was too old for this, I told myself, but I couldn't stop crying. I couldn't stop worrying.

I hid in my cabin out of shame and hurt until my grandfather called me to come make dinner, since Marilyn was hurt. I made tacos. I put on a pleasant face. I was solicitous to Marilyn, whose hand was swollen and throbbed. I answered questions with one-word answers. I smiled politely when my grandfather made jokes to lessen the tension. But I wasn't really there—only an empty, armored shell. It was the closest thing I could muster to being brave. My worry had moved on to anger.

I hated the boat. I hated my grandfather for making us take the trip. I hated Catalina. I hated the rope. I hated Pete for not moving faster. And what hurt most and made the least sense: I hated Marilyn for getting hurt. Why had she grabbed the rope? The answer was that anyone would have; it was an instinct. But I told myself it was because she was clumsy, stupid. The angry armor clunked around and cleared the table, got Marilyn more ibuprofen, made my grandfather his tea, gave him his insulin shot, hoped it hurt.

As I got ready for bed that night, I hated the toilet I couldn't flush because my grandfather was worried we'd fill our holding tanks too quickly. I hated the cats for throwing up and making the cabin stink. I also hated them for being able to hide and get away with it. I hated the rocking, even at anchor. I hated wanting to throw up and not being able to. I hated myself, my worry. I hated missing swim practice. For this. I hated my bunk, which was suddenly uncomfortable.

I couldn't sleep. What if a boat hit us? What if Marilyn's hand really *was* broken? What were we going to do tomorrow? I was tired and sleepy in the way seasickness makes one, but all I wanted to do was pace. I needed to get outside. I thought of Richard Henry Dana sleeping on the deck of his ship. I grabbed my sleeping bag and Marilyn's old camping pad.

Outside on the top deck, it was better. No one was around. The breeze was almost cold, but it felt good against my flushed face and warm limbs. Dew had already slicked the rails and furniture, and this made everything seem fresher. I rolled the pad out on the rough, blue paint, then covered it with my sleeping bag and pillow. I leaned against the rail and stared back toward the mainland. The stars floated in the sky above me—nothing like the sparkling swathe of stars near Yosemite or in the desert, but more than at home, where I could only see two or three through the smog and terminal lights. The water around us sparkled too, with the reflections of lights from Avalon and other boats. A faint, red glow in the distance was the only sign of LA. I was in a wide-open space, and my spirit expanded to fill it. I felt my shoulders melt, the long-held tension in them float away.

Even though I still hated the boat and its loud engines—the way the furniture flew around while we were underway, the alarming lurch and creak of the hull—I suddenly understood the lure of the sea. Not the lure of yachts and powerboats, of varnished teak and the latest GPS, but of this: the fresh breeze at night and a dark horizon, the feeling of being away from land, of having cut the ropes that bind us to the cares of a teeming world, of floating free in the dark.

I lay on my sleeping bag. I could still feel the motion of the boat, but up here I could imagine it as the rock of a hammock, the gentle rock of our boat at Donahue's. I closed my eyes and tried to sleep. From the beachside bars and clubs, I heard the sounds of revelers, a quiet roar punctuated every so often by a scream of laughter or the shout of men arguing. During the day, the shore had seemed much too far away for me to hear anything from it, but now, at night, without the engines and only the 8kW running, the sound from shore seemed close by. Perhaps it was only a trick of the wind. All day I'd thought that I wanted to get away from people—from my grandfather, Roger, Marilyn, Pete—but as I listened to the burble of voices, I realized the opposite was true. The voices comforted me, the way that when you're lonely, the play-by-play of a ballgame on the radio can make you feel less alone. I realized that all day I had actually just been lonely. It wasn't, I realized, that I wanted to get away from people; I just wanted to get away from *these* people, because as much as I loved them, I didn't belong with them anymore. I didn't want to worry about them anymore. I realized, suddenly, that I was ready to leave home. I belonged somewhere else—maybe not on that beach with the drunks laughing and shouting—but on some distant shore, somewhere as of yet undiscovered by me. I looked again at the stars, sequins and glitter scattered across black velvet. I imagined Michele and Spence behind the sky, looking down, keeping silent watch over me, wishing good thoughts for me. Did they know where I belonged? Could they tell what my future held?

When I grew up, I decided that night as I fell asleep in the damp salt air, beneath the wide, starlit sky, I'd make a normal family. I decided I wanted this more than I wanted anything in the whole world. First I'd go to college and live somewhere green and leafy, like Alabama. Then I'd marry someone my age, and we'd have normal jobs, and we'd live in a real house on land with normal toilets and a basketball hoop. We'd have kids and grill and go to baseball games and play catch in the yard, and our life would be really, really, gloriously boring. I fell asleep to that happy thought.

28

"WHERE THE HELL WERE YOU?" MY GRANDFATHER ASKED ONE day when I got home from helping Annie in the garden. He was drinking a mug of tea.

"Working in the garden." It was getting late in the summer, mid-August. There'd only be a few more weeks of helping, maybe a month, before school started again.

"Bloody waste of time. *I'm* your father, you should be helping *me*."

I moved Stormcloud from a chair and sat down.

"Don't move the cat! She was sleeping!" my grandfather growled.

"Sorry," I said.

Stormcloud toddled off to find some food.

"There's plenty of stuff that needs doing around here, instead of wasting your time in a fucking garden."

"Like what?" I couldn't think of anything that really needed to be done at home. Roger did the sanding and varnishing and painting; Pete repaired anything that needed repairing. Although my parents talked about firing our cleaning lady to save money, they hadn't done so. Once a year, I helped Marilyn enter data into an aging computer for the business's taxes, for which she paid me. I cleaned the kitchen most nights and usually once during the day.

I did laundry sometimes. Between visits from the cleaning lady, I swept up the cat litter and animal hair. I *was* lazy, though, so it wasn't as if I did these chores eagerly or with gusto. Sometimes I took on projects like scouring and shining the ship's brass bell, work that I actually enjoyed. But usually there was nothing that needed doing except schoolwork. In the summers, I made up my own homework to keep busy—doing grammar exercises in an old grammar text of Marilyn's, giving myself vocabulary quizzes, reading *Discover* or *National Geographic* and novels from various schools' summer reading lists, memorizing definitions out of the dictionary, drawing, once in a while trying to write a story.

"Well, why the hell am I paying Roger to do the brightwork around here?" my grandfather huffed. "I'll get him to teach you how to sand first thing in the morning."

The thing was, I actually wanted to learn how to do that. I wanted to learn something practical, to work with my body, to feel the way I did after a morning of gardening. And I wanted my parents to think I was worth my keep.

Once when I was little, maybe nine or ten, my grandfather had screamed at me for not cleaning up my room and for not helping enough around the house. "You're nothing but a parasite!" he'd shouted at me, his face red with the exertion, his hand holding my arm so I couldn't move. "Do you know what a parasite is?" I did. I'd learned about tapeworms at school; I'd seen the leeches in *The African Queen*. When he said that, I felt as small as a parasite, as vile as something that sucked a nobler animal dry. Years later, part of me still felt that way. I was fourteen, and I felt completely useless.

But my grandfather's threats always fell through. The next morning when I reminded him about learning to sand, he said, with genuine surprise, "Why would you want to do *that*?"

What my grandfather really wanted me to do was sit by him

in the dining room while he watched TV or read or, at the very least, to be within earshot in case he wanted a cup of tea. I couldn't really blame him. He needed us to help him dress. Marilyn or I needed to help him test his blood sugar and shoot him with insulin. We needed to trim his nails and get him in or out of a bath. If he wanted to go somewhere, he needed someone to drive him. Sometimes he needed help dialing the phone. When he counted quarters for the store, he needed me to haul the heavy sacks to his desk and dump them into the counting machine, which we'd bought after his accident. He needed me to carry away the wrapped bags of counted quarters. He needed me to bend over and pick up the things he dropped, to find his glasses, his slippers, his books, his watch, his billfold. As much as he pretended not to need Marilyn and me, summoning or dismissing us with a gruff command, I knew that he knew he was helpless without us. Somehow I understood that it terrified him.

Marilyn, too, needed me, although helping her was not as easy as helping my grandfather. Now that my grandfather was incapacitated, she did almost everything for the business. She ran errands all afternoon, then came home, rolling groceries and tape boxes along the long dock with her hand truck, then made dinner, then worked on accounts or tapes until two or three in the morning. She'd sleep in late, and when she woke, she'd wake up angry, slamming shampoo bottles and trash cans, kitchen pots and pans, screaming "shit" and "fuck" to no one in particular, although I knew the noise was directed at all of us. My grandfather, the cats, the dogs, Pete, the boat, and I—we were all burdens on her, things that just created more work. Anyone could see that. And even when we tried to help—doing the cat boxes or cleaning the kitchen or having Pete run errands—nothing we did met her standards. Five minutes after I started the dishwasher, she'd open it and completely reload it, slamming plates between the metal prongs of the rack. She'd sweep the floor again after I'd just swept and mopped it, muttering under her breath about dirt I could not see. She'd refold her laundry before she put it away in her drawers. Helping around the house seemed pointless when it simply created more work for her.

Nothing helped Marilyn, unless you counted coffee—which she drank all day, toting it around with her in thermoses, premixed with NutraSweet and cream—and wine, of which, I realized that summer, she'd been drinking a lot.

Since finding the two bottles stashed among the groceries, I'd begun to pay attention. I'd found where she'd hidden the bottles: they were under the kitchen sink, tucked way in the back. She used them to refill the small bottle she kept in the fridge, so it looked like she'd been working on the same bottle for weeks, when she'd really been drinking something like a bottle a day. It was hard to keep track, though, because she mixed her wine with sugar-free cran-apple juice, which she also kept in the fridge. She'd buy three bottles of juice at a time. But I'd only ever seen her bring home the wine that one time.

She drank the mixture out of red Solo cups instead of wine glasses and called them "fruity cocktails." They'd taken the place of Engineer's Specials, and instead of just drinking them before dinner, she drank them all evening once she got home. She rarely got obviously drunk. Instead I started to notice how she just got slower in speech and movement, happier—unnaturally chipper— and then sleepy. But if she fell asleep at the dining room table or later on at her desk, it was easy to credit it to her long days working, the late hours she kept.

It would be easy to miss what was happening if you didn't notice how the cork in the wine bottle in the fridge was dried out and stained red on both ends. Or if you never looked under the sink for scouring pads and saw the wine bottles gleam faintly in the shadows. My grandfather couldn't bend down that low and wouldn't have seen well enough anyway. As for me, I saw it all, but it still took me a few years to understand what I was seeing and longer to say something and even longer to try to do something about it. I'd like to think it was because I was young or because she hid it so well, and perhaps that was part of it. But even then, part of me knew that she needed her fruity cocktails to function. And we—my grandfather and I—desperately needed her to function, so much so that we both turned a blind eye. And in some way I could not fully fathom, I knew that she needed us to need her just that much.

They both needed me to keep them safe: him from tripping, falling, illness, stroke, heart attack; her from him, from herself.

In the face of so much need, nothing I could do seemed adequate.

"You see, you have to make skirts either very short, so you can see lots of leg," Josette said, "or just below the knee, to hide the knee. The knee is so ugly, don't you think?"

I didn't. But I didn't want the skirt she was making—a beautiful straight one out of camel-colored wool—to be too short, and so I'd chosen the longer option. A couple of weeks before school started again, Josette decided I needed new school clothes, clothes for a young lady. I was standing on her trampoline—a small, black-and-metal device meant for exercise, not fun—while she squatted beneath me, her silver head bobbing up and down while she worked to pin the hem. Sometimes she dropped a pin, and they'd tinkle-bounce beneath the couch or into the sewing room's dim corners. When I'd been little, my favorite thing to do at her house was take the yardstick that she'd attached a magnet to and sweep for pins.

"*Tiens, c'est fini*," she said. "You can take it off now. I'll sew the hem, and it will be all done. You can wear it the first day."

I knew already that the skirt would not be a "cool" thing to wear at school; but I loved it, and I loved Josette, so I'd wear it anyway. Maybe not the first day, though.

I changed in front of her, pulling my jeans under the skirt, then wiggling the skirt off, careful not to jar the hem.

She talked to me as she sewed by hand. I sat cross-legged on the trampoline and answered her questions. I liked spending time at Josette's, how absolutely quiet it was, except for the ticking of her grandfather clock, the hyperdrive purr of her cat. I liked browsing the endless shelves of books, classics of literature in English and French, cookbooks, and tomes on gardening.

I don't remember how we got to it, but I said, "My grandfather doesn't like it when women wear pants. He says it makes our bottoms look too big."

"Well, your grandfather is from another time and place," she replied.

I figured she knew what she was talking about. After all, she'd been a child in France during the war; she understood his time and place more than I did—only she wore pants all the time.

"I guess that explains the shouting," I said lightly, realizing as I said it that it must have seemed to come out of the blue. But in my head, it made sense. The shouting had something to do with his having been of another generation, of having been born in 1917— almost a Victorian. Or perhaps the shouting came from his having been a naval officer in the war. I meant it as a joke.

Josette raised her gray eyes to look up at me over her sewing, as if she were deciding whether or not to tell me something, and then looked down again.

"Do you remember Nancy?" she asked. "She worked for your

grandfather and Marilyn a few years ago. Right before you moved on to the boat."

I did remember Nancy. She'd had short, blond hair and was always cheerful. Josette had gotten her a job with us, helping Marilyn do the bookkeeping at the video store. I'd been under the impression that Nancy needed the job as much as Marilyn needed the help. But she hadn't lasted long—maybe a few months—and then Marilyn was back to doing everything on her own.

"She told me about the way Richard shouts." Josette kept sewing, her eyes securely locked on the needle and camel-colored thread, and I watched, too, the glint of the thimble as it bobbed and darted. "How he screams at Marilyn, especially. She said, 'Josette, it's verbal abuse.' That's one of the reasons she quit."

I'd never heard the term "verbal abuse," or at least never in the context of a family, of *my* family. The way Josette said it, it sounded like a husband beating a wife or child, someone out of control, someone drunk or violent.

"Do you think she's right?" she asked. The thimble kept moving.

I looked up from her lap. "I don't know." I wanted to say, "But what about me? He shouts at me too," but I didn't. I felt guilty thinking it. He shouted at Marilyn a lot more than he shouted at me.

My grandfather shouted at everyone, though; it was just how he was. He shouted at people on the phone, the dog, Roger, even the traveling freelance porn salesman who brought tapes to the boat for us to buy. I thought of the way he used to shout at Guillermo— the way it made Guillermo physically sick—how Roger sometimes shook after my grandfather was done screaming. How I sometimes shook. I thought of the way Marilyn often sat before him while he shouted, her head bowed like that of a child being scolded, waiting for it to be over.

So very many things could upset him: not being enthusiastic

enough about a gift from him, forgetting to make him a cup of tea or to get a roast out from the freezer, preparing dinner too late, being too excited about anything, seeming to favor Marilyn over him. But I thought, too, of the times he was loving and funny and generous and silly, and how very few things felt better than being with him at those times.

I thought of the knot in my stomach when there was a chance he might be upset: the suspense of getting home late with Marilyn and opening the door to the boat, sliding it slowly, waiting to discover the first signs of his mood, whether it might be anger or forgiveness. And if the former, the tension-filled, careful dance of anticipating his desires in order to prevent an explosion.

But he'd never hit us, not once. He'd even stopped Marilyn from spanking me after I'd moved in with them. Spence had spanked me when I lived with her, and I still remembered the relief I felt knowing I'd never be hit again. Verbal abuse wasn't as bad as physical abuse, was it? Surely what he did couldn't be that bad.

I thought again of Marilyn sitting at the table, her head bent like a little child, the way she sometimes agreed with whatever he said, even if it was something bad about herself. "Okay, okay, okay," she'd say. "You're right. Okay."

I thought of how helpless I felt watching her, that painful knot in my stomach. I thought of the glasses of wine. I looked up at Josette, who sat with her soft hands folded loosely in her lap.

"It's okay," I told her. She nodded and waited for me to say more, but I didn't. It was okay. It wasn't a big deal, not a big enough deal to have a name like that. After a moment, she smiled.

"Your skirt is ready, dear," she said and held it up to me with her strong hands.

29

O UTSIDE IT WAS GETTING DARK. THE FLUORESCENT PV
Barbers sign glowed orange through the window. Moths
were starting to flock to the lit barber pole, the mesmerizing swirl
of blue and white and red. Some of the stylists were getting ready to
go home, sweeping up their stations and folding towels. The clock
above the long mirror said it was ten till six.

My swimsuit was itchy under my clothes. I wished I'd changed
after the meet instead of just throwing my shirt and shorts on over
it. When I moved, the backs of my thighs stuck a little to the
vinyl bench. I looked up to make sure Gil hadn't heard the little
fart sound my legs made when I moved, but he was sitting in his
empty chair by the window, reading glasses perched on his nose,
the sports section spread before him. My anthology for English lay
open across my thighs, but I'd stopped reading. The short story for
tomorrow was about a boy giving his dying father a shave; I didn't
much like it.

Gil let me sit in his shop every day after school or swim
practice. It was the spring of my sophomore year. PV High had
closed in 1991, after my freshman year, along with another high
school on the peninsula. That fall, three thousand other students
and I started at the remaining high school in the district, a school
designed for one thousand. The traffic around the new high school

was horrible, so Marilyn picked me up at the shopping center across
the street. Every day I walked across the expanse of its parking
lot, dodging sixteen-year-old drivers screeching through parking
spaces in BMWs and groups of plaid-shirted stoners headed for
Burger King. For most of the fall, I'd sat on a bench outside, next
to Mayer's bakery, which was two doors down from Gil's shop. I'd
wait there for Marilyn, my stomach growling every time someone
opened the door to Mayer's, releasing the vanilla-sugar smell of
baking cookies and cakes. I did homework. Sometimes I watched
children come out of the Stride Rite shop clutching balloons in
their hands, moms running errands at Thrifty's. When we lived on
the peninsula, Marilyn had taken me to get shoes at Stride Rite,
then ice cream at Thrifty's. The Jolly Roger and the bookstore my
grandfather used to take me to were just on the other side of the
mall. They all seemed to belong to another lifetime.

One afternoon during a rainstorm a few months earlier, when
I'd sat bundled in my swim parka after practice, dodging the
sheets of water the wind blew under the eaves, Gil had waved at
me through the glass window of his shop. When I didn't come
immediately, he poked his head outside the door.

"Well, don't you want to come in where it's dry?"

"Me?"

"You're the only one stupid enough to be out there." He flung
the door open. "Come on!"

I grabbed my backpack and jogged into the store. I stopped on
the welcome mat; I was dripping wet. Gil threw me a towel.

"Thanks."

"I see you out there every day. You waiting for a ride?"

"Yeah."

"Well, you can wait in here now, if you want."

"Are you sure it's okay?" I asked, looking around the shop for permission. A silver-haired man in an old-fashioned barber's jacket was cutting hair two stations down from Gil.

"Hey, *I'm* the boss," he said. "What I say goes. Now, you sit down there. You can read the paper, if you want."

Gil spoke with a faint accent, something like Ponch's in *CHiPs*. He was in his fifties, I guessed, his black hair receding a little on top and graying at the sides, a neatly trimmed mustache above his lips. The skin on his muscled forearms was tanned dark; an old Marines tattoo rippled with each snip of his scissors. When he smiled, which turned out to be fairly often, a glint of gold flashed from somewhere inside his mouth.

I'd made the high school swim team again that spring, even with all the other students trying out, having improved my fifty free time by about ten seconds. I'd worked all summer and fall to make it happen; I'd never wanted anything so much.

At the end of the first day of high school tryouts, Coach Terry had taken me aside and put her arm around me. "I'm so proud of you. I know how much you wanted this, and you worked so hard to get it. You can be proud of this forever."

Even though I would quit high school swimming the next year, when no one would drive me to early morning varsity practice, she was right. I'm still proud.

———————————

That night, just after I'd looked back to my book, the door jingled. Gil's last customer of the day walked through the door and raised an eyebrow at me on his way to the chair.

"You waiting for a haircut?" he asked me as he stepped onto the steel ledge and eased his backside onto the vinyl seat. He was wearing brown slacks and smooth, mahogany loafers; his tan socks peeked out beneath the cuffs of his pants. He'd slung his jacket on the chair next to him.

"No," I said, smiling a little and drawing my feet under my body.

Gil snapped the cape like a crisp sheet over the man's stomach and chest. "Nah, she's just waiting on her mom to pick her up after school. I let her cool her heels in here, if she's nice. She gives me grief, I kick her out into the street." Gil winked at me over the man's head.

The man's shaggy, brown hair was flecked with gray; it looked wavy and coarse. I didn't suppose it mattered much. As far as I could tell, Gil cut every man's hair pretty much the same way: trimming with scissors, buzzing their neck with clippers, and then finishing off with some tonic that made the shop smell a little like Noxzema and Pine-Sol.

The two men started talking about golf. I knew better than to interrupt.

Now it was five after. Marilyn was late picking me up. She almost always ran thirty to forty-five minutes late, but an hour wasn't entirely unheard of. I wasn't worried yet, I told myself. I'd start to worry if she wasn't there before Gil closed his shop.

After the man in the brown suit had paid, Gil threw his scissors and comb in a jar of Barbicide, then began to sweep up. It was twenty after.

"You wanna call your mom?" he asked.

"No. She'll come."

"Why'd you get here so late anyway? You had a meet today?"

"Yeah."

"You do well?"

"Yeah. I won my race!" A smile spread across my face. It was the first race I'd ever won. I'd been ecstatic that afternoon, but by the evening, I'd almost forgotten it. I'd moved on to the next day's homework, watching Gil's customers, trying not to worry about Marilyn.

Gil stopped sweeping and grinned. "Well, why didn't you say something? That's great! What'd you swim?"

"Fifty freestyle. It's just frosh/soph. It doesn't really matter."

"Course it matters! You won! Good job."

Gil went back to sweeping. He and I often talked about swimming. It was one of our favorite subjects, followed by his stories from the marines and his take on life. He was right; the race did matter. It mattered to me. Telling him made me proud again, happy. His praise made me glow.

"You sure you don't want to call your mom?"

"No. She's probably on her way."

"Well, I'm not going to stay late if she doesn't get here."

He did anyway, finding something to do until six thirty, when Marilyn's minivan finally pulled up.

I piled into the passenger seat and threw my duffel bag and backpack behind me. I waved at Gil, who was watching us through the big window.

"I'm sorry I'm late. I got stuck at the store, and then there was the traffic, and then there was a line at the post office and then another one at the bank," Marilyn said as she pulled away. "Poor thing, you must be starving!"

"That's okay. They had food at the meet."

"It's so nice of that guy to let you sit in his shop. What's his name?"

"Gil."

"Gil." She took a puff from her cigarette. "Right."

I waited for her to ask about the meet. When she didn't, I turned to tell her about my race, but she'd already replaced the white earpiece of her pocket radio, and I didn't feel like shouting.

Marilyn had started listening to the radio a year or so before. At first she'd only listened in the car to Dennis Prager from one to four in the afternoon on KABC. I didn't mind listening to him when she picked me up from school. He didn't spend too much time on politics; he mostly talked about personal issues and ethics. He was a Jew, and I liked hearing about what it was like to be a practicing Jew. Of all the religions I knew about, Judaism made the most sense to me because it was about being a good human being and repairing the world.

Dennis encouraged his listeners to participate in any monotheistic faith. Marilyn listened to him, but she didn't convert to Judaism. Instead, she started going to Calvary Chapel, a big auditorium of a church in a strip mall by the 110 Freeway. And now she also listened to Dr. Laura and Rush Limbaugh. Rush was always shouting about Bill and Hillary Clinton, and Dr. Laura kept telling women not to move in with men before they got married. In the mornings before Rush came on and in the evenings after Dennis had signed off, she started listening to Christian talk radio and praise music on stations like KFSH. She listened to the radio all the time, everywhere—in the car, while she cooked, in the shower. She started carrying a small radio in her pocket, which was connected to her ear by a tiny, white earphone so that she could listen to shows without interruption while she bought groceries, went to the bank, walked from the car to the boat. Soon she stopped taking it off. She wore it in the car or at home, in the kitchen while she made dinner, occasionally taking it to the dining table with her, nodding and harrumphing while we ate.

Sometimes it felt like when Marilyn had started listening to the radio, she stopped listening to me. Most of the time she didn't hear me when I tried talking to her through the earphone. And if I raised my voice, she'd hiss, "Shh! I'm trying to listen to this!" It was as if the white earphone were a door she'd shut between us, a Do Not Disturb sign hanging on its knob.

30

DINNER WAS LATE THAT NIGHT. MARILYN COOKED WHILE I worked on biology at the dining room table. I did my homework at the table now instead of in my cabin. I liked being able to spread my books and papers out beneath the bright fluorescent lights, to listen to the burble of PBS or CNN on the TV behind me. My grandfather sat at the other end of the table, wearing a white undershirt and boxers, his dressing gown draped haphazardly over his belly and legs. It was what he'd worn all day. Since he seldom went out into the real world, he rarely dressed to face it.

He huffed. I didn't look up. He drummed his dirty fingers against the wood of the table. He sighed. I turned a page in my biology book—a section of woody stem seen beneath a microscope, hundreds of circular vessels, xylem and phloem colored like stained glass. My grandfather rolled his chair back, crashing into the bulkhead behind him. "Goddamn it," he grumbled. I pretended not to hear. He sighed again, slammed his hand against the armrest, then got up. He cinched his dressing gown closed as he shuffled past the galley toward his cabin.

Ten minutes later, he came out and leaned into the galley to shout at Marilyn.

"I can't sleep with all that goddamn chopping of carrots and pots banging. Christ!"

He went back into his cabin, slamming the door.

When dinner was ready, I went in to tell him. He lay in the dark room with his back toward me.

"Dinner's ready, Daddy," I said softly.

Only the dog moved.

"It's too late," came a petulant voice from the pillows. "I'm not hungry anymore."

Marilyn and I ate in silence. Carrots with dill and butter. They were really good. Afterward, she went back to her office to work, taking with her a red cup of fruity cocktail. I cleaned the kitchen, then went back to biology.

Around ten o'clock, my grandfather came back out of his cabin to find something to eat. He plopped down in his seat at the table, spooning leftovers straight from the Tupperware to his mouth, dribbling bits of sauce on his shirt.

"I just can't eat dinner that late. I lose my appetite," he explained between slurps and smacks of food.

I stared at the Tupperware.

"This swimming shit. It's ruining our family meals. It's very selfish of you."

I said nothing.

"I never see you anymore. You're always off swimming."

With a heavy sigh, I put down my pencil.

"And I'm paying for it! How much does this cost a month?"

I shrugged.

"I asked you a question, how much does this cost a month?"

"High school swimming is free," I finally answered. "I don't remember what the Y team costs."

"That just shows how spoiled you are. I'll tell you how much. Too goddamn much is how much."

I knew he wanted me to volunteer to quit swimming. He'd

been complaining about it for months. Our conversations would sometimes end with him stomping downstairs to Marilyn's office to talk to her about it. I'd hear their muffled voices—his usually accusatory, hers usually conciliatory. She never let him make me quit, though. I think now that Marilyn must have known that swimming was important to me, though at the time, I probably never considered how many times she'd stood up for me against him. I took for granted how she drove me back and forth to practices. Instead, I compared her to the swim team parents—the ones who brought brownies for the whole team and volunteered at meets, who asked me sometimes where my parents were, a subtle reproach in their voice. Sometimes I told them that my dad was an invalid, and that his wife was too busy looking after him and earning us a living to help at meets. It was close to the truth, but it felt like a lie when I said it. Secretly, I reproached my parents too.

But that night my grandfather didn't go downstairs. Instead he got up to go to the bathroom, dribbling pee on his way. I could hear it splatter on the floor. He'd started having accidents a while before. When he got back, he changed tactics.

"You shouldn't be spending this much time swimming. You need to be getting ready for university. You should be studying!"

I looked at the papers and books spread before me. I could get away with the arch expression on my face because he couldn't see it, even with his glasses.

"Now, you've got to start thinking about this. What are you going to do with your life? You've *got* to plan for the future."

It was clear there would be no more studying that night. I closed the biology book with a loud thump he either could not hear or chose to ignore.

"I think you should apply to the service academies—well, Annapolis and the Coast Guard Academy, wherever the hell that is.

I think there's an academy for the merchant marine. I don't think the air force would have you, and I don't want you joining the army. You'll be an officer like I was. Then, when you get out, you can get a job on a cargo ship, travel the world. You'd like that."

I picked at the cat debris on the table, sorting fur, cat litter, and tapeworm eggs into little piles. It seemed like no matter how often you wiped the table, the stuff was always there.

I imagined my life as one of the lonely sailors I'd seen walking the decks of the tankers docked at the oil farm next door: men away from their families and friends, stuck in a treeless world of sea and harbor and metal decks. I couldn't think of anything I'd like less.

I knew that my grandfather had gotten the idea about the Coast Guard Academy from spending time with the Coast Guard Auxiliary. Even though we'd only gone to a few meetings, the idea of the Coast Guard Academy had lodged in his mind, remaining long after he'd forgotten where it had come from. For a while, I'd felt obligated to apply there, if only because of the free pencils and T-shirts they'd given me, but it only had majors like "seamanship" and "marine engineering"—nothing I could force myself to get excited about.

"Whatever happened to the Coast Guard Auxiliary people?" I asked. "You don't go to meetings anymore."

"The who? What meetings?"

"Nothing." I went back to popping tapeworm eggs. Sometimes you could see the tiniest of dark specs in the liquid that oozed out. I wondered if it was the larvae or something else.

If I didn't receive an appointment to one of the service academies, my grandfather's Plan B was business school: "You'll go to UC Irvine and study business. Then you can get your MBA at Pepperdine. I keep hearing their ads on the radio. Then you'll help Mommy with the business and live at home."

"Why would I need an MBA to work in a porn store?"

"Well, you won't work *in* it; you'll run it! You can buy another store or branch out into other businesses. For instance, Mommy and I've been talking about buying a Laundromat. The point is I've built this business for you, so you'll always have money. You need to keep the family business going."

I didn't know what I wanted to do with my life, but I knew I didn't want to spend it in business, especially *my* family's business. The porn store wasn't a bakery, after all, or a hardware store, or a fishing boat, or any other family tradition worth keeping alive. I couldn't imagine working all my life at something of which I was so ashamed; I couldn't imagine explaining the business to my children.

But most of all, the idea of living at home after high school made me want to cry, and I couldn't explain, even to myself, why I felt that way. But I didn't argue with my grandfather. I nodded my head, said nothing, and moved my hands to my lap. He couldn't see how hard I dug my fingernails into my palms, the beginning of tears in my eyes.

"Well, you don't seem very excited. Maybe you should be a doctor, then. *I* was going to be a doctor, you know, but the war took that away from me. You'll never be out of work if you're a doctor. You could be like Josette's daughter—join the navy and get them to pay for medical school. Then you could be a doctor *and* an officer! Yes, that's what you'll do!"

"I don't think that I really want to be a doctor," I began.

"Why the hell not?" His voice had started to rise.

"I...just don't."

"Well, what *do* you want to be?"

"I don't know. I thought I'd major in biology. Or history." I loved biology and history. I liked English too.

"And what would you do with your degree? What will you do for a living?"

"I don't know yet." I thought those were the things you figured out in college.

"Well, I'm not paying for college unless you know what you're going to do with the rest of your life. I'm not sending money down the drain like that. I need a return on my investment." He punctuated the last few words by jabbing his finger on the table.

It was news to me that he'd even thought about helping to pay for college. Most of the time he told me we couldn't afford college, that I'd be on my own when it came to paying for it. The boat had to be finished, and that was where the money needed to go. The boat was a good investment, after all. It was a gift from him to us, security for Marilyn and me after he died for which we should be grateful. Never mind the fact that we were tens of thousands of dollars in debt because of the boat. Or that to maintain it so that it would be around for Marilyn and me to live on, we'd need to stay in debt. Never mind that it had been him who had really wanted it. But part of me still thought it was my fault. If only I'd said no to moving on board that day at the Flower Drum.

When my grandfather finally went back to bed, I went down below to my cabin, stopping to clean up his urine on my way, soaking up what was still wet with dry paper towels, then wiping with wet ones. Our boat had begun to smell like urine—the dog's urine outside on the deck, my grandfather's and the cats' inside—no matter how many times we cleaned.

Marilyn was asleep at her desk, her upper body sprawled across its surface. Her sun-spotted arms lay across papers; one red cheek was pressed against the wood. Puffs of air broke through her pursed lips after every snore.

I shook her. "Go to bed, Mommy." An empty red cup sat by the adding machine.

"Okay, okay," she mumbled thickly. I knew she wouldn't

move. I used to panic when I found her like this, but now I just wanted to cry.

I got into my pajamas and brushed my teeth. Marilyn hadn't moved. I closed my cabin door and climbed into my top bunk to think.

Across the room on my bookshelf, snug behind the pin rail, sat *The National Review Guide to Colleges*. Marilyn got a lot of "free gifts" for subscribing to various conservative causes and publications, something she'd done for the past year. One of them was the *National Review's* guide. According to Dennis, Rush, and various hosts on Christian talk radio, it was imperative I not go to any of the UC schools, most of the big state schools like UW Madison or SUNY, and absolutely, under no circumstances, any of the Ivies or Seven Sisters. At those schools, I would be brainwashed into an Unthinking Liberalism That Hates America, Capitalism, and the Canon; I would turn into an angry, possibly braless, woman who protested things—a little like what Marilyn herself had been during the '60s, when she had journeyed to the South to register black voters in Mississippi. She still believed that the original civil rights movement was good and was inspired by the Christian leadership of Martin Luther King Jr., but she hated what she thought the movement had long since become: a mix of divisive identity politics, government handouts, and bean counting. Now, it seemed to me, most of the other things she'd done as a young person—the values she'd taught me as a child, the values her generation had fought for—were wrong in her book, or were at least code words for more sinister ideas. Peace, diversity, and tolerance really meant moral relativism and anti-Americanism; environmentalism was an excuse for government regulations that devalued human lives and progress. All the things she and her friends had once believed, she now regarded with scorn. "Fucking hippies," she'd mutter. "I can't believe we fell for that shit." And even though I followed the radio hosts' logic to a point, Marilyn's change of mind, and the passion it inspired, left me confused, disoriented.

"Here," she'd said when she'd given me the college guide. "You can apply to any school you want in there."

They were almost all private schools. How could we possibly afford any of them? I turned toward my portholes and curled my knees against my chest.

My grandfather wanted me to be everything he'd wished to become when he was young but hadn't been. Marilyn seemed to want me to be the opposite of the person I thought she once was. As for me, I had no idea what I wanted to be. Surely, I thought to myself, I should be able to choose for myself. Wasn't I supposed to decide what I wanted to do with my life? I started crying at the thought. Wasn't *I* supposed to decide what kind of person I wanted to be? All I knew was that I wanted to be far from home, from LA, from California. I wanted to live somewhere with trees, green grass, and bodies of freshwater, somewhere too far to come back home. I looked across my room to the pictures of Michele and Spence. Wasn't *I* supposed to get to decide?

Outside my porthole, the lights from shore shone across the black mirror of the water. My tears blurred them into smears of pink and green and white light. In English class, we'd read an account of Gertrude Ederle's swim across the English Channel. There was a line in the story about how the water in her goggles made little patterns and eddies; I thought of it now as I stared into the black water outside my window. Ederle had started her swim at night. Since I'd started swim team, I'd dreamed of swimming across the Catalina Channel, but I knew I'd never be able to. I was just too slow. And that night, as I looked out my window, living my own life and leaving home seemed just as impossible. How could I pay for college on my own? Dear God, I thought, I don't want to live here forever. Dear God, I want my own life. I bit my pillow so Marilyn wouldn't hear me sob. Soon the pillowcase was soaking wet.

Twenty years later, my despair is difficult to understand, even for me. I had parents who wanted me to go to college, after all, and who, in the end, would be able to pay for it. But to dismiss my fear and pain merely as the troubles of a privileged child is somehow to betray that fifteen-year-old girl, that girl who really thought she'd never escape, who really thought it was the end of her world.

Sometime that night, I got down from my bunk. I looked for a second at Michele's picture, then turned it facedown, along with Spence's. I took a scallop shell from the bric-a-brac on my shelf and cracked it against the pin rail until it broke into jagged pieces. I sat down at my desk, wedged at the very point of the bow, cradled by slanting walls. I dragged a sharp fragment of shell hard against the soft skin under my wrist, down along the vein. It scratched but didn't cut. I put it down.

I dug my nails into my veins until red crescents appeared. They weren't sharp enough.

I looked through my desk drawer, the dozens of pencils and pens and markers I'd accumulated over the years. A beautiful fountain pen my grandfather had given me, its point long broken. Nibs from pen-and-ink sketching. My old X-ACTO knife, its point still encrusted with hobby glue from some long-forgotten project, a space shuttle perhaps. I took it from the drawer and patiently picked the glue off. I'd stopped crying.

I pressed the knife's edge against the blue vein and held my breath. For a moment—from when pressing harder would have drawn blood to when I lifted the blade—I wanted it to work. I wanted to die.

But I lifted the blade. I exhaled. I put the knife back in the crowded drawer. Marilyn would be sad if I died, after all, and I didn't want to hurt her. So would my grandfather, whom I knew loved me, even if right now I wasn't sure I loved him. Pete would be sad, and Gil. Coach Ron at the Y and the little kids I swam with there. Coach Terry. Dee. Somewhere in heaven, Spence and Michele, who surely were watching. I felt suddenly tired. Besides, the next day I'd go swimming. Nights like that night—there were only a few—always ended with that thought: the muscle memory of arms pulling and hips rolling and legs kicking a strong rhythm, the happy solitude beneath water, the oblivion of exercise.

Sometimes my grandfather tried to enlist Pete in his antiswimming campaign.

"She spends all her time swimming," he'd start.

Usually Pete would nod politely, but I knew he was on my side. Every morning on the way to school, he'd ask me how swim team was going. He'd pretend to understand when I told him about my times or races. He'd act impressed if I'd show him an eighth-place ribbon I'd won at a Y meet. When I lost weight, he told me, "You really look like an athlete now! You just wait, those boys are gonna finally wake up!"

But one morning a week or so after that night, Pete was quiet as he took me to school. He tailgated more closely than usual, honked his horn for no good reason. After a while he said, "Richard tell you what happened yesterday?"

"No. What happened?"

"Well, I kind of told him off. I'm not really looking forward to seeing him today."

This couldn't be good, I thought.

"He was going on about your swimming again. *She spends all her time swimming,*" he imitated my grandfather, making his voice sound like a spoiled child's. *"She doesn't spend any time with me. All she cares about is swimming!* So I told him what I thought: Swimming's the best thing that's happened to you. You love it. It's not your job to spend time with him anyway—you're in high school. You're supposed to be going to parties and meeting boys and making friends. And it's not like you're doing drugs or sleeping around or getting into trouble—you're *swimming*. And you get all As. I see those report cards on the fridge. He should just be so proud of you."

I didn't say anything. At a stoplight, he turned to look at me. My eyes were full of tears, and when I smiled at him, I felt one dribble down. I wiped it off quickly with my sleeve. He punched my upper arm lightly then pointed a finger at me.

"Don't you dare quit, okay?" he said. "You swim as much as you want." He handed me a Kleenex. The light turned green.

31

S OMETIME THAT SPRING, I'D STOPPED BEING ABLE TO SLEEP. I'D
stay awake until midnight, and after a few hours of sleep, I'd
wake again—suddenly, irreversibly alert, the previous day racing
through my head like an erratic film loop, running at fast speed
one moment and slowing down to obsessive-replay another: classes,
conversations, algebra problems, novel passages, poems, lab experiments, but most of all, swimming sets, sprints, races. I wouldn't fall
asleep again until four or so; my alarm went off at six. I'd sleep four
or five hours a night. Sometimes I'd fall asleep when I was doing
my homework; it was difficult to stay awake in math and French.
Marilyn tried to help, buying me chamomile tea and heating up
milk some nights, rubbing the back of my neck before bedtime.
It was like I was little again, sick, and she was taking care of me.

I started watching old movies in the middle of the night,
infomercials, reruns of *Star Trek*, *Bewitched*, *I Dream of Jeannie*. I
dug out my old books on tape, listening once more to Sherlock
Holmes, *Murder in the Cathedral*, James Herriot, *The Green Hornet*.
I'd watch *The Twilight Zone* and *Perry Mason*, waiting for my grandfather's name to appear in the ending credits. Anything to keep me
distracted from my thoughts long enough to sleep. On Friday or
Saturday nights, though, I slept soundly.

Insomnia made me a night watcher. I knew how many times

a night my grandfather got up to go to the bathroom, how many times he sat at his desk above my head, how many times he left his bedroom. I knew when the tugs brought a new tanker to the oil farm in the middle of the night. I learned that sometimes, just after dawn, a crew team would come sculling down the basin, rowing in time to the coxswain's angry bark. I knew what time Marilyn finally left her desk to go to bed, what TV programs she fell asleep to. Sometimes when the boat was quiet and I was sure everyone was asleep, I'd make rounds, wandering like a ghost, to the pilot-house and deck, the dining room and lazarette, not really seeing anything, just walking, just passing through.

On a few of those sleepless nights, I read passages from my grand-father's book on the Hillside Stranglers, Michele's possible murder-ers. It was Darcy O'Brien's *Two of a Kind: The Hillside Stranglers*. I'd looked at it before, when I was eleven or twelve, reading snippets on the fly, nervous I'd get caught. I learned how Kenneth Bianchi and Angelo Buono had raped, tortured, and killed ten women and girls in Los Angeles in late 1977 and 1978, strangling them and dumping their naked bodies on hillsides. I learned that they'd been a media sensation; a whole city lived in terror. I read bits about sadistic beatings and dead bodies left spread-eagled, injections with Windex, electrical burns. I thought of my mother's body, of her being hurt. Had she been hurt? Had it been that bad? I hoped she hadn't really been killed by them.

And now, at night, I read in earnest. I read about Bianchi and Buono blindfolding and gagging a fifteen-year-old girl—a girl my age—stripping her naked and then flipping a coin to decide who got to rape her first, how Buono won. I read about Bianchi getting hard as he listened to her muffled screams, how they took pictures of themselves with her, and then how Bianchi forced himself into her anus. How Buono seemed to teach Bianchi how to strangle her and dispose of the body, like a master coaching an apprentice. I thought about my mom with every word, just as I had when I was eleven. I felt an intense desire to know more about her death and an intense shame of that desire, because to read about these things in this book was like uncovering my mother's most private parts.

When a passage was hard to read, I clapped the book shut and tossed it onto the shelf as if it had burnt me. I'd pick it up again a few weeks later.

Over the years, I had imagined what had happened to my mother, what her body looked like when it was found. I'd been building by accretion, every detail I learned added to the ones I already knew. I pictured my mother naked, spread-eagled, her foot touching a crumpled bag of Fritos, an empty can of beer by her side; it was 1976, and so I figured it must have been one of those steel cans of Bud with the pull-away tab, the kind I'd found in the woods buried under layers of leaves. I saw my mother lying in that empty lot overgrown with weeds, littered with trash, within earshot of the 101. I'd looked up the address on one of Marilyn's city maps.

I imagined my mother's hair, brown like mine, long like in her picture. I saw it spread around her head, a halo in the grass. Her death certificate says she was found at 8:10 a.m., and so I always pictured her an hour or so before she was found, in the quiet hush of morning that can happen even in LA. I always tried to give her a little beauty before I got to the hardness of her death: sun shining through beads of dew on a blade of grass, a ladybug, a birdsong, and then…I imagined purple bruises around her neck, her lips torn, rope burns around her wrists, her eyes, hazel like mine, filled with hate.

But now, on those sleepless nights, I uncovered more and

more questions. A lot of the Stranglers' victims were prostitutes. Was my mom a prostitute? Prostitutes. I thought of the Old White Man and his black girlfriends who weren't, I'd finally realized, his girlfriends at all. I thought of the tattooed white woman who'd lived behind our boat and sold herself for drugs.

And if Michele was a prostitute, how had she gotten to be one? What had happened between that birthday party my grandfather had pictures of and that day she ran away? Between the picture of her as an adult that Marilyn had given me and the motel room where she'd left me? I thought of Tracy who used to live at the marina, what her mother had said about her—how Tracy had "found an old man" who gave her things. Marilyn said it meant she would trade sex for money, for a place to live or new clothes. That's how it could happen, just like that. You just left home. Tracy left home. Michele left home.

If my mother hadn't run away, would she still be alive? Is that what my grandfather was trying to tell me when he told me about her walking in on Dee and Spence?

And who was my father? My grandfather said the birth certificate didn't mean much, that "Archibald" was just a name Michele had written down to give me a father. But if my father wasn't some guy named Archibald, was he just some guy who'd paid my mother for sex?

Did that make me something different from what I thought I was? I thought of that word from old movies and books, the word my grandfather used all the time: bastard. Was that me?

Did the man who'd killed her also rape her? Was my mother raped before she died? I didn't want her to be raped. The moment from *Frenzy* flashed before my eyes. I closed the book when I thought about her being raped. I shut my eyes and thought of something else.

And another question: The book said the Hillside Strangler

killings started in 1977; my mother was killed in 1976. Why did the detectives and my grandfather think they were related?

Who could answer these questions? I couldn't imagine asking my grandfather or Marilyn. Dee didn't know. I thought of that brunch when I was eight, with the detective I couldn't really remember the name of. Barney. Varney. That was it. I wished I could talk to Detective Varney.

"The last time I saw you," he'd said that day, "you were just a bitty thing."

I imagined his gentle smile, his hands spread a baby's length apart—those hands that had picked me up from the dresser drawer, that knew where I'd come from.

I wished I could find him. I wished I could ask him to tell me every single thing he knew.

32

ALTHOUGH I TRIED TO AVOID HIM, SOMETIMES ON MY SLEEPLESS rounds I'd meet my grandfather. Sometimes he'd come out of his room naked and shout at me for being there to see it. Some nights, equally naked, he'd ask me to help him find Stormcloud. Once in a while, he'd put his dressing gown on and try to get me to sit and talk.

One night he told me for the hundredth time how Marilyn wouldn't sleep with him, had never slept with him, and how, even if she would sleep with him, he didn't think he could get an erection, but wasn't entirely sure.

"If I could just get with a real woman, I'd be able to tell if everything still worked. It's different with a real woman than when you jerk off to a magazine or a movie. You know?"

I didn't.

"No, Mommy's really a very selfish woman. Self-centered."

We sat at the dining room table in the near dark, the fluorescent light sputtering and blinking on the weak shore power. Everything was cast in an unsteady, blue-green glow.

I was fifteen and starting to feel uncomfortable—angry, even— with these conversations. When I was younger, I thought we were just talking about the facts of life. I thought I was special because he was talking to me about grown-up problems. I tried to under-stand; I tried to comfort him.

But that night I did not commiserate, because now I was fifteen and I understood a few things. I understood, for instance, what sexual attraction was in a way I could not have when I was younger. I understood, for instance, how I felt about Tom Heath, who was a year ahead of me and on the swim team—tall and dark, the muscles on his back rippled like sand on the beach—and completely out of my league. I understood, too, why Marilyn wouldn't want to have sex with my grandfather. He was so much older than she was. He was fat; he had always been fat. His chest looked like an old woman's, only covered with graying, matted hair. There was a crust of black dirt behind his knees because he couldn't reach back there to wash. His toenails were thick and yellow, and his heels were cracked and dry like an elephant's. Hair like steel wires grew from his ears and nostrils. He'd leave a trail of urine along the hall and a puddle around the toilet, and Marilyn or I would have to clean it up because sometimes he didn't notice what he'd done—and even when he did notice, he couldn't bend over to reach it. Instead, he'd haphazardly lay a paper towel over the puddles and drag it along with his foot, smearing the urine across the floor and leaving damp footprints.

But it wasn't just these things, things he couldn't really control and for which I knew I shouldn't judge him. It wasn't just the incontinence; it was also his refusal to wear Depends. It was also his reluctance to wash his hair more than once a week or to get dressed. It was the way he complained about the pain in his back but refused to lose weight—although perhaps I shouldn't judge him for that, I thought, his having been in a concentration camp and all. If, in fact, I really believed that.

I was fifteen and I understood these facts about my grandfather—whatever their causes—to be incompatible with sexual attraction, especially if the attraction hadn't been there in the first place; I was pretty sure it hadn't been there in the first place. I remembered that time when I was little, at the park, when I'd asked Marilyn why she'd married my grandfather, the pause when I asked her if she'd loved him too. And I thought about what Josette had said about verbal abuse: the screaming, the shouting, the way he said things to hurt her. Why would you want to have sex with someone who treated you like that?

It was somewhere around two or three in the morning that night when my grandfather told me again how infuriating it was that he could not fuck a woman. How difficult it was.

"If I could just get with a real woman," he said, "things would be different."

He turned those thick glasses straight at me; he looked at me. And in the pause after that statement, I felt something I had never felt before. I wondered if he was hinting that *I* should help him, that *I* should sleep with him. He hadn't asked this of me before—and he would never ask this of me—but suddenly I was scared. And because I was only fifteen and really didn't understand everything as much as I thought I did, that fear didn't leave me. For years afterward, some part of me confused a man's healthy desire with that frightening, angry need of my grandfather's, of the men who went to our store, the man in the restroom at the beach, the man in the car, men everywhere it seemed—the man in *Frenzy,* perhaps even the man who'd killed my mother. When men wanted me, even those I loved, I wanted to run away.

And I was scared of me, too, and of my own desire, because that time I watched *Frenzy* hadn't been the only time violence had turned me on. Sometimes when I touched myself, I imagined men hurting me. Faceless men slapping, hitting, choking. And then at the end, besides the usual guilt accompanying such activities, there was this: *That's how your mother died. How could you?* Her picture sitting across the room from me, her eyes staring down at me. Sex and violence and fear and guilt—I couldn't separate one from the others.

And then, that night, my grandfather told me this: "It isn't as if Marilyn doesn't like men, you know. She had that affair with a nigger a while back. She was fucking him. I had to put an end to that! She's not the saint you think she is."

I winced at the n-word, although it wasn't the first time he'd used it; I winced at what he'd just said. My grandfather stared at me expectantly, looking with his one good eye through his thick glasses to see if his arrow had hit home. I didn't say anything. I'm not sure I even breathed.

"She had an abortion too, you know. She got pregnant from that nigger, and she had an abortion to get rid of the kid."

This last was too much. These were not his secrets to tell. Something snapped in me; something popped into place. The way he said things to hurt her, to hurt me. The only reason he could have for telling me that was to make me love Marilyn less. Fear gave way to anger.

"I don't care," I said through gritted teeth.

"What?"

"I don't fucking care."

"Well, you bloody well should," my grandfather hissed.

"No," I screamed back. "All Marilyn does is cook for you and work for you and clean for you. All she does is look after you. And all you do is bitch about her. You should be so fucking grateful, you fucking asshole." I had never cursed my grandfather to his face before.

And with that, I got up and pushed my chair in. I stood right before him for a second and stared, just so he knew I meant what

I'd said. It was the bravest thing I'd ever done. He sat in front of me stiffly, spraddle-legged and fuming. I saw his hand rise from his side, and I turned to go down to my cabin. I felt the breeze of his hand by my hip as he missed. On the steps, I heard him hiss after me, "Goddamn it, get your ass up here." I kept going. By the time I got to my cabin, I was crying, stifling my sobs so Marilyn wouldn't hear me. He stomped upstairs. He pounded on the hatch. I ignored it.

"Go to hell," I told my empty, dark room. I thought that I'd stopped loving my grandfather that night.

As I cried in my bunk, holding Applesauce the Bear as if I were a little girl, I thought about what he'd said about Marilyn. I didn't care if she'd had an affair with a black man the way he, in his own prejudice, assumed I would; I didn't care if she'd had an affair with anyone. I didn't even know if it was true, but I decided that even if it was true, I couldn't really blame her. Instead, my grandfather's revelation just made me feel sorrier for her that she was stuck on the boat with us, when she'd had another, happy life I'd never known about, when she'd actually been in love. I was sad that she'd given it up.

Many years later, I'd connect my grandfather's revelation with Marilyn's "nervous breakdown" when I was little: that day she went on an all-day drive, that day I thought I'd lost her, that summer I'd found her diaphragm. But, no, she says when I ask her now. The affair he told me about was something that had happened in the seventies—a fling, really, she says, just a few weeks with a grad student at USC.

I'd always assumed my grandfather was telling me about something that had had happened relatively recently. But it was something he'd dug up from twenty years earlier, something that happened before I was even born. If there is anything I haven't been able to forgive my grandfather for, it is for that night, for his jealousy; it is for trying to separate me from the woman I called "Mommy," the only mother I had.

33

IN MRS. MILLER'S ART CLASS THAT SPRING, WE HAD TO DRAW mandalas. We were all juniors and seniors, upperclassmen taking an elective art class. The other kids at my table were two Korean American guys and a white golfer. The Korean guys were always talking about their Korean Catholic church. They also talked about rap, their ball caps turned backward on their heads. The golfer would insert himself into those conversations. Except for passing art materials, they ignored me. They didn't make fun of me and for that, at least, I was grateful to them.

Some people made their mandalas abstract and geometric, more or less well-executed imitations of Tibetan and Indian patterns. I made mine a circle of angels dancing around a central golden orb. Mrs. Miller had said that some artists and monks made mandalas as a spiritual practice; making my mandala—the angels as graceful and flowing as I could muster—felt spiritual to me. I concentrated on my project, my focus drowning out discussions of Cypress Hill and Tupac.

"Why are you drawing angels?" one of the Korean boys asked one day.

I thought he was going to say something mean.

"Because. I don't know," I said quietly, looking up and smiling. I thought a submissive smile might stave off an attack, in the way a dog crouches low and wags his tail.

But he wasn't making fun of me.

"Do you go to church?" he asked gently.

"No."

The golfer and the other boy were now watching us.

"Do you believe in God?"

"I don't know."

"Do you want to?"

"Yeah, I think so."

"You should just believe then." He shrugged his shoulders and went back to his painting. The rest of the semester, I smiled shyly at him when he sat down at the table, but we never talked again.

Sometime that fall, Marilyn had gotten saved. She had not officially declared this to my grandfather and me, but I could tell from not-so-subtle signs that she had: She never missed a Sunday at her warehouse church. She began going to Bible study on Tuesday nights. Every evening, she read from her brand-new Bible and laboriously filled out her Bible study guide. She began reading books with showy clip art and words like "discipleship" and "spirit-filled" in the title. She wrote scriptures on white index cards and taped them to the bathroom mirror so that she could memorize them while she brushed her teeth.

Even though she was saved, she still worked for the store, ordering pornographic tapes and sex toys, labeling them, counting money—all the things she had always done. But now she did them while she listened to Christian talk radio, Christian easy listening, *Focus on the Family*, and *The Word for the Day* with Dr. McGee. And because she listened to these shows all the time, it meant I did too.

Marilyn's Christian radio poured from the kitchen, her cabin, the car. It assaulted my ears with a trained interrogator's incessant repetition: *Are you saved? Would you like a closer relationship with God? Do you know where you will spend eternity?* Words rang in my head like the echo of a bell: sin, hell, salvation, spirit, and above all, Jesus. *Jesus*, the refrain of soft-rock songs. *Jesus,* the repeated exclamation of preachers during broadcast sermons. *Jesus*, the person I was supposed to pray to for the forgiveness of my sins, redemption, eternal life—the list was endless.

Even though she was saved, Marilyn still drank. I thought she drank because she was unhappy, because she was a Christian stuck running a porn store. I thought she drank because my grandfather was so hard to live with. I thought she drank because she didn't love him. Part of me thought she drank because I did not love her enough.

Every afternoon as I walked from high school to Gil's barbershop, every evening as I tried to sleep, important questions wrestled each other in my mind: If people who don't believe in Jesus go to hell, why should I believe in Jesus just to be safe? Isn't that like supporting a tyrant? And how can you start believing in something you already don't believe in? And why is it your fault you can't believe in something? If God is good and fair, why would he send you to hell for not believing in something you tried and failed to believe in? And if he'd send you to hell for it, why would you want to believe in him anyway? They were not questions that answered themselves easily; I fought belief and unbelief simultaneously. I was tired, worn down by the fight.

———————————

One night I lay in my bunk watching *Casablanca*. I'd watched the video so many times I almost had the script memorized. Sometimes I mouthed the words along with the movie, gesturing with the actors. I would have been mortified if anyone had ever caught me:

RICK: How can you close me up, on what grounds?

CAPTAIN RENAULT: I'm shocked, shocked to find that gambling is going on in here.

WAITER, *handing Renault money on a silver tray*: Your winnings, sir.

RENAULT: Oh, thank you. *Renault pockets the cash.*

But that night, the radio from Marilyn's office blared into my cabin. The later she stayed up, the more she drank—and the more she drank, the louder the radio got. Christian talk show mixed in with the movie's soundtrack until the film was finally overwhelmed. Instead of Bogey and Bergmann, all I could hear was *Focus on the Family,* or something like it, and I found myself listening:

"I was addicted to pornography," a husband haltingly admitted. "I watched it in hotels every time I traveled for business. I found it in magazines. I called 1–900 numbers. I was squandering my beloved family's precious resources on this filth, this degrading, ungodly pollution."

"I prayed for my husband every night," his wife piped up, her clear voice trembling a little at the edges. "He thought he was keeping it a secret from me, but of course, I knew."

"You were saved at this time?" the host gently asked.

"Yes, I was. And I just prayed every night that the light of Christ would enter my husband's soul and show him the way to Salvation."

The host asked, "And it did?"

"Yes, it did," the husband said. "And the moment Christ entered my life, my addiction to porn vanished."

I listened to this, and then I went to Marilyn's office. She sat crying at her desk, and soon I was crying too. I turned the radio down, and we moved to her bed and sat down next to each other, our feet dangling off the edge. Her eyes were trained on her bookshelf, looking at nothing. I watched her, the way her face had taken on a weathered look over the years, the way her jawline was puffy now, bloated, the way her eyelids sagged over her sad eyes, the way she always slouched now, the way her stomach sat on her thighs, the way her mouth had melted into an almost permanent frown. I thought for a second of her affair, back when she was younger, back when she was maybe still happy.

"Why don't you just leave?" I asked her. "You should just leave. You should divorce Daddy."

"Oh, I couldn't do that," she said, still staring straight ahead.

"Yes, you could."

"Well, what about you?" She looked at me.

"I'll be okay." I pulled my legs onto the bed, glad that she was considering leaving. "We can still see each other. I just want you to be happy."

"I can't leave Richard."

"Yes, yes, you can. I'll look after him."

"No, I can't ask you to do that." She turned back to the bookshelf. "He's my husband. It's my Christian duty to take care of him." Language like that was still new out of her mouth; I wasn't used to it.

"No. I can look after him. We'll be fine," I said. I tried to smile. "Please, just leave him. I want you to be happy."

I knew I could look after him: I was sixteen. I was almost done learning to drive; I could get my driver's license. I could pick stuff up at the store. I imagined the happy life Marilyn would lead on land, in a house or an apartment, how we'd visit each other on weekends. I was desperate for her to leave.

She interrupted my planning. "What'll I do for money?"

"You could get a job."

"I don't know how to do anything."

"Yes, you do! You run a business. You know how to do lots of stuff!"

"No, I couldn't get a job, not one that would make enough money. Besides, I'm too old. No one would hire me."

"You're not old." I sighed. My happy vision for her was fading.

She put a soft arm around me. "Besides, I can't leave you alone to look after him. You need to live your own life. You need to go to college and meet a good man and everything. I'll just live through you."

I didn't say anything, but I knew that she was giving me permission to leave her—to, as she said, live my own life. I also knew that to leave home was to abandon her, to give her up to her unhappiness with my grandfather, her unhappiness with her life. I knew that she was making a sacrifice for me and that to take her up on it would be a profoundly selfish thing for me to do. But before I made it back to my own cabin, before I'd even gotten up from my seat beside her, I already knew what choice I was going to make. I was going to be selfish. I was going to get away from home. I was going to live.

Marilyn got me to college; I wouldn't have gone without her. She helped me pick four schools from the *National Review* guide: Notre Dame, University of Chicago, University of San Francisco, and Sewanee. I picked Notre Dame because it had a history I knew from movies and because I knew Dee would be excited about it, being Irish and quasi-Catholic. I picked Chicago because they had small classes and gargoyles, and Marilyn said it was a good school.

I picked San Francisco because it was closer to home, and it would make my grandfather happy; I had no intention of ever going there. I picked Sewanee, a liberal arts college in Tennessee, because its campus was in the middle of ten thousand acres of undeveloped forest on the Cumberland Plateau and had a student-staffed volunteer fire department, which for some reason tickled my fancy. She let me apply to two UC schools as backups.

Marilyn took me on a summer trip to visit colleges, driving us from Chicago down to Tennessee in a rented car, stopping in Kentucky to see Mammoth Cave, while Pete looked after my grandfather. She was patient when I was too shy to talk to college tour guides or ask admissions counselors important questions, patient when I cringed with embarrassment. After we returned, she sat at her desk late in the night, navigating her way through financial aid forms (we didn't qualify) and loan applications (no one would give my parents one). She proofread my essays for me. Most importantly, she convinced my grandfather to set aside the rest of his eye settlement for college and to use some of the money they made on the store for school instead of the boat. She finally wore him down. If I got enough of a scholarship, she told me, and the store income kept up, and they kept juggling credit cards, we'd be able to afford a private school or, failing that, a UC. She didn't want me to be distracted by a job during school because she'd had to work to put herself through Berkeley. It was one of her biggest gifts to me.

I filled out admission and scholarship applications. I listed awards that I'd won: Most Inspirational in swimming, National Merit Commended Student, a writing award from the National Council of Teachers of English, prizes in French, memberships in honor societies, and so on. I listed honors and AP courses, extracurricular activities, and service groups. My transcript was a line of As, interrupted only once by a B. When I held those applications—stacks of paper clipped neatly together—it was like I was holding someone else's achievements, someone else's life. That person seemed smart, industrious, normal. Was that really me? But then I'd see my name typed at the top of each form: Kelly Michelle Grey. That was my name; that person was *me*. I was proud of her.

In the spring of my senior year, a series of thick envelopes arrived in the mail at Josette's house: acceptances from everywhere I'd applied and an invitation from Sewanee for an all-expense-paid visit to compete for a scholarship.

That weekend in March, I wandered through Gothic build-ings swarmed with ivy, hiked through damp woods to waterfalls, attended classes about the French Revolution and cellular respi-ration, listened to the lilt and melody of a half-dozen different southern accents. I climbed stone steps worn down in the middle by generations of students before me and thought of a line from MacLeish's "Ars Poetica," which we'd read in sophomore English class: "Silent as the sleeve-worn stone / Of casement ledges where the moss has grown." I interviewed with men who wore bow ties. I'd never seen someone wearing a bow tie before.

The night before I flew home, I walked in a warm rain on a deserted street in the dark and felt completely safe. I passed an old cemetery, groves of hundred-year-old trees, the Episcopal chapel with its intricate rose window—something I recognized as a mandala—shining like a jewel. Standing in front of it, I felt warm and light, close to God, to my real self. I was free to stay out and walk as long as I wanted to; there was no need to call home or to worry about my grandfather being angry about dinner, no way to monitor Marilyn's alcohol intake. I didn't have to look after them because there was no way I *could* look after them. The night was truly dark there, not the orange-hued twilight of the harbor. The clouds cleared. I could see stars.

As I walked that night, I cried for love of a place I'd only just met, for a life I'd only just begun to imagine. If I got a scholarship, I could come back to this place. Never had I wanted something so desperately. Is it possible to pray without having been conscious of the prayer?

I got a scholarship.

———————————

Marilyn, Pete, Josette, my best friend from kindergarten, Jill, and my grandfather, on his scooter, all came to my high school graduation in 1994. Dee flew out especially for it, staying with us on the boat. Marilyn took a thousand pictures; I still have one of them. We're all in it—my grandfather, Pete in his driving cap, Josette, Marilyn, Dee, Jill, and me. It sits in a cheap, wooden frame in my study, next to a picture of my husband and me in college and a tiny portrait of Marilyn. I remember when those graduation pictures first came back from Sav-On, all I could think of was how ugly I was, chubby cheeked and fat in my gown, my long hair a straggly mess. But now when I look at the picture, all I see is a happy girl and the people she loved, all of them overjoyed for her and proud.

———————————

That summer after graduation, I got saved at a Harvest Crusade at Anaheim Stadium. Marilyn and I went down to the outfield with the people who wanted to be saved, thousands upon thousands of them. The stadium lights dimmed. A pastor prayed over the loudspeaker, telling us to repeat after him. He told us to really, really mean what we said; I really, really meant it.

During those few months before I left for college, I was closer to Marilyn than I ever would be again. We went to services at Calvary Chapel, perused Christian bookstores together for dorm room décor and clever T-shirts, studied the Bible. I took on the political and moral beliefs that, according to the radio and our pastors, were the sine qua non of being Christian. I was going to save myself for marriage; I opposed the "homosexual lifestyle;" I hated "big government" and Planned Parenthood. In spite of the beauty and truth I'd once found in the theory of evolution and the scientific evidence supporting it, I convinced myself that God had made zebras and flagellates the same week he'd made Adam. I believed that every single word of the Bible was God's Word and that there was no interpretation of those words besides what other fundamentalist Christians approved. I was willing to defend these opinions and beliefs to anyone who would listen—Jill, shocked friends from high school, strangers in the public bathroom. I took these beliefs on suddenly, like magic, not because I'd necessarily thought them through, but simply because I believed I was a Christian, and I believed that Christians had to believe those things.

I thought my life had changed that summer, and I was right—but I am a different person now. The politics, the black-and-white judgments, the homophobia, the fundamentalism, the guilt, the fear that unbelievers would go to hell—all of that would eventually fall away like dead skin, like scales on eyelids, except for a faith in God through Christ, except for an abiding love and hope. But that summer, that summer before I left her, I was everything I thought Marilyn wanted me to be.

34

ANNIE'S TRAWLER SMELLED A LITTLE LIKE CIGARETTES AND dust, but it wasn't an unpleasant smell, because most of the cabin was taken up with her galley, and so it also smelled like a pantry, mixed in with the breeze that came through the back and side doors. Bob had covered the back deck with a plastic tarp for shade, and she'd hung a wind chime, and so if you sat at the high table of the galley, you could hear the plastic rustle and flap gently in the wind, the clicking of seashells on strings. The day I said goodbye to Annie, we ate cookies and Ritz crackers at her galley table, so tall it came up to my chest. My cola can and her beer can sweated in the warm air. She rubbed a dry, cracked foot along Spot's back while we talked about her granddaughter and her garden, her husband, Bob, me.

"What's Marilyn going to do while you're at college?" she wondered, leaning her head against her clawed hand.

"I don't know."

"Well, she's got plenty to look after, with Sir Richard and all. You be sure to write her."

"I will. I'll write you too," I finger painted loop-de-loops in the condensation on the Formica. I don't remember if I kept that promise.

"Now, what you going to study at the university?"

"I don't know yet. Maybe biology? I think I'm going to major in biology or history."

"Well, you do good. You be careful too." She took a drag off her cigarette.

"Careful of what?"

"Just be careful. Don't do anything stupid." She looked at me seriously, conveying a deeper meaning in her blue eyes, one I didn't understand. Did she mean sex? Alcohol?

Annie was one of the smartest people I knew at the marina. She'd been a tennis star in high school. Bob said she had flaming red hair when she was younger, a real beauty. I wondered if she'd ever wanted to go to college. If something had gotten in the way.

Sitting there, looking at her, I didn't realize how much of a difference she and the people at the marina had made in my life. They gave a child attention and a listening ear when she needed it most. When I was young, I thought people like Annie—and Josette and Pete and Gil the Barber and countless others—took an interest in me because I was a special person. But now I know it was actually because *they* were special themselves. They helped raise a child not their own.

"I'll try not to do anything stupid," I smiled, "but that might be hard for me."

She snorted at the joke.

"I'll see you when I come back at Christmas," I promised her as I got up to leave.

"That'd be real nice," she said. "If we're still here."

"Well, hopefully everyone will still be here."

Annie said she doubted it.

All through my senior year of high school, there had been rumors that Donahue's was going to close. Even though Sonny and Gunner owned the marina, the city owned the actual land—as it did for all the harbor—and leased it to the marina. The American President Lines cargo terminal that abutted the marina needed to expand; people said that when Donahue's lease was up, the harbor department would grant the land to APL for sure. Worse yet, the city had begun to limit the number of liveaboards in the harbor. No one at Donahue's knew where they would move to or if they'd be able to keep their boats. Where would they find the money to rent an apartment in LA when they could barely afford the three hundred dollars it took to rent a slip each month?

I hugged Annie goodbye, the skin on her arm dry and fragile as I held it, the muscle beneath strong.

"Bye, sweetheart," she said. "Don't forget I love you."

IV

The Ends of Things

35

FOUR YEARS HAD PASSED. I CARRIED MY ROLLED-UP COLLEGE degree on to the plane with me, still tied in its purple ribbon and stuffed into a plastic Kroger sack. It sat on my lap the whole trip because I didn't want it to get smashed in the overhead compartment. In my backpack were pictures from graduation two weeks before: me standing in the university quad in my long, navy, floral dress, my academic gown draped over it, holding my diploma. My grandfather hadn't been able to come to commencement with Marilyn. I was taking the pictures and the diploma to show him, even though I already knew I'd be wearing that navy dress to his funeral.

That morning, Marilyn had called with the news I'd dreaded in childhood but had grown to expect as a young adult: my grandfather was dying. He'd had a massive stroke; he was in a coma, still connected to machines at the hospital, but brain dead.

We had talked only a few nights before. He'd been ebullient.

"I'm going to buy one of those new Lexus cars," he'd told me. "When you get back, I'll take you for a drive up the coast!"

"Daddy," I reminded him. "You can't drive."

"Who says I can't drive?" he wondered. "Well, if you want to drive, just say so. I don't care." Dementia seemed to make him happier than he had been in a long time.

On the plane, I was lonely, lonelier than I had been in the past four years. After graduation, all of my college friends—the closest friends I'd had in my life—had dispersed across the country. I'd just left my boyfriend, Ben, at the Atlanta airport. I didn't know when I'd see any of them again. I didn't know how I'd be myself—the true self I'd found at college—without being at college, without my friends.

And then there was the loneliness of grief, something I'd never understood before, the way it makes you feel profoundly different from everyone around you. That evening, as Ben and I hugged goodbye at the gate, I wanted nothing more than for him to come with me. Now as I flew west, curled in the window seat in my empty row, I stared out the window into the dark. The galaxies of small towns and highways, country roads and big cities, marked the path back home. I looked at my fellow passengers in the dim cabin, asleep or reading, old and young, carrying on inner lives of joy and struggle I could not begin to fathom. No doubt a few of them had just lost someone too, only I'd never know. I understood then that no one could come with me through this, not even Ben, not really. I wondered, too, when I would start crying. I'd packed tissues in my carry-on for the tears I was sure would come; I held one crumpled in my hand, but so far there was nothing. I wondered what that meant.

Pete picked me up from the airport in his van, giving me a hug on the curb before he helped me with my bag.

"How you doing, Peanut?" he asked when I got in.

"I'm okay," I said. "Just tired."

He looked tired too. "I know you're okay now," he said. "But stuff like this is never easy. It's always harder than you think it's going to be."

At the hospital, Marilyn waited in a hall outside my grandfather's room, slumped on a bench, sleeping or thinking; I couldn't tell.

"Oh, honey," she said, when she saw me. I didn't cry when she hugged me, not even when I saw her tears or how tired her face was, her unwashed hair.

Together, we went in to see his body, draped in sheets and penetrated with thick, plastic tubes and wires. His face was different without his glasses on—vulnerable, soft. His hands were the same, though, his big bear claws that still dwarfed my own.

The next morning, we signed the papers to remove life support.

My grandfather's body was strong. After the ventilator was removed, he kept breathing. It took four days for him to die. I stayed with him the whole time, except for quick trips home to shower. Marilyn came to visit us for a few hours each day; it was too hard for her to be with him much longer than that. In some way I could not understand, she loved him too.

The Filipina nurses who cared for my grandfather talked to him, even though he was brain dead. "Mr. Grey," one would say, "I'm going to give you a sponge bath now," before she gently lifted his arm.

"You should talk to your grandpa," a nurse named Emmie told me, patting me gently on the shoulder as I sat by his bed. "The hearing is the last thing to go. He can't understand you, but he'll hear your voice and know he's not alone."

I imagined my grandfather's spirit locked in his dying body, listening to the outside world but not understanding, longing for a word of comfort, of explanation. And so I talked to my grandfather. I told him what was happening to him. I showed him my graduation pictures, wrapped his limp paw around my diploma. I told him things I would never have told him while he was alive: things about Ben, books I'd read in school, ideas I had about God. I stroked his hand.

Sometimes I sang to him. I sang him hymns out of my Episcopal hymnbook—ones I thought might be familiar from his English childhood, ones that were my favorites from the college chapel. I sang a setting I'd learned that spring of Tennyson's poem:

> Sunset and evening star,
>> And one clear call for me!
>
> And may there be no moaning of the bar,
>> When I put out to sea...

It was a poem my grandfather had recited to me when I was little. "It's about dying," he'd said, though I couldn't understand why at the time. I read him the last rites and burial of the dead from my Episcopal prayer book. I couldn't do much for my grandfather, but I could give him words, sentences of comfort and hope. I realized then that death could have its own beauty: my grandfather's death, in old age, with the company of someone he loved, who, in spite of everything, loved him.

It was a Catholic hospital. When the nuns—older sisters in full habit, the sacred heart embroidered on their chests—asked to come in to our room, I always said yes. Together we prayed, my hand touching his, a sister's hand touching mine.

"You're a good girl," they often said when they left.

I didn't understand what they meant until I walked the ward one evening. Old men and women sitting up in bed—living ghosts, blue from the TV's light, calling out to family that wasn't there. But now, I think, I understand how that happens too. How families fracture, the distance between loved ones that seems impossible to traverse, even when someone is dying. It wasn't that I was particularly good; it was just that I didn't mind being there.

At one in the morning on the fifth day, I woke to a hissing sound. The oxygen tube had come out of his nose, and I couldn't figure out why. I put it back, then realized the room was perfectly quiet. His raspy, uneven breaths had stopped. His chest was still. There was a peace in death I did not expect. I went to the nurses' station where Emmie was working.

"My grandfather's dead," I told her.

"I'll come make sure," she said, just as calmly. We returned to the room and stood in the dim light.

"There," she said, putting her stethoscope away. She touched his head. "It isn't so bad to be dead," she said, whether to him or to me or to herself, I could not tell. "I'll tell the physician on duty. He's going to have to sign some forms. I'm going to leave you here with your grandpa, okay? But I'll be back." She touched my shoulder on the way out. "You're a good girl."

In the shadows, I reached for his hand, the skin already beginning to cool, and told him I loved him. I told him I'd miss him. I kept talking to him because the hearing was the last thing to go. I talked to the body in front of me, but already I felt his gaze at my shoulder, his eyes at the back of my neck.

I cried for my grandfather only once, on the night before his funeral, as I sat in his cabin on the boat, writing his eulogy. I wrote about how he used to carry me to breakfast in the mornings when I was very little, breakfasts big enough for two adults to share. How he packed my lunch boxes full of candy so that I'd make friends at school. How he made funny fish and toad sounds to cheer me up when I was sad. I wrote of garnish-sword fights at the Jolly Roger, old black-and-white movies, how we both loved to read. I thought of how he'd promised to come back as a ghost. *I miss my Daddy,* I thought to myself. And after a few minutes of quiet tears, I realized that I had missed him for a very long time, for years, maybe even for a decade. I tried—and failed—to think of a good memory of him from high school or college. I found instead arguments and shouting. Late nights and his bare, hairy flesh standing in a wedge of the refrigerator's light, eating. I thought instead of the empty bottle of Viagra I'd found in the spice rack in the kitchen when I came back from his hospital room. The old spanking magazine I'd found on his desk, still turned to the Readers Write page. I thought of those thick glasses, now folded on his bedside shelf, the way they hid his eyes.

I lay across his bed, the spot where he'd collapsed, and held the sheets to me. They still smelled vaguely of him, even after they'd been washed. I cried harder, loud sobs—not for the person who had just died, but for the person who had vanished long before: the exuberant, silly, loving, difficult man who'd fed me Cadbury bars and treacle, who told me amazing stories about the war and Hollywood, who'd taken care of me when I was little and alone, who'd called me "Little Toad," who'd promised to haunt me after he died. Where had he gone? How had he been replaced by the grandfather who was angry with me more often than he was pleased, selfish more often than caring? Had I changed to make him that way? Had he changed all on his own? Or had he always been that way, and I'd been too little to notice? I wanted my Daddy back, the one who'd died years before and for whom I'd never mourned. That was the person I cried for that night.

His service was at a funeral home in Long Beach. Pete and

Roger came, as did my grandfather's old lawyer; Norm, the store's manager; Josette and her husband; Marilyn's relatives; the traveling freelance porn salesman. Marilyn chose the music: American hymns my grandfather would have hated, broadcast over a tinny speaker, the cassette tape old and wavering.

A few nights later, I heard a noise upstairs on the main deck: the scramble of claws, an animal scream, a thump. More scrambling.

Two cats sniffed at something on the deck, their bodies blocking my view; two more stood on the cap rail, staring intently into the narrow space between the bulwark and the cabin wall. They scattered as I approached.

A night heron lay on its side, the smooth steel feathers of its back like a cape, the downy cream feathers of its belly ruffling gently in an imperceptible breeze. One of the ghost birds of my youth, the silent beauty that appeared as if my magic outside our kitchen window when I washed dishes. I'd always thought their colors looked like a stormy seascape—pumice and gunmetal clouds, the gray-blue of a dark, brooding sea. For a moment, I couldn't breathe. I had never seen one so close. How did the cats take it down?

I squatted next to its head. Its wings seemed askew. Yellow legs curled tensely against the belly. The red eye, like a jasper bead, stared at me then blinked. It was still alive. I noticed the abdomen floating and sinking against the rough blue paint. What should I do?

The cats circled behind me, trying to insinuate themselves between me and the wall, anxious to get at their prey. I couldn't see any blood. It was eleven at night; what vet would be open? Was the bird suffering? I couldn't stand the thought of it suffering. The eye blinked again.

"What is it?" Marilyn called from the door, her consonants softened, the way her voice sounded at the end of the day.

"A bird," I said, the tears beginning to form in my eyes. "It's still alive. I don't know what to do."

She came to look. "Shit," she said, then stood there.

I ran downstairs for an old, frayed towel to put him in. I still had no plan. The furthest I could see into the future was the bird wrapped in the towel, ready to be taken somewhere.

When I got back, it was still lying on the deck. It hadn't moved at all. The cats had inched closer.

"What should we do?" I asked Marilyn.

"I don't know, honey."

I trembled as I picked the bird up in the towel. There was no struggle, no protest, not even the twitch of a muscle. It was a dead weight, but light as air—all hollow bones and feathers, lungs filling and emptying. I held it close to me; I wanted to throw it far away from me. I couldn't stand the thought of it suffering. The thought of it suffering was intolerable; I did not know how to save it.

"I'm sorry," I said, my voice cracking. I ran a finger along its perfect head.

I carried the soft cloud of feathers and willow bone, the miracle of beauty and flight, its beating heart and filling lungs, to the varnished rail. I let it go.

The bird tumbled then splashed into a circle of water lit by our deck's light. I watched the trail of air bubbles as it sank, the air it had just breathed. I gripped the fluttering towel in my fingers. For a moment I contemplated jumping in to rescue the bird, to undo what I had done, but it was too late.

"I didn't know what else to do," I told Marilyn as we went back inside.

36

A NNIE WAS RIGHT THAT AFTERNOON WE'D SAID GOODBYE; THE marina did close.

That fall, during my first semester of college, my grandfather and Marilyn moved our boat to another marina—one on the Cerritos Channel, on the border between the LA Harbor and Long Beach. You had to drive through an oil field to get there. It had better electricity and sturdy docks, a real office and a nice café, but no garden.

When I went back to visit Donahue's over winter break, everything had changed. The breeze kicked up small clouds of dust around the abandoned office. Annie's green garden was nothing but a few dried plants and a forlorn wishing well without its phone. She and Bob had moved to a trailer park in Long Beach. Jerry had packed up his RV and chickens and left for parts unknown. The only person I found still there was Wade, less than a year before his death, but at the time, still doing well. He didn't know where he was going to live, he told me, but not to worry, he'd find a place. Oh, and hey, he had kin in Tennessee, not too far from my university, and did I want their number in case I ever needed help out there?

Years later, as I write this, I find an article that ran in the *LA Times*. Under the headline "Sea-Goers Seek to Keep Berth 117 Alive," it describes how twenty marina residents and fishermen had spoken before the Board of Harbor Commissioners, asking them to keep the marina open. I didn't know they'd fought the closure.

"'A few of the people docked at this marina live on their boats and will be homeless if it closes,'" their attorney told the reporter.

"'When boats are torn by weather, they either need to be destroyed or restored,'" Gunner had testified. "'Without this marina, as boats get old, they will have no choice but to die.'"

I imagine Annie and Bill and Catherine and Wade and people like them, dressed in their best clothes, standing up, one by one, to speak to a panel of men in suits and fine shoes, some of the most powerful men in their world. They were never going to win. Closing Donahue's was just one part of a city plan to industrialize the Southwest Slip and gentrify the harbor. Over the next decade, the city would make it impossible for poor people to live on their boats by imposing size minimums, safety inspections, licenses, and fees.

In the article, the reporter keeps referring to the Donahue's folk as "sea-goers." It makes me think of the Old English poem "The Seafarer": "My soul roams with the sea, the whales' / Home," the seafarer laments, "wandering to the widest corners / Of the world." I think of the marina people who had to leave their homes, imagine them wandering alone, trying to find another place to dock their boats, keep their cats, plant their gardens. I wonder where they all are now, how many of them are still alive.

If you take the 110 Freeway south to the Los Angeles Harbor and cross the Vincent Thomas Bridge, you can look down on to the Southwest Slip. All the dusty shores and reedy marshes are covered in impeccable asphalt and millions of neatly stacked shipping containers. And where there had once been a little dock and all manner of boats and people, there are massive cargo ships laden with goods imported for Walmarts and Targets and Walgreens. You would never know what was there before.

37

I LIVED WITH MARILYN FOR A YEAR AFTER MY GRANDFATHER'S death, working as a ticket agent at Northwest Airlines and using my employee standby tickets to visit Ben in Lincoln, Nebraska, where he was in graduate school. I stayed because I thought she might need help finding her own life without my grandfather. I tried to convince her to join AA and to sell the Laundromat—a business my grandfather and she had bought while I was in college and which caused her endless stress. I tried to convince her to sell the porn store and to file amended tax returns. I tried to convince her to sell the boat and move on to land, something I knew she wanted to do. Sometimes she'd say yes, then not do anything about it, not even let me do anything about it. Most of the time she'd shake her head or say, "I'll think about it, honey," then go back to work or talk radio or Fox News, a cup of fruity cocktail close at hand.

I was right; Marilyn did need help. But what I didn't realize then was that I wasn't the person who could help her. We were too close, and at the same time, had grown too far apart. I'd changed a lot in college.

Now so different from each other in outlook, Marilyn and I couldn't talk about much of anything. I couldn't talk to her about art or music or literature, pursuits which were to her a frivolous waste of time, the domain of the idle rich or the liberal indolent, but which had become my life's passions, pursued with all the fervor of the young. I couldn't talk about faith with her, because although I was still a Christian, I wasn't a conservative Christian anymore. All she seemed to be able to talk about were politics, turning conversations with me or her friends into one-sided, angry fusillades of talking points lifted straight from the radio. My politics had changed too—not drastically yet, but enough so that talking with her about anything became a minefield. We couldn't even stand to go to the same church—although, to our credit, we both tried.

After a year, Marilyn told me I should leave LA to start my own life. She said it out of love, concern for me, but we both knew she wanted to live her own life as much as I wanted to live mine. What we didn't know then was that we'd reached the end of the closeness we'd always had, of the intimacy we'd shared since she became my mother. And we didn't know that the gulf between us was only going to widen or that we would both help it grow.

In the years that followed, Marilyn would remarry without inviting me to the wedding—most likely because I didn't especially like her new husband. She'd fire Pete after his fifteen years of work for us, when he was too old to get another job. She'd dump all of the cats at the pound, only to adopt different ones a few years later. She'd get into arguments with most of her friends over politics and stop talking to them, even Josette. She'd sell the Laundromat and borrow thousands from her mother and brother to fund her new husband's business plans. She'd stop filing taxes. She'd be close to homelessness but refuse to let me send money. She'd go months without calling me or her mother; she wouldn't return our calls. I'd be sick with worry; I couldn't get my work done. When she did call, she'd often be drunk, telling me how horrible my grandfather was, as if somehow I didn't know. She'd scream at me about politics, long after I stopped replying, until she was debating the static between us, talking over the sound of my tears.

When we talk about that time now, Marilyn tells me how desperate she was then—to get off the boat, to get out of porn and the Laundromat, to get out of the life Richard had trapped her in. She just didn't know how, and this was the best way she came up with. Hearing her say that now makes her actions more understandable, although at the time, they seemed erratic, irrational, selfish. I didn't know how to help her, and so I spent sleepless nights worrying instead.

Somewhere along the way, I realized if I kept worrying about her the same way I had as a child, I'd ruin my life too. And when I gave up on saving her, it was as if our biggest bond had been severed. We'd still talk on the phone every few months, visit every few years, but I'd built a wall around my heart. I let her go.

Marilyn would move off the boat eventually. The *Intrepid* would fall into disrepair, her hull covered in algae, her brightwork faded and peeling. She and her new husband wouldn't be able to afford the liability insurance required to keep the boat in the new marina, but instead of selling it to the first buyer, they'd wait for one with more money, and then for another with even more money, one who never came. And so they'd decide to leave the boat mostly unattended at Cat Harbor, the windward harbor at the Isthmus of Catalina Island, with just an anchor to hold it against the Pacific storms. Ten years after my grandfather died, the *Intrepid* would slip its anchor in a storm; the wind would drive her ashore and smash her against the rocks.

When I heard, all I could think of was the wood—forests of teak, mahogany, oak—splintered and waterlogged. I saw water pouring into my cabin with no one to close the watertight door, no one to use my escape hatch. The engines flooded and ruined. I mourned a whole forest of wasted wood, a thousand fixtures and components that might have been salvaged but now never would be: portholes, pin rail, compass, bell, swim step. I imagined our dishes, broken, their jagged edges wedged in tide pools and sand. Books and papers and pornography rolling in the surf. The emerald ring my grandfather gave me when I was a little girl—long outgrown—half-buried in sand; the picture of Michele, its glass cracked, her face covered in water; Spence's badge wedged among the rocks; my Pallas Athena pendant washing away. What had happened to her ship's bell? I imagined it clanging violently as she was pushed closer and closer to land, ringing an alarm no one heard. The way her hull groaned before it snapped. *I want to go home*, I thought for the first time in a very long time. *It's not there*, I reminded myself. I felt unsettled, nervous for days, dwelling on the absence of a place I hadn't been to for years—a place, I realized now, I'd loved as well as hated.

It was worse for Marilyn: with the loss of the boat, she lost everything. She couldn't pay the Coast Guard–mandated environmental cleanup for the crash. She abandoned the video store, whose mortgage she'd long ceased to pay. She and her new husband moved to a trailer with no running water or electricity in the Mojave Desert, miles away from the nearest town.

But that fall when I still lived with Marilyn, a year after my grandfather died, before any of those other things happened, I loaded up the cute, used Saturn she'd generously given me for graduation, filling it with books and clothes, a stereo, my teddy bear Applesauce, and my pet rat, Gizmo. I left my little altar—the pictures of Michele and Spence—planning, always, to take them with me the next visit. I don't know why I chose to leave them; they were some of the most valuable possessions I owned. I gave Marilyn a long, long hug, memorizing how it felt, the contour of her arms and shoulders, the smell of her hair, storing the memory in case I should never see her again. And then I headed to Nebraska to be with Ben. I left her once more—the way I'd left her when I went to college—and again, I felt as if I were abandoning her, as if I had failed to save her. And perhaps I was right.

On the first night of my road trip to Nebraska, as I drove along I-70, the road rising over the Wasatch Plateau in Utah, I felt homesick. I was at that part of the journey where home is too far away to return to, but the destination still seems impossibly far to reach. My stop for the night, Green River, was still a ways away, and the night was especially dark—there were no lights from towns; the only billboards advertised a watermelon festival that I had missed. My radio had been useless through most of Utah and was now only picking up faint static. Gizmo was asleep, quiet in her cage. I wondered if I was doing the right thing: a twenty-two-year-old moving to Lincoln with no job prospects, no idea of what I would do. I missed Marilyn, the boat, even the orange light of the harbor. Suddenly, as I fiddled with the AM dial, a familiar voice came over the speakers. It wasn't a pastor expounding on the fate of unbelievers or a political commentator calling for Bill Clinton's impeachment.

"On, King! On, you Huskies!" it urged instead. "On!"

It was Sergeant Preston of the Yukon, hot on the trail of some Canadian evildoer. Suddenly I was a girl again, washing dishes in the galley, at home with parents who loved me—even at our worst, I always knew my parents loved me. I listened raptly, corny as it was, staying in the car to finish even after I'd reached my motel's parking lot.

After the closing music came the radio's call sign, a simple "KNX 1070, Los Angeles." I couldn't believe it. How could that radio station have found me so far from home? I now know that this is a common phenomenon—AM radio waves, reflected by the ionosphere, can travel randomly for hundreds of miles, especially at night—but back then it seemed like a sign, a valediction from my childhood, a farewell from the city itself. I wiped a tear from my eye, stretched, then went in to the Super 8 to check in.

The next morning when I got back into the car, the signal was gone.

V

Where You Come From

38

Twenty years after that brunch with Detective Varney at the Yankee Whaler, in 2004, I find myself at the library of the University of Nebraska, where I am in graduate school. But today I'm not studying. Instead, I carry a spool of microfilm in my hands like a bird's nest and follow a student worker to a microfilm reader. I am in my late twenties, newly married to Ben and quietly grieving the distance that has grown between Marilyn and me. Although I will only realize it in hindsight, it is these two facts that have led me to this place, the beginning of what will be a long search for my past. But by now, I've realized that my grandfather was wrong when he told me, "Where you come from is important; it's who you are," because it was only partly true. "Who you are" also happens after you leave home. You are turning into "who you are" your whole life.

The student leads me into a dim room, made even darker when he pulls the thick shade across the only window. Patiently, he threads the spool of microfilm into the viewer, turns the machine on, and shows me how to work the controls: forward, backward, focus, zoom. He doesn't talk much—eager, I think, to return to his computer game. I am glad he doesn't ask me what I am looking for in these old newspaper reels, but part of me wants to tell him. I am afraid of what I might find, and I don't want to search on my own.

He leaves me alone with the sound of the machine, the hum of its fan, the clunk and whir of the film as I advance it. Two weeks' worth of the *Los Angeles Times* blur in front of me, the motion making me slightly queasy, until I reach November 29, 1976—three weeks after I was born. I read through headlines, glance at ads for J. C. Penney's Thanksgiving sale, Safeway's holiday specials. And I laugh a little because not much has changed in all that time: Donald Rumsfeld is once again Secretary of Defense—this time under George W. Bush—and depending on whom you ask, Elvis is still alive. I realize that what I'm looking for isn't in the big headlines or the ads, so I go back to the front page and read through the smaller items—articles about Amy Carter's high school, a robbery in Fullerton, a blind drum major—but I still can't find it. I read on to the next day and then the next, but still there is nothing. Pretty soon I reach the end of the film: a blank screen and the jarring clack, clack of the tape flapping on its spool.

My mother's body was abandoned in an empty lot near downtown Los Angeles, about a half mile away from *LA Times* headquarters. Her death didn't even make the paper. The only notice I can find is a one-line obituary that appeared a couple of weeks later, the kind the funeral home puts in the paper for free. My grandfather didn't pay for an obituary, and neither did Spence, as if they were ashamed of her.

There is nothing about the Hillside Stranglers, either, but this makes sense. She died almost a year before their spree began.

Because there is nothing in the *LA Times* about Michele's murder, I decide to call the Los Angeles Police Department to request a copy of her file. It takes me days to work up the courage to make the call, and I shake as I dial, but the lady in the cold case department who answers the phone is kind.

"All I can do is give you the case summary," she says when I've explained my situation, "because your mom's case is still open. We can't release any other details. Can you hold for a second? I have to go pull a book from the shelf." I imagine leather-bound folios gathering dust on a shelf or, more likely, huge three-ring binders stamped with LAPD. I hold the phone with both hands, then tuck my elbows into my chest, so that the receiver doesn't shake right out of my grasp.

"Okay," she says when she gets back on the line. I hear the thump of the book on her desk. "What I have here is a case summary of your mother's file. It's not... It's pretty ugly, okay? I really wish you were here in person so that I could be with you to tell you this, but I'll try to read it over the phone."

She pauses a second as if trying to control her emotions, but perhaps she is simply reading ahead. "I really wish you were here in front of me."

I had steeled myself to talk to a burned-out detective or a calloused bureaucrat; I'm not prepared to talk to someone kind. It is her care—and not what follows—that makes me cry.

"Okay, in the upper left-hand corner it says, 'Beating–blunt instrument–unknown. Strangulation–ligature.' That means she was strangled with a ligature, like a rope or a cord or something. Then it says her name: Michele Ann Grey. Your mom was murdered between November 28 and 29, between 10:00 p.m. and 8:10 a.m., when she was found. It lists the suspects as unknown. Okay, then it says—you're gonna hate me"—I hear her mutter under her breath, then she continues—"'Victim is a Hollywood prostitute who was living with three companions at the Hollywood Center Motel. At 10:00 p.m. she told her companions she was going next door to turn a trick to help pay the rent because they did not have enough money. Her friends thought she meant a hotel up the street. They did not see the victim alive again.'"

She clears her throat. I remind myself to breathe.

"'The victim was discovered by a gardener in the vacant lot at 610 North Hill Place. An autopsy revealed the victim had been beaten and strangled with an unknown ligature. She was fully clothed except for her right shoe. There were no witnesses to the body being dumped or the homicide occurring.'

"'Status: Investigation Continued.'" She takes a breath. "That means your mom's case is still open. And it always will be until... until it's solved. And I'm actually the investigator for homicides in 1976, so I'm the detective on your mother's case. My name is Vivian Flores."

I don't trust my voice, so all I can say is "thank you."

Detective Flores takes down my contact information and tells me she'll read through my mother's file to see if there is anything else we can do. When we hang up, I am still trembling.

She faxes me the one-page case summary she'd read me over the phone. It is signed by two detectives: Detective Orozco and Detective Varney. Detective Varney—his name floats back to me across so many years—and I remember the detective my grandfather took me to meet when I was eight years old. *I knew you,* I think, as I touch his name on the form.

That evening, I think only of my mother, so alone, so desperate. Her body beaten before the life was choked out of it. She'd had plenty of time to suffer, to be terrified. I try to imagine those last moments, but I can't. My mind refuses.

A week later, Detective Flores calls me to tell me that she has sent the available physical evidence to be tested for useable DNA. If they find any, they will compare it to the DNA of known murderers and rapists to try to find a match.

When I ask her about the Hillside Stranglers, she says they were eliminated as suspects long before. She says it easily, as if they weren't ever seriously suspected. I wonder if my grandfather knew that. I'm disappointed. I hadn't realized how much having someone to blame had meant to me, even if it was just a guess, a possibility.

I ask Detective Flores if my mother was raped.

"They did a rape kit on her body, but it doesn't look like she was."

I'm relieved. At least there wasn't that.

"This isn't like *CSI*, okay?" she warns me before we hang up. "It'll take four to five months for the test to come back. And we're probably not going to find anything."

But at least, I think, *you're trying. At least you care.*

That night I think about the physical evidence in my mother's file, evidence I didn't know still existed. Her clothes, I imagine, maybe jeans and a sweatshirt, underwear. Perhaps her wallet or a watch or earrings. Her left shoe, her socks. I keep thinking about her right shoe, the one that was missing. I wonder what happened to it, where it is now. I imagine they store all the items in a big cardboard box in a temperature-controlled warehouse, the kind you see on TV mysteries. I think of how more of her belongings are in that box than I will ever possess. The only thing I've ever owned that was hers was the Bible she had when she was a child. I remember how I used to touch that Bible, rub my finger along its spine. I think of the evidence in that big cardboard box, and I want to touch it too, run my finger along the jeans my mom once wore, the hem of the sweatshirt that once kept her warm. I lost that Bible somewhere along the way to adulthood. I wish I had it back.

After the first round of tests, the lab finds no useable DNA on Michele's evidence; there is no way to use DNA to trace her killer. A break in the case will have to come from somewhere else: a confession, a connection Detective Flores might be able to make where the original detectives had not, someone coming forward with new information. *You knew the odds were slim from the beginning*, I tell myself.

Detective Flores has been trying to locate all the principal witnesses to the case, people my mother associated with around the time of her death, including my dad.

"I'm still looking for him," she tells me the day the results come back. "He's out on a warrant. I've left a note with his probation officer that I want to talk to him if he turns up. I can't tell you his name because of privacy rules. Do you know his name?"

"There's a name on my birth certificate—Archibald? William, Richard? Something like that."

"Yeah, that's him."

I wonder where my father might be, out on his warrant, out on the lam. Is he alive or dead? I remember what my grandfather had told me about Archibald: that he probably wasn't my father anyway, that he just wanted to use me to get out of jail. I find myself still scared of the man named Archibald, scared he'll take me away from my family—from my grandfather, long dead, from Marilyn, from Ben.

"Keep in touch," Detective Flores tells me before she hangs up. "Send an email every once in a while. You never know. The technology is changing all the time."

It seems like such a small nail to hang my hopes on.

39

WHEN I ASK HER TO TELL ME ANYTHING SHE CAN REMEMBER about Michele, Marilyn shares this story:

A few months before Michele died in 1976, she called my grandfather from a pay phone on Sunset Boulevard and asked for help. She was pregnant with me and alone. She asked her father for a place to stay, for some money. It was only temporary, she promised; she'd get a job; she even promised to stay sober—a promise both of them knew she couldn't keep. He heard her crying on the other end of the phone, the catch in her voice as she tried to muffle her sobs. She begged him; she pleaded with him. My grandfather said no. I like to think he was just hurt, angry, when he said, "You've really fucked up now, haven't you?"

It would be their last conversation—not that he didn't change his mind a few weeks later and try to get in touch with her. He called her last known number, but the man who picked up couldn't speak English. My grandfather even called my grandmother, Spence, and asked if she knew where their daughter was. She hadn't heard from her in a while; she'd said no too.

Marilyn says my grandfather was devastated when Michele was killed. He blamed himself for not having helped her when she asked; he blamed himself for her death. For months afterward, he spent nights driving around Hollywood, searching for the man who had killed her.

I imagine those nights, go with him from place to place: He'd drive down Sunset and La Brea and every street and alley in between. He would slow down his car and peer into the dark places behind dumpsters and into doorways, rolling down his window and shining his flashlight on sleeping men, or whores shooting up, or dogs digging through trash. Some nights he would sit in a vinyl booth at a Denny's on Sunset, drinking coffee and watching. He watched the cops come in for their meals. He watched bums try to come up with change for coffee. Sometimes he bought them dinner and plied them with questions they never knew the answers to. He read the graffiti in the john—names and numbers scratched in the stalls—looking for a clue. He looked for an answer in the mirror while he washed his hands; he saw only himself. And then he would head back into the dark to search some more. He never found what he was looking for.

I think of that picture I have of him holding me as a baby, the one where he looks so tired.

Sometimes I imagine my mother in the months before her death. I imagine, for instance, that it was raining when she finally went to the clinic. This isn't likely, because she probably went in May or June, months when it doesn't rain in LA. But I like the rain, and I like to think she did too, and so I always make it rain as she waited at the bus stop. It was 1976, and so I imagine Chevettes and Galaxies driving by on the busy street in front of her, their tires kicking up a fine mist. Her jeans were probably too long for her, as mine are; their hems were frayed and wet. Perhaps she leaned back against the smoky, translucent plastic of the shelter, then touched her stomach. Just a faint, quick touch, as if she were checking to make sure her top button was fastened, but it wasn't that. She hadn't fastened that button for weeks.

She rode the bus for a long time; she knew if she had a car, it would only be a short drive. As she walked from the bus stop to the clinic door, she passed a little store. It was closed, and the only reason she stopped to look through the dusty window was because the things there caught her eye: a painted Virgin of Guadalupe, small candles, glasses and vials, metal implements, figurines she didn't recognize. The sign painted on the glass of the window was in Spanish, a language she did not speak. She recognized the Virgin of Guadalupe, though—no one who lives in LA does not—and it made her smile, just a little bit. My mother liked to stop and look at things. I know this about her because I am her daughter and I do it too.

At the clinic, men and women sat in hard, plastic chairs, rustling magazines and talking in hushed voices. A little boy, four or five, was running through the aisles of chairs, but slowed and stared when he got to her. For the first time that day, she felt self-conscious about her torn jeans, her stringy hair, the stain on her shirt. After a lot of waiting, she was led into a room where they gave her a test, and then she waited some more. She already knew what the test result would be, but someone told her that if she got the test, she could get money for the baby. But that isn't why she decided to keep her baby, just for the money.

When the white coat came back in—doctors, nurses, assistants, they were all the same to her—he told her that she was pregnant. He told her they didn't do abortions there; she'd have to go somewhere else. He told her there were many organizations that would make it possible for her to bring the baby to term, that they'd help her put it up for adoption. He told her if she was going to keep drinking or doing drugs or sleeping around or whatever, though, she might as well just have an abortion. She stared at the dull metal of his stethoscope while he talked. She wondered why he thought she didn't know these things already.

He asked her if she had any family.

"Yes," she answered, then said nothing more.

She took the paperwork they gave her, clutching it in her hand all the long bus trip back, keeping it dry under her poncho; I don't suppose she carried a purse. She kept her wallet tucked in her hip pocket, perhaps, safer there than in a purse.

Before she went to sleep that night—wherever she slept in those days—my mother thought about her child. She imagined the dark world inside her: the little girl—she had always known it would be a girl—floating in a shaded pool, the cord keeping her from floating away into the darkness. Or was it, she wondered, the other way around? Maybe the cord kept *her* tethered to the child, like a boat at anchor. She liked to think that, that the cord kept *her* tied down, stopped *her* from floating off into some dark who-knows-where. She thought about the child inside her, made a little promise that she'd look after her, no matter what. She wanted to do right by her little girl, whom she'd already named and already, long ago, decided to keep.

She'd call her father in the morning, she thought, just before she dozed off. Surely, he'd help. But of course he didn't.

One night, three weeks after she gave birth to me, my mother left me with some friends in a motel room they shared on Wilcox Avenue in Hollywood. Before she left, she laid me in a dresser drawer, nestled me between some socks and jeans and a dirty T-shirt and tucked my baby blanket around me. I like to think she kissed me before she left. I like to think I made her happy.

40

I REMEMBER THE FOLDERS IN MARILYN'S FILING CABINET, THE WAY I snuck into them at night or when she wasn't at home, looking—always looking—for answers. I wish I had them now: Michele's death certificate, Spence's birth certificate, anything with more information. When I ask, Marilyn readily agrees to send me all of them. I wonder, then, why I'd thought they were such a secret, why I'd felt the need to sneak.

In the package she sends me are all the ones I remember—the death certificates, the birth certificates—but also one I don't remember: the probate report for Spence's estate. It is signed by her executrix, Yvette P. Genovese. Who on earth was Yvette Genovese? I wonder. Why wasn't Dee Spence's executrix? Then I remembered what Dee told me, how Spence had a sister: *Yvette* to go with *Yvonne*. The sister my grandfather said had wanted to steal me from him. I had forgotten that I once knew all of these things.

I am sure she must have died long ago, but I google her name anyway: she is not dead. In fact, she has just won a national bowling championship for seniors. I am delighted. All this time I'd thought I had no living blood relatives, and here is one padding around in bowling shoes. I imagine she is spunky. I imagine her brightly colored bowling shoes moving gracefully at the head of the polished lane.

But I am scared to call my great aunt because of what my grandfather told me. I'm scared she won't want to have anything to do with me. I'm worried she will think I want money.

"It won't be that way," Ben says, so I send her a letter.

We talk on the phone only once, but for a very long time, well into the night. It is so strange, I think as we talk, to find her alive when her sister has been dead twenty-five years. I sit on the floor of our apartment, my knees drawn to my chest, the phone cradled against my ear. It's cold in Lincoln, but that's not why I'm shivering. Yvette has a kind, warm voice on the phone—an old voice, spunky, opinionated. She tells me how she'd wanted to adopt me after my grandmother, Spence, died. She's been wondering about me for twenty-five years, worrying about me, hoping I was okay. She tells me how she and Spence had not gotten along very well; they weren't speaking when Yvonne died. She tells me how glad she was to find out that I'd turned out okay.

"Your grandfather had nothing to do with raising your mother, Michele" is the first thing she wants me to know. She is adamant about this, her voice hard-edged. "Your mother was mostly raised by *my* mother, Irma. Yvonne was too busy to really look after Michele, you see. She was busy with her friend Dee and work. To be honest, she was into the drinking pretty heavily too. Your mom came over to visit my house a lot, but with my husband being disabled and my own children, it was too much for her to live there. So she moved back and forth between Yvonne and our mother when she was a little girl. But your grandfather, he never saw your mother."

According to her, my grandfather and Spence met in New York after the war. When Spence returned home to Los Angeles, my grandfather came with her. But the minute Spence got pregnant with Michele, my grandfather abandoned them. It is almost completely the opposite of his story.

"I think he saw her at least a few times," I say, trembling harder, wanting to defend my grandfather. "At least that's what he told me." I am shaking so badly that I can't hold the phone still against my ear.

"No, he was lying. He never saw her, not even once."

I wonder who is right. Perhaps he never did see her, although I wonder how he got those pictures of her, the ones in his desk. The stories he told, about how she picked my name? He couldn't have made them all up, could he? I suppose it doesn't matter; the outcome was the same: Michele was alone.

"And then, of course," she says, "there was that horrible car accident, when your mother was killed."

The hairs on my arm rise. I stare out the window into the dark night. The trees, barely lit by our porch light, are bare of leaves; the branches rattle together in the wind.

"Well, actually, you know. She wasn't killed that way."

"No?"

"No, actually, she was murdered."

"Oh…all right." She doesn't sound surprised. She changes the subject.

She tells me how Spence served in the SPARS during the war, then took ten years to finish her BA. It only took Yvette four years to get her nursing degree from Stanford. When she says this, she sounds like a young woman again, the little sister feeling superior. She tells me how Dee and Spence used to live together in a trailer in her mother's yard.

I ask her the question that I've wondered about for so long. "My grandfather always said that Yvonne and Dee were, well, um, maybe intimately involved." I do not know how to phrase this question for someone of her generation, someone whom I barely know.

"No, that is not true!" It is the only time during the

conversation that she raises her voice. "I know your grandfather said that, but it was a lie. They were just friends, very close friends!"

I decide not to push. It doesn't really mean anything, anyway. I remember what Dee said about Yvette, so long ago: "Personally, I couldn't stand the woman." But I want it to be true; I like to think that two women I loved found true love at least once in their lives.

I learn from Yvette that their parents had both worked in film: their father was a half-Hawaiian casting director at MGM and a movie extra specializing in nameless parts like "Hawaiian peddler" and "Indian." How her father was a friend of Duke Kahanamoku, the Olympic swimmer and trailblazing surfer; how our family was descended from Hawaiian nobility. Their mother had been a film editor at Warner Bros. Yvette tells me how she and my grand-mother spent a month on location on Catalina Island, working as child extras for *Mutiny on the Bounty*; how Clark Gable came over to her house for dinner—stories that are wonderful to listen to and border on the unbelievable, stories not so unlike the ones my grandfather told me about his own connections to the movie business, his own noble blood. Not too long after I talk to Yvette, I'll discover that my grandfather did, in fact, write a few episodes for *Perry Mason*, that his parents really were killed in the Spanish flu epidemic. When I write to the Royal Navy for his war record, they'll inform me, very politely, that they've never heard of him.

Yvette and Spence also wandered between homes, Yvette tells me. Their parents were divorced too. Three generations of women, I think as Yvette talks, left to raise daughters on their own.

At the end of our conversation, she promises to mail some pictures. "I went through her house, you know, after your grand-mother died. I knew Richard and Dee were coming to clear it out to be sold, so I went in before they did. I took all the pictures I could find. Someone had to save them for you. They were important."

Later on, I will think of how, for twenty-five years, Yvette did nothing to try to find me. I will think about how many times, for how many years, I looked for pictures—anything—having to do with my mother and did not have them because she took them. But at the end of our call, I am grateful to her.

When I come home from work a few weeks later, my great-aunt Yvette's package is waiting for me.

Most of the pictures are of Michele. Even as a little girl in her frilly dresses and perfect curls, she wasn't all that cute; she was chubby and stubby and very pale. She smiles in none of the pictures. My five-year-old mother frowns as she sits in her shiny fire truck. In the picture of her on Santa's lap, she frowns, and in a picture of her with a new doll, she also frowns. But it could be that Santa scared her, that she didn't like her new doll. Because I know how Michele's story ends, I want to read loneliness and sadness into these pictures. But maybe she was just spoiled; maybe she was just a brat. Maybe she just didn't like to have her picture taken.

And perhaps I would really believe this if the sadness stopped at her mouth, but it doesn't. Even as a four-year-old, her eyes are the eyes of an adult, staring off into the distance at some sadness just beyond the frame.

As I look at the pictures, I think of what Yvette said—that my mother bounced between Spence, Yvette, and their mother, with little or no contact with her father. Perhaps it isn't fair to say that Michele was unloved; perhaps it is unfair to say that neither Spence nor my grandfather wanted her or that her grandmother or aunt did not love her. But surely it is fair to say that no one seems to have loved her enough to keep her—or to let her stay with someone else who loved her more.

My mother, Michele, got pregnant three years after *Roe v. Wade*. She was broke; she was alone; she was a prostitute. I've often wondered why she kept me, and perhaps the answer is in her wandering, unloved childhood. She wanted a baby to make a family; she wanted someone to love who would love her.

If there is any redemption in my mother's story, it is this: when they got a second chance, my grandfather and Spence took care of me.

Stuck at the bottom of the package is a small, white envelope; it is a letter from Michele. I handle the yellowed pages gingerly, touching the paper my mother herself touched, tracing the loops of her cursive with my finger. Her letter is written on lined tablet paper; the pages are still bound together with brittle adhesive from where she tore them off the pad. It is written to her mother, Spence, and mailed from her grandmother Irma's house.

My mother wrote the date as "9/ /67," starting the letter without knowing the date and forgetting to fill it back in. In 1967, she would have been fourteen. The upper right corners of the pages are stained with coffee. Who spilled it—Michele when she wrote or Spence when she read?

"Dear Mom," she begins, "Chiou! As usual I shall start off with a boring 'How are you?' At any rate I'm fine, and feeling quite chipper."

I recognize the affected, breezy style of a young person—or at least the same breezy style I affected when I was her age—complete with misspellings.

As I read, I realize she has not seen her mother for months: "I had a very eventful summer: Summer School, my first printed reviews, and the weekends with Helen and Treat…I started school approximately two and ½ weeks ago."

For a moment I wonder who Helen and Treat were—but then

I remember my grandfather telling me that Michele had called him Treat before she knew he was her dad. And I remember my grandfather talking about his girlfriend Helen, whom he'd always called "The Mexican." Later on, Michele writes about Treat's boat, and I know for sure then that it is my grandfather. She *had* spent time with him. He'd owned boats, large and small, all his life.

My mother continues: "I was seriously considering marine biology as a career but gave it up as science and its perpetual experiments, and formulas got to be a drag. But I will always love the ocean where we came from. As my new career unfolds (journalism), I find myself more and more wrapped up in it…after a four-year-college education at UCLA, I'll probably go to the Columbia Graduate School of Journalism in New York for my master's."

I think of my love for the tide pools and marine animals as a child, how I'd wanted to be a marine biologist for a while and almost majored in biology. And how strange that she was interested in a writing profession, when I'm a writer too. Are these things genetic, I wonder, like the weight problems and asthma we also share? If journalism was really her heart's dream, I wonder, why did she let go of it? What happened?

My mother writes: "To get back to the present, I'm really going on an appearance campaign. You see, I'm getting a small trace of acne on my chin and I most certainly don't want to go through that troublesome stage of adolescence. Between Clearasil and just Jell-O for lunch, I'll get rid of my pimples and weight in about two months. Wish me luck!"

One of the pictures Yvette sent is of Michele in her early teens. She is overweight, and her hair hangs shaggily in her face. She wears thick glasses in heavy frames, and acne dots her shiny face. Her smile is faint, self-conscious, almost a smirk. When I first see the photo, I am dismayed. But then I realize how similar she and

I were in high school. When I was a teenager, I couldn't imagine what my mother could have been like; I didn't know I had only to look in the mirror.

In the margin of her letter to her mom, Michele has drawn a little picture of someone who looks like Ginger on *Gilligan's Island,* but with glasses, which is apparently meant to be her in a few months. "I'm going to grow long hair too" is the caption. *No, no, not Jell-O,* I tell the picture, *that's not the way.*

Michele closes the letter by describing the crush she has on a twenty-eight-year-old man: "Treat introduced him to me and said he liked him as much as if he were his own son. I agree. Paul is kind, sensitive, and considerate. He loves horses as much as I. He respects me. He also is born under my sign!" She signs her letter with a flower and "Chele."

Something about the way she talks about Paul bothers me. Is it the way she knows he was born under her sign? Is it that she thinks he loves horses as much as she does or that he respects her? Did he tell her those things? Did something happen? Or is this just the way a fourteen-year-old girl writes to impress the mom she's been trying so hard to impress for the past five pages?

As I write this, I look again at the picture of Michele as a teenager. I want to show the girl in the picture how to eat and exercise. I want to take her for some new clothes, a better haircut, some Retin-A. I want to take her on a tour of the Los Angeles Times Building, help her with her writing, show her what books to read. I want to be her friend, to show her she's not alone, to love her. I want to mother this child in the picture, this child who is my mother.

I look at another of the pictures Yvette sent me. It shows an eleven- or twelve-year-old Michele standing outside a Chinese restaurant, circa 1965. But I realize now that it is not just *any*

Chinese restaurant: Behind her are red-lacquered columns and a stone lion I know well, a familiar parking lot. Above her head, a sign for the Flower Drum, the Chinese restaurant a few blocks away from my grandfather's video store—the one we used to go to together, the one where he asked me to move on to the boat. "I've been coming here for years," my grandfather always said. I hadn't realized he meant *decades*.

The photograph of Michele in front of the Flower Drum makes me even more certain that my grandfather had known his daughter while she was growing up, that Yvette was wrong when she said he'd completely abandoned her sister and niece. Because why on earth would Spence, who lived in West Covina, ever go to Inglewood for a Chinese lunch?

But my grandfather, who owned a business just down the street from there, certainly would.

What, I wonder, happened between the time she wrote this letter and the day she called my grandfather from the phone on Sunset? Did she run away from home suddenly—as my grandfather said—when she walked in on Dee and Spence? Or was it something else? Or dozens of something elses? What was her life like before she got pregnant with me? How do you go from an unloved, unmoored child to a runaway, a prostitute, a murder victim? I suppose it's not an uncommon story, but I don't want to know the common story; I want to know hers.

41

I'M FIVE MONTHS PREGNANT WITH MY FIRST CHILD. IT'S JANUARY 2011; I'm in Los Angeles for a job interview. On the day I'm supposed to fly home to Ben, my cell phone dies. My flight has been delayed because of a storm in Atlanta. Somehow I've also managed to lose my phone charger. I don't want to fly without a phone, so I decide to walk the mile to the nearest Sprint store before my shuttle leaves for the airport.

I grew up in Los Angeles, but I've only been downtown a handful of times: a few visits to Olvera Street, center of the old pueblo, with Le Lyçée and Marilyn; once to catch the train to go to college almost twenty years ago. For the past few days, I've walked around my downtown hotel in the sun, relishing the January weather I remember from childhood—not the Midwestern snow and ice I've lived in for the past ten years. I've had fun reading directional signs meant for tourists and commemorative plaques, learning things about my hometown I never knew. I'm enjoying my walk this day, pausing to contemplate old buildings and their architectural details, smiling at excited Clippers fans headed to the game at the Staples Center. And that's when I see it.

It's a sign for South Hill Street, and I realize it must be the same one: the street name printed in mimeograph ink on Michele's death certificate, the address of the empty lot where her body was dumped. I'd known it was close to where I'd be staying, but I hadn't known it would be this close. It hadn't occurred to me, until now, that I should visit it. Actually, if I'm being truthful with myself, it had. While I was packing, I thought I should take a copy of her death certificate, just in case—but something in me was too scared; something in me had refused. And now here it is.

I turn left and am suddenly in another world. There are no Clippers fans, only a few homeless men asleep on the sidewalk, a private security guard trying to rouse them. The tall buildings block out the sun, and in the shadows, I'm cold. I stick out with my interview suit, shiny new red shoes, the little pregnant belly. This is the Jewelry Mart district, but none of the stores are open on a Sunday. The restaurants and cafes are closed too; only the occasional car drives by. My pace slows; it's as if I'm walking in a fog—an invisible fog noticed only by me, but still thick and hard to get through. I am suddenly, completely, deep within myself. I walk toward the 600 block. Will the empty lot still be there, or will something have been built over it? How will I know when I've gotten to the right place? There will be no marker to tell me that I've found it, no memorial plaque or tourist-information panel with a friendly icon. No knife and fork for "restaurant" or wineglass for "bar." I smile a little, even in my trepidation. What icon would they use, anyway, for a crime scene? A chalk outline, a knife, a hangman's rope?

How many other bodies, I wonder, have been found in this area, the Fashion District, the Jewelry Mart, the Historic Core? What other unmarked spots are there in the history of this place? No one has put up a plaque at the spot where a girl bought her *quinceañera* dress, or where a shopkeeper had a heart attack, or where a small boy discovered his love for wonton soup. I wonder what it would be like to mark them all—all the moments of all the lives lived here. The street takes on new color in my imagination: I see it plastered with Post-It notes—blue and yellow and pink sticky notes on every door, every inch of sidewalk, all the light posts— commemorating first kisses, purses stolen, ears pierced, hearts broken. Lives begun, lives ended.

I can't find 610 South Hill Street. There is a building at 620 and one at 608, with only a small, sealed-off space in between. The buildings look to have been built in the 1920s or '30s, long before my mother's death. Perhaps I have the address wrong, although it is burned into my memory: 610 South Hill Street. Perhaps I've already passed it somehow. Was it that parking lot a hundred yards back— the earth on which she'd lain paved and repaved, the lines repainted a dozen times in the thirty-four years since she died, the asphalt once more cracking, the lines once more fading? Should I double back?

I realize then my mistake. I summon the image of the death certificate in my mind, its slightly blurry type. It was 610 *North* Hill Street *Place*. Another twelve long blocks away—something like a mile—and still I'm not sure where it would be. I consider walking there to look, but I don't know the neighborhood between here and there. Already on this empty street I've felt like an easy target with my suit and my pregnant belly. The new shoes gave me blisters yesterday; now there's a little pool of blood at the back of my shoe, and the raw spot on my heel stings with every step. And I have a flight to catch.

I'm furious with myself. Why hadn't I planned this? Why hadn't I packed the address after all, ordered a cab, driven there? What kind of daughter am I? Suddenly I want nothing more than to be at that spot—that spot where my mother's broken body, fully clothed but for her missing right shoe, was discarded like trash. But I have a flight to catch, a stupid phone charger to buy, a mile to walk back to the hotel.

I turn on Sixth and resume my walk to Broadway, coming to

the suddenly bustling blocks that surround Grand Central Market. I hope the Sunday crowds of little children and their parents, the cops on their bikes, the street vendors, the tourists, don't notice the tears in my eyes. I keep imagining my mother, Michele, walking these blocks. I imagine her spirit beside me, seeing what I see; imagine her noticing the sweet little girls in frilly dresses, the wood shavings on the sidewalk outside the Central Market, the sweet smell of a *panadería*. But of course she probably never had reason to walk these streets. Her ghost isn't here, I remind myself. Why would it be here any more than it would be at her grave, if she had a grave, or the place she died, or the Hollywood Center Motel where she lived, my first childhood home?

But then I think perhaps she is here somehow; perhaps the very act of searching, of thinking of her, has summoned her to my side. I stop in the middle of a busy sidewalk in downtown LA, on Sixth Street, somewhere between Hill and Broadway. I imagine her next to me, in front of me, behind me; I imagine her where she is as close to me as she can get, where she can see and know everything there is about me. I want her to know every good thing that's happened to me since I last saw her. I close my eyes for a second and stick my hand out a little, as if to hold hers.

Mom, I think, but that doesn't sound right. *Michele, I'm here. I'm going to have a baby. It's a little girl. I just wanted to show you.*

I wait a moment, then walk on, leaving no mark behind me.

42

It's the Sunday of Memorial Day weekend, a few months later. At two in the morning, the OB ward is quiet. Light filters into our dark room from the hallway, making a dim twilight around bassinet and bed. My mother-in-law and Marilyn have not yet gotten into town. Ben, too tall for the creaking recliner, has gone home for a good night's sleep. Our little girl, Milly, is twenty-seven hours old. It is our first time alone together.

She's just finished nursing, and her sleeping body lies between my breasts. I am getting used to the sounds she makes, little gurgles and sighs. I can barely feel the weight of her six pounds, but I feel her warmth, the soft puff of her breathing, the occasional twitch of her tiny, curled fist. The curve of her rump fits perfectly in my hand, so also the back of her head. I am so full of love for this creature, this small body, barely human. I am so full of love that it overflows in tears that meander silently down my cheeks.

I wasn't *that* sentimental during my pregnancy. There was rarely any sighing over tiny pink socks in stores, no letters written to my daughter in utero (as my pregnancy book suggested), no deep meditation on the meaning of motherhood or womanhood. On most days I had to remember to talk to her, remind myself to tell her I loved her—unsure, sometimes, that I really, actually did.

But on this night, there is no doubt about my love. I would give anything, do anything, for her and her happiness. Every part of me, every humble cell, every higher thought, loves her, wants her. This is the surest truth I know. And it is because of this, this flood of love, that I know, beyond doubt, that Michele loved me too.

Tonight, as I hold Milly, I wonder who was in the room with my mother when I was born. Not my father. Not her parents. I imagine she was alone. Were the nurses kind when they told her to push? Or did they smile tightly when they said, "It's a girl," and judge her with cold eyes? There were no flowers in my mother's delivery room, as there are in mine, no cards or gifts, hand-knitted blankets and hats. There was nothing. Her own worn clothes folded neatly on a chair.

In my hospital room at two in the morning, I imagine my mother nursing me, holding me to her chest afterward. When I feel Milly's soft breath against my breast, I know what Michele felt when I was born. I know how much she loved me: with every bit of herself, every cell, every higher thought.

I think, too, of how my mother only had three weeks of this: of baby in arms, gurgles and sighs, whispers of smiles in sleep. Only three weeks of this pure, pure love. I sob at the thought of only having three weeks.

All of my life, I've thought her murderer's greatest crime was taking my mother from me. But here, holding my little girl in a darkened hospital room, I know better. The true crime was taking a mother away from her baby, stripping her of the love she'd bravely made for herself, crushing it with the brutal force of blunt fists and tight rope.

And I know now what my mother's thoughts were as she died; I don't need to imagine them anymore. In her last struggles and shudders, in that terrible moment before she blacked out, when she knew she wasn't going to get away, my mother thought of her baby girl. My mother thought of me.

43

THE FALL AFTER MILLY'S BIRTH, I CHECK ON MY MOM'S CASE again. Detective Flores has left the cold case department; Michele's case has a new detective now. When I ask her if I can see the material in my mother's file, Detective Estupinian says no, unequivocally. "The detective takes quite seriously the responsibility of being the victim's voice since they are no longer able to speak for themselves," she writes. "Letting someone from the outside view the case might unintentionally influence a witness's testimony or give false witness to facts." But she also says that she will review the case again and, if warranted, send the clothing out to be tested once more. "The science is always changing," she says. "You never know."

You never know. I let myself hope a little.

Two months later, in December, I receive an email at work from Detective Estupinian:

Good Morning Kelly,

I wanted to let you know that I will be submitting some requests for your mother's clothing to be examined for DNA. This might take several months for results but I will let you know.

Your mother's case was immediately assumed by my Division, Robbery/Homicide in 1976. The Division investigates all high profile cases and serial murders within the city. Your mother's case was thought to be possibly linked to the Hillside Strangler Series. I don't know if you have ever heard of these murders but they were committed by two cousins in the late 70s. The pair were picking up prostitutes and dumping their bodies on the hillsides of Hollywood area. Are you aware that your mother was found on a hillside just off Sunset Blvd. It is entirely possible that she was also a victim of the series but Detectives could never link her case to any solid evidence and unfortunately Angelo Buono and Kenneth Bianchi did not give any information which could have linked it.

I wanted to ask you how much you know about your father or if you have had contact with him? Would you let me know?

Additionally, I am sending you a picture of your mom. This picture was used in the LAPD bulletin asking for public assistance. I think she looks especially sweet in the photograph. It was taken on May 29, 1976.

At the bottom of the message, I see my mother's piercing eyes, her mouth set firmly in a straight line. The photo startles me. I hold my breath until I'm done looking; I haven't seen her adult face so closely before. Her hair falls in loose waves at the side of her face and on her shoulders. Her cheeks are full but not fat—she's lost weight since she was a teenager. Her skin is clear of the acne too, although there are gray marks on her cheeks, either scars or freckles. Her nose is a little wider than mine, her eyebrows thinner. She seems at turns defiant or quietly happy; I cannot tell. I run my finger along the screen, the curve of her jaw, the side of her cheek. I take a breath: May 1976. Already she was pregnant with me.

Later that night, when I show the picture to Ben, my mother's face staring out at us from a computer screen, he will say, "She looks just like you." No one will have ever told me that before.

"No," I will say, "she's beautiful." I'll hold a sleeping Milly in front of the screen. "Look, it's your third grandmother," I'll whisper.

But earlier that afternoon, I am restless in my office after I get the email with the picture. I write back to the detective and tell her everything I know about my father: that my grandfather said he was a criminal who didn't care about me; that he just wanted to use me to get out of jail, that Detective Flores said he was a material witness and that he'd been out on a warrant for a long time.

Detective Estupinian writes back quickly:

Well I, too, have tried to find your dad. You are correct, he was in prison at the time of your mother's murder. He appears to have struggled with drug addiction for many, many years and was in and out of prison up until 1994. He was listed as a parolee at-large after that, apparently, because he didn't check in with his parole officer, but that warrant is no longer in the system. He does not show up on any of my radar, even when I search with a social security number. My gut feeling is that he may be deceased, but he does not show in the death index as well. I would like to speak to him about the people that surrounded both your mom and himself.

I am sending you a letter, which your father wrote

while still in prison. I believe that God has a purpose for every person on this earth and that every person should know that they were loved. Your mother and father made some bad choices in their lives but from what I can gather they both wanted you very much. I think you should know this. The letter your dad wrote is to Detective Varney. I am sure that whatever your grandfather told you, it was out of love and wanting to protect you. However, I also believe you should be entitled to see this letter. It does not appear that he was trying to use you to get out.

I stand up from my desk, put my hands to my head and close my eyes, then sit down again to open the file she has sent me.

It is a scan of a photocopy of a neatly typewritten letter. There is the gray shadow of a punch hole in the left margin where someone—Detective Varney or a secretary—filed it away in a binder. Up in the right, my father has typed, "RE: Michele Grey Archibald," and I realize then that he regarded her as his wife. Already this is different from the story my grandfather told me.

"Dear Mr. Varny," it begins, "This letter is in regard to the whereabouts of my daughter, Kelly Michele Archibald." My father explains how the minute he'd found out about Michele's death, he'd contacted his married sister, who lived in New Jersey. She had agreed to take me in. She was "even now awaiting only communication from the childcare agency that my baby will be delivered to her when she arrives before beginning the trip out here." But "as late as Friday, December 24, 1976," he'd been told that "no caseworker had been assigned and there was no one my sister could contact regarding the child." My father was writing three days later, on December 27, because he had only that day found out that my grandmother Spence had already picked me up from McLaren Hall,

LA County's foster care center, on December 13. The childcare agency had misled him, and now no one there would give him Spence's address. "This action was taken without my knowledge or consent," he tells the detective, and asks him to intercede with the childcare agency on his behalf. He also asks for a birth certificate for me, pictures of Michele. In a sentence that will always haunt me, he writes about Spence, "I certainly do not want that woman to have custody of my baby for any period of time at all…she did enough to Michele." I wonder, what, exactly, he meant.

I sit at my desk. For a few minutes, only one thought courses its way through my mind: my father wanted me. My father wanted me. My father wanted me. I walk out of my office and down the hall and back again. My father wanted me! Somehow—I don't know how—I manage to pack my bag and drive home. I am in a daze all the rest of the night, cooking dinner, nursing and bathing Milly, cuddling with Ben after she's gone to sleep, reading and rereading my father's words.

All my life I'd thought he didn't care about me or my mother. But when I read his letter, I hear a man calling me "my baby." I hear the desperation of a father who does not know where his child is, who is powerless to help her. I hear the love he held for my mother and me, and I hear him realizing that both have been taken away. I am a mother now; I can begin to imagine how he felt.

Later, Detective Estupinian tells me she thinks my mother and father were a couple of street kids, hooked on drugs and surviving the best way they could. Michele had started with prescription pills, drugs she'd found at Spence's house or her grandmother's. She might have run away, she thinks, but she also might have been kicked out.

"Your dad," she tells me, "he was taking care of your mom right about until the sixth month of her pregnancy. He was breaking and entering and selling stuff to make money for them. But then he got caught."

I realize now, why my mother called my grandfather for help that day from a pay phone on Sunset Boulevard, that day he said no.

"She probably started turning tricks to support you guys," Detective Estupinian says, and now I understand. She sold herself because of me, for me.

It does not occur to me to judge her; I understand without questioning. If I had to, I would do anything for Milly.

The detective continues, "That might even be why she went with him, the man who killed her. She didn't know what she was doing."

She didn't know what she was doing. I picture him, some faceless man, leading her away into the dark, her silently following him. Together, they disappear.

He supported her; he loved us. This means more to me than I ever thought it would. Now I can imagine my father. I imagine him sitting in a jail cell, surrounded by metal painted gray, metal painted white. I imagine him sitting on the lower bunk, staring out into the space between heavy bars, out into the hall, past the steel doors between him and the outside world. Even if he could get through the bars, there are the armed guards in blue uniforms, their black billy clubs and saps, their guns. The mattress is thin on the steel bed and he can feel his bones against the slats.

He is thinking about the woman he calls his wife, pregnant with his child, who visits when she can. She was as big as a house the last time he saw her, her shirt stretched over her stomach, her jeans held up by a belt, a used wool sweater keeping her warm against the October chill. With his eyes closed, he conjures the reddish brown of her hair, the spark of her eyes, the sudden gaze of her smile. In this dark world all his own, he recreates her hands, their warm fingers, her soft breasts—pale white, the nipples rose—her hips. He puts them from his mind just as quickly, though—not with the man above him, who grunts when he is awake and farts loudly in his sleep, who jacks off to girlie magazines smuggled in from outside.

He thinks instead of her hair again, the smell of it sweet to him, even when it's greasy. He imagines the life they will have together when he gets out, and they both go straight, clean. He has talked to her about this. After the child comes, they will have to try. If not here, someplace else. Nevada, he thinks. Texas.

"This is no way to bring up a kid," he'd told her the last time she visited, reaching his hand toward hers, stopped by the glass.

He falls asleep, and when he wakes it is mail call and there is a note for him. He recognizes the still-girlish handwriting, the flower drawn in the corner of the envelope.

"It's a girl," she says. "Her name is Kelly, like we said. She is beautiful. I can't wait for you to meet her."

He is not a passionate man but a cool one, inclined to deliberate action, but the letter makes him slam his hand against the thick bars, enough to score a reprimand from a guard, a hoot from his neighbor. He wants to know how the labor was, how they're doing, how she paid for the hospital. He wants to know if she's okay, if she's healthy, sore. Where are they staying? He is maddened by what isn't in the letter.

———————————

Later I ask Detective Estupinian if she thinks he ever saw me, his baby. "I guess it's possible. She'd have had to have taken you down to Central after she had you. She might have. I don't know."

I imagine her there in the visiting room holding me, wrapped in a blanket, a quilt, and I wonder if there was glass between them this time. Could he reach out and touch her, me? Would he have been permitted to hold his only child? I imagine her cooing at the baby as she passed her to him. I imagine the almost electric jolt that went through him when his hand touched the back of her head, when he assayed his child's light weight. I think of the look on Ben's face the first time he held Milly and transfer it to my still-faceless dad: the smile of wonder, the eyes blinking with tears. I imagine the pain, too, in that moment—of knowing he'd have to give up that warm, light bundle in his arms in just a few minutes, that his wife and daughter would leave and he could not join them. I imagine him studying that tiny face, its closed eyes and pink lips, trying to burn it on to his retinas, to etch it permanently in his mind. I know this because I do it all the time with my own child, in case somehow she is taken away.

And then it's time. He hands the baby back, dashing tears away from his eyes with the backs of his hands, wiping them on his pants. He embraces Michele and his baby tightly for one more warm moment, and then the guard calls angrily, and he is led away. Back in his cell, he sobs, his mouth against the thin mattress. He couldn't give a single fuck that the man on the top bunk is laughing at him, calling him a pussy.

Or what if Michele didn't visit him? What if it was too hard? If she couldn't afford the bus fare, if she wouldn't take her baby to a place like that? What if she just didn't want to go, sending excuses whenever he asked?

The selfish part of me would like to think my father held me at least once, that we laid eyes on each other, however briefly. But wouldn't it have been less painful for him if we hadn't? Wouldn't it be better for him if I had remained an abstraction—an idea—instead of the warm, small body, flesh of his flesh, embraced then surrendered?

I imagine, too, the day he found out about Michele's death, although I do not know how or when it happened. Was he told by his caseworker? Was it by letter? A phone call? A visit from Detective Varney? Really what I imagine is the moment after he found out. The closed eyes, the clenched hands, shaped something like my own. The shortened breaths, the pacing, the physical energy of an enraged, grieving man in a confined space.

And then, the moment of panic. What about the baby?

———————————————

I know I was better off being raised by my grandfather and Marilyn. If I were a social worker and had to choose between him or my grandmother—the probation officer with a house—I would have picked Spence too. But it breaks my heart a little, to know that my father spent his life wondering what happened to me. I wish I could tell him that I turned out all right.

44

MY HUSBAND AND I SIT IN THE DARK WATCHING *Frenzy,* Alfred Hitchcock's second to last film, released in 1972, four years before my mother's death. Ben gave me a boxed set of all his films, and we've been watching them in order. Milly is upstairs asleep, and I lean against Ben, but not in a romantic way. I'm nervous. I've loved all of Hitchcock's films since I was a girl, but I'm scared of *Frenzy*. It's the one that really scared me when I was young; the one with the rape scene—the first sex scene I ever watched—the one that ended with him murdering her.

Tonight, when I watch that scene as an adult, it is as I remember it: she screams and fights; her breast lolls out of her bra; he comes as he throttles her. I am repulsed, and even though I am safe with my husband, I am scared—body scared—the kind of fright that makes you curl into a ball. My eyes tear up, angry tears. I'm mad. I know so much more than when I first watched that film, when I was twelve.

I'm angry on behalf of that twelve-year-old girl—me—whose first and formative understandings of sex were the brutality of that scene, the degradation of women in porn, her grandfather's inappropriate revelations, the sexual nature of her mother's murder, which she intuited even before reading her grandfather's books on the Hillside killings. I am angry at her grandfather—his own daughter strangled—letting *her* daughter watch that film. I am angry that after his own daughter was murdered by a sexual predator, he sold porn, including images of women beaten and humiliated and fucked—sometimes raped—to feed the violent fantasies of certain men. I am angry on behalf of the porn stars whose painful careers made my easy childhood and my education possible. I am angry on behalf of Marilyn, who had to look at those soul-deadening images day in and day out.

But I am angriest at the world that made all that possible, the world where women have been, for so long, eminently disposable. I am angry for the women whose first understanding of sex was rape or incest, girls devastated simply to satisfy the desires of strangers, brothers, fathers. For every woman raped or touched or flashed. For every girl made to feel ugly for not looking like a Victoria's Secret ad. For women who have never enjoyed sex because no one bothered to make it feel good for them or to teach them to expect it to feel good. For girls and women everywhere objectified and harassed, pursued and hunted, followed on the street. For the dead female bodies on the news, more and more of them: women butchered by men, killed because their lives were deemed less valuable than a man's pride, convenience, desire. Here are some of their names—names you've likely never heard: Natalie Chavez, Karen Perez, Victoria Brown, Renee Perez, Alice Faye Chatman, Surrie Perry, Susan Berman, Kathleen Durst, Patricia Warrington. Perhaps you have your own names, names of women and girls you loved or knew or went to school with. Here is one more: Michele Ann Grey.

I'm angry at TV shows and films that make these deaths entertaining and sexy, giving them innocuous names like "mysteries," "thrillers." I'm angry at this world where women's lives are less valuable than cheap entertainment.

My own little girl, sleeping sweetly upstairs—innocent, tiny. This world waiting for her to step into its maw.

I bury my head in Ben's warm side and breathe deeply, let him hold me and comfort me and keep me safe. I have married a good man, I remind myself, a loving man. A good man is my husband. A good man is my daughter's father.

And, I think too, a good man was my father. I know that now.

45

I T IS THE SUMMER OF 2013. I GET A VOICE MAIL FROM A
California number that is not Marilyn's: "Hi, Kelly, this is
Detective Estupinian, well, Camacho now. I was wanting to talk
to you about your mother's case, Michele Grey?"

I had always imagined that if they ever solved my mother's
case, I'd find out with a call like this one. I call her back, but her
voice mail picks up. I leave a long, confused message. I email her
too, just in case. And then I wait.

It is a busy day. Tonight, Ben and I are going to buy a car to
replace the twenty-five-year-old hand-me-down Nissan Stanza that
has seen us through college, grad school, our lives in Tennessee,
Nebraska, Iowa, and now Texas. I get caught up with last-minute
financing details, online transfers of money, two-year-old Milly, who
wants me to play dress-up with her. Just as we are about to leave for
the dealership at 4:00 p.m., my phone rings.

"It's the detective," I tell Ben. "I have to take this." The car
will have to wait.

Milly plays in my office as I talk to Detective Camacho. My
hands are shaking. I cannot find a pen. I take notes on an envelope
with a stubby, blue crayon.

She wasn't calling to tell me they'd solved the case, not really.
Instead she was calling to say that the results had come back from

when she'd sent my mother's effects to the lab again. There was blood, but only my mother's. There was DNA, but in fragments too small to produce a match.

But she'd spent a good amount of time reviewing the file: "The original detectives on the case, Detective Varney and Detective Orozco, thought it was the Hillside Stranglers. You know who they were, right? In fact, Detective Varney was one of the investigators on those slayings, so he probably had a good idea. They were excellent detectives. Legendary, really. And now, when *I* look at it—the MO, the details of her body—it fits. They might have worked together, or Bianchi may have worked on his own, trying to impress Buono, before they got together. But neither of them mentioned her, and, of course, Buono's dead now. If I had more funding, I could go up and interview Bianchi. He's still alive, up in Washington, but I can't, not without more evidence. And right now we don't have any."

"My digger is broken!" Milly interrupts to tell me. My hands tremble as I snap the truck's plastic cab back into place.

Detective Camacho doesn't say it, but I understand. This is my answer. She sounds as certain as she can be, with no evidence and no confession and no way of finding either. This is the best we can do with what we have, and I trust her and Detective Flores and Detective Varney and Detective Orozco. She cannot tell me, but I tell myself: my mother was an early victim of one or both of the Hillside Stranglers. Their names were Kenneth Bianchi and Angelo Buono. They weren't prosecuted for my mother's death, but they were prosecuted for the deaths of ten others. One is in prison; one is dead. It is okay, I tell myself, to hate them. But at the moment, I feel nothing. The hate will come later, in flashes, for weeks and months. It is not a burning hate or an angry one, as I expect it to be; it is cold and hard when it comes, sharp and fleeting.

Later on, I will look at their pictures online. Buono's curly hair, his insouciant stare as if he'd just told someone to go fuck themselves; Bianchi with his thick mustache, looking for all the world like a used-car salesman. But you can't do a Google search for their pictures without also coming upon crime-scene photos of young women, their legs splayed, a pulp novel with a soft-porn cover—things that make my insides lurch. I will think back to the Darcy O'Brien book I'd read on those sleepless nights as a teenager, how Buono almost seemed to be teaching Bianchi how to strangle a woman and dispose of her body, as if he'd killed before. Had he? Had my mom been his practice?

That afternoon, Detective Camacho continues, "I also thought you might want to know more about your dad. He was in the Navy from 1960 to 1963, and he was honorably discharged. It looks like he only went to school up to eighth grade, but he was really smart. You can see that in the letter I sent you. Really articulate. And he was with your mother until he got put into jail. Anyway, I have a picture of him. Would you want to see it? I can try and email it before I leave today."

Would I want to see it? I don't know how I keep talking, but I find the words.

"Yes," I say. "I really would. I've never seen him. I have no idea what he looks like."

I can't stop pacing. Milly amuses herself by tangling herself between my legs. "Shh," I whisper to her, even though she isn't making a sound.

Before we hang up, I tell Detective Camacho, "I don't know how I'll tell my little girl all this. You know, like—just. About everything."

"You'll tell her when the time is right," she says, calmly and professionally, and in her calm professionalism, she is comforting. "And you'll tell her the best way you know how."

At the car dealership, I cannot think straight. I sign forms I do not understand, because I cannot parse the words that come from the salesman's mouth. I want to answer every question the financing lady asks us with "I don't care. I want to see my father." Milly squirms on my lap; I shift under her weight. On the financing lady's desk are family photos: dark eyes stare out at me, their white ceramic frames gathering dust.

And when we get home after dinner, it is there, waiting for me in my email. In the photo, from 1993, my father is in his fifties and wears the cheap, oversized eyeglasses you probably get in prison. His hair is thinning and his skin is orange from the lights at the DMV. He is completely ordinary looking. I search his face for signs of my own. The eyes, perhaps? The nose. It's hard to tell, because his face is too old compared to mine. I cannot imagine him as a young man, the street kid who loved my mother. I was a senior in high school when that photo was taken. If things had been different, he could have come to my graduation.

I hear a creak behind me, and before I can close the photo, Milly asks, "What is that?"—because that is how she asks, "Who is that?"

"Oh, he's just a man," I say.

When she catches me looking at it again, just before bedtime, she reassures me, "He's just a man, Mommy."

"Yes," I say. I touch the screen, run my finger along his pixilated face. "Just a man." I sigh. "Let's go to bed, Babycakes."

After Milly has finally fallen asleep—tucked safely into bed and provisioned with water, her stuffed lobster, Freddie the Dinosaur, and Applesauce the Bear—I lie in my own bed and listen to the sounds of the night. Ben is asleep next to me, and I slide my hand between his arm and shirtless side so that I can feel the gentle motion of his warm chest, the filling and emptying of his rib cage, the steady pulse of his heart. The fan whirs gently over our heads. Crickets chirp outside, a rhythm section for the high-pitched songs of frogs. A bird cries, disturbed from its sleep, then quiets. I can't sleep.

I can stop wondering who killed my mother; I know my father's face.

I think of how today I lied to Milly about the picture—her family—something I'd promised myself I would never do. I don't want to lie to her again. I want her to know where she comes from.

From across the hall, I can hear her rhythmic breathing. My husband turns in his sleep. The dog, curled into my side, twitches. The coolness of the sheets, the whirl of the fan, my daughter's breath from the other room. My sweet family, the family I dreamt of when I was young, here in our peaceful home. Everything I care most about in the world.

I think again of what the detective told me: "You'll tell her when the time is right, and you'll tell her the best way you know how."

46

By the time I find Detective Varney, I already have the answers to most of my questions. So instead of asking him anything, I write him a letter to say thank-you: *Thank you for working on my mother's case; thank you for being the friendly face I remembered all those years. Thank you for taking the time to come to brunch.*

When he gets my letter, he has his daughter call me back because he cannot. Detective Varney is dying. He remembers me, she says. "He remembers finding you in that motel room in the drawer. He remembers the brunch. I remember it too, when he and my mom came back from it."

I don't remember his wife being there. My memory of that day shifts again: five people at the table, Detective Varney's wife, also named Marilyn, sitting at the end, smiling.

"My dad had a hard job, you know," she goes on. "It wore on him. On all of us. That was a really nice thing your grandfather did. It meant a lot to him. He got to see a happy ending."

Acknowledgments

I AM GRATEFUL TO THE FOLLOWING FOR THEIR SUPPORT— material and moral—during the long process of writing this book:

Jonis Agee, Grace Bauer, Sidnie White Crawford, Ted Kooser, Hilda Raz, Timothy Schaffert, Gerald Shapiro, Judith Slater, Janet Carlson, Elaine Dvorak, Susan Hart, Linda Maloch, and Leann Messing and other faculty and staff of the University of Nebraska-Lincoln, *Prairie Schooner*, and the University of Nebraska Press. My teachers at NSWC: Meghan Daum, Debra Earling, Jesse Lee Kercheval, Marjorie Sandor, and Judith Claire Mitchell.

The editors of various magazines in which parts of my story have appeared, in different forms: Roxane Gay at *The Rumpus*, Carolyn Kuebler and JM Tyree at *New England Review*, David Leavitt at *Subtropics*, Joe Oestreich at *Waccamaw*, Joe Mackall at *River Teeth*, Richard Mathews at *Tampa Review*, and Ladette Randolph and Patricia Hampl at *Ploughshares*.

My wonderful and very patient agent, Emma Sweeney, who encouraged me for ten years. My brilliant editor, Anna Michels, and everyone at Sourcebooks who made this book better.

My colleagues and friends at Trinity University, especially Jenny Browne, Ruby Contreras, Casey Fuller, Anne Graf, Laura Hunsicker-Wang, Michele Johnson, Nicole Marafioti, Maria

Paganelli, Andrew Porter, David Ribble, Claudia Stokes, Angela Tarrango, and Harry Wallace.

The Virginia Center for the Creative Arts, for time and hospitality.

My friends emily danforth, Carrie Shipers, Gayathri Prabhu, Pat Emile, Kati Cramer, Daryl Farmer, Erin Flanagan, Kate Flaherty, DeMisty Bellinger, Adrian Koesters, Holly Heffelbower, Haley Holmes, Jill Schwartzberg Bickel, Catherine Salmon, Cheryl Sheehan, and Chris and Abigail Cudabac, as well as many too numerous to name here but for whose support and friendship I am grateful.

The people and clergy of St. Mark's on the Campus Episcopal Church, Lincoln, Nebraska. The Diocese of West Texas and the Bishop Jones Center, especially Laura Woodall. The people of St. David's Episcopal Church and the Reverend Lisa Mason.

My family, especially Marilyn Grey Warner, Susan Carlisle, Callie Welden, Anthony Genovese, and Yvette Genovese.

The dedicated and compassionate men and women of the Los Angeles Police Department's Robbery-Homicide Division and Cold Case Homicide Unit, especially Detectives Orozco, Varney, Flores, and Camacho. I am most grateful to Detectives Flores and Camacho for the care and time they spent on my mother's case and for answering my questions. Because of them, I know my parents' faces.

My husband, Ben, who taught me how to be normal, and who taught me that there's no such thing. Without your support and love, I would have given up on everything. My sweet Milly.

Finally, I am grateful to the people mentioned and unmentioned in this book who in large ways or small, took care of me as a child, especially Marilyn. Thank you.

A portion of the author's proceeds from this book will be donated to the work of Thistle Farms, an organization that supports the survivors of prostitution, trafficking, and addiction. Visit thistle-farms.org for more information.

Reading Group Guide

1. Throughout the memoir, Kelly's grandfather tells her that it is important to remember who you are and where you come from. Think about where you come from, whether that be your family or the town or home where you were born. How has it shaped who you are today?

2. When Kelly is young she asks her grandfather questions to try and learn what her mother, Michele, was like. Imagine that you are in Kelly's shoes and have never met an important member of your family. What would you want to know about him or her? How would not having this person around affect your childhood?

3. Describe Kelly's relationship with Richard versus her relationship with Marilyn. Do you think Richard and Marilyn were capable guardians for Kelly?

4. Richard seems to be full of contradictions, sending Kelly to an expensive French school while also running a porn business. Overall, how would you describe Richard's character?

5. Many sections of *We Are All Shipwrecks* talk about Kelly's

struggle coming to terms with her burgeoning sexuality, especially in regards to the violence and pornography she has come to associate with sexuality. How do you think Kelly's grandfather owning a porn store affected her? Do you see any lasting effects of this association?

6. How would you feel if your family had decided to move on to a boat for the greater part of your childhood? Would you look at it as an adventure like Kelly did, or would you dread the move like Marilyn?

7. Describe the community down at the marina. Were there any characters you particularly liked? Any that you disliked? Why?

8. Why do you think Kelly found solace through swimming during high school? Have you ever had a hobby that has helped you escape the world? What was it?

9. If you could give high-school Kelly one piece of advice, what would it be? If you could give the high-school version of yourself one piece of advice, what would it be? Do you see any similarities between teenage you and teenage Kelly?

10. How did Kelly and Marilyn's relationship change over the course of the memoir? What caused those changes?

11. Why do you think Kelly seeks out Michele's new detective and pushes for the open case to be closed? Do you think she finds closure in the end?

12. Do you think it is important to remember where you come

from? Why or why not? What's more important, where you come from or who you become in the end?

A Conversation
with the Author

What made you decide to write this memoir? What are you hoping to share with readers by telling your story?

I first started writing about my childhood because I wanted to explain why I was so different from other people. My other personal motivations were to show the love of all those people who helped me grow up—from Marilyn and Richard to Pete, Dee, Josette, Gill, and Annie—and to inspire others to participate in the lives of children not their own. I also wanted people to know about the LA Harbor where I grew up, because this is a part of LA that is largely gone now. Finally, I wanted to tell Michele's story, my birth father's, and Marilyn's, because to me they exemplify the bravery of parents trying to do their best by their child, even if their own lives were messy.

What I realized as I wrote the book was that I wasn't that different from other people and we all have experiences that provide us with a unique perspective and personality. As I've published parts of my story and have talked to readers, I've also realized many people have families or childhoods that don't fit a traditional definition of "normal." So there are a lot of truths I wanted to share with readers, but the most important ones are these: The first is that if you're in the middle of a painful, weird, or difficult childhood or recovering from one, there is hope. You might need a lot of help, but you can find your way to the life you want to lead. The second is we all have stories of where we come from that matter and that others can learn from. Sharing our stories and our vulnerabilities actually makes life easier for other people.

Describe your writing process.

This book me took a long time to write, and my process changed as I went along. In general, I wrote first to remember important things—sort of like a diary of thoughts and realizations—then I transformed the important moments and ideas into scenes. Usually I could rely on vivid memories of events, but sometimes I had to recreate scenes through my knowledge of the people, places, and historical and emotional context involved. Sometimes that transformation didn't happen until the fourth or fifth draft. A memoirist can't tell the whole story of her childhood in one book—there are too many experiences and moments and too many ways of interpreting them—so a large part of my process was actually eliminating material so that I could focus on the plotlines, themes, and experiences important to *this* telling of my story. A lot of people helped me in that process through their feedback.

Did you find it painful to talk about the more difficult times in your life, or was it a cathartic experience?

A lot of authors write about childhoods that were much more painful than mine. There were only a few passages that were really hard to write—the scene at the airport restaurant when I called Dee, the scene when my grandfather told me about Marilyn's affair, and writing about the strained relationship between Marilyn and me. I wrote the scene with my grandfather's revelation at a writer's retreat. When I was done drafting it, I was so upset I got up to leave my studio…and walked straight into a wall. Writing about this has helped me process my childhood, but that was a side effect of the writing, not my intent. My intent was to tell a story others could enter into and experience.

It is apparent that, as a child, you believed your family and home life were fairly normal. Now, looking back, how would you describe your childhood?

Children don't often think to question their family situation; they assume what they have is the norm. And I think almost every teenager believes their family is unusually weird. As an adult who has spent a lot of time thinking about her childhood, I think my upbringing was eccentric in its circumstances, but that a lot of the dynamics within my family—loss of birth parents, being raised by grandparents, marital discord, a wife's unrealized dreams and isolation, a husband's manipulations and borderline abuse, alcoholism, and my reactions to them—are fairly common, even if they don't all happen in the same family.

Describe your family in one word.

Loving. Marilyn and my grandfather loved me and did their best by me, working within the limitations of their own personalities, circumstances, and neuroses. I count all the other people in this book who took care of me as family too. My childhood was full of love, even if I didn't always recognize it.

If you could go back and give teenage Kelly one piece of advice, what would it be?

Hang in there, be yourself, and keep swimming. Also, get your eyebrows waxed, because you have no idea how such a trivial thing will improve your self-confidence.

What is your happiest memory from your time living on the *Intrepid* with Marilyn and your grandfather?

Seeing the natural beauty that found a way to survive in the very industrial harbor. The harbor was a place of constant wonder, mystery, and beauty.

What is your favorite place you've ever lived?

I've found a way to love every place I've lived, although I prefer green, undeveloped places.

Your mother's murder was a horrific event that has changed the entire course of your life. Have you found any closure over the years?

I think of closure as something you seek after traumatic loss and grief. I didn't experience trauma or grief about her death because I was so young. Many readers of this book will have experienced greater grief at a loss of a parent than I did. But I do feel closer to her than I did before I started writing the book, and our best guess as to who did it—Bianchi and Buono—satisfies me. But because the case is not officially solved, part of me still worries that her killer has gone free.

How do you think you will tell your children about your own childhood experiences?

I don't know. I'm following Detective Camacho's advice and telling them as they're ready to know and in the best way I can. One is still very young, and one is still unborn. If they care to read it when they're older, there will be this book.

Who are you favorite authors?

How long do you have? There are probably a hundred or

so. Maybe a better answer is to list a few of my favorite books off the top of my head: *White Teeth* by Zadie Smith, *To Kill a Mockingbird* by Harper Lee, *In Cold Blood* by Truman Capote, *The Devil's Highway* by Luis Alberto Urrea, *Atonement* by Ian McEwan, *Pearl* by the Pearl Poet, *Absalom, Absalom!* by William Faulkner, *Americanah* by Chimamanda Ngozi Adichie, and *Beowulf*.

Describe your writing style.

This is a really hard question. I like to think my style changes depending on the material I'm writing about and the situation in which I'm writing. In this book, I tried very hard to sound like myself telling a story, my truest and best and clearest self.

About the Author

Kelly Grey Carlisle's essays have appeared in *Ploughshares, Salon.com, The Rumpus, New England Review, The Sun, The Touchstone Anthology of Contemporary Creative Nonfiction,* and others. She teaches writing at Trinity University and edits *1966: A Journal of Creative Nonfiction.* She lives in San Antonio, Texas, with her family in a house with conventional plumbing, a backyard with a grill, one dog, and a basketball hoop.